Validating Violence –
Violating Faith?

William W Emilsen
John T Squires
editors

The PACT Series

The PACT series is a set of publications of the Public and Contextual Theology (PACT) Strategic Research Centre, Charles Sturt University, Australia. Each volume in the series focuses on an issue or series of related issues in the disciplines of public and contextual theologies. The series explores how public and contextual theologies are worked out in the Australasian region, in collaboration with similar centres in South Africa, Western Europe, and North America.

Editorial Committee:
Dean Drayton
James Haire
Elizabeth Mackinlay
David Neville
John Squires

1. *Dodging Angels on Saturday*, Graeme Garrett, 2005
2. *'Into the World You Love'*, edited by Graeme Garrett, 2007
3. *From Resurrection to Return: Perspective from Theology and Science on Christian Eschatology*, edited by James Haire, Christine Ledger and Stephen Pickard, 2007

Validating Violence –
Violating Faith?
Religion, Scripture
and Violence

William W Emilsen

John T Squires

editors

ATF Press
Adelaide

First published 2008

National Library of Australia Cataloguing-in-Publication entry
Title: Validating violence- violating faith? : religion, scripture and violence / editors: William Emilsen, John Squires.
ISBN: 9781920691899 (pbk.)
Series: PACT series
Subjects: Violence--Religious aspects--Judaism.
             Violence in rabbinical literature.
             Violence--Religious aspects--Christianity.
             Violence in the Bible.
             Violence--Religious aspects--Islamic.
             Violence in the Koran.
Other Authors/Contributors:
             Emilsen, William W.
             Squires, John T., 1954-
             Australasian Theological Forum.
Dewey Number: 205.697

Published by ATF Press
An imprint of the Australasian Theological Forum Ltd
PO Box 504 Hindmarsh
SA 5007
ABN 90 116 359 963
www.atfpress.com

Typeset in Times 10/14pt
cover design
by Astrid Sengkey
based on
The Entombment by Chris Wyatt (2007; gouache and ink on paper). Painted for the exhibition Stations of the Cross at St Ives Uniting Church, NSW, curated by Dr Douglas Purnell, Easter 2007.

Contents

Foreword

The closely related disciplines of public and contextual theologies represent a new and significant way in which theology is being carried out around the world. They presuppose the classical inheritance of the Christian faith and of Christian theology, but recognise the need for a hermeneutic that is responsive to a changing world. We no longer inhabit cultures that take for granted a working knowledge of Christian belief and practice. Our societies are now subject to global movements and are a diverse mixture of cultures, faiths and secularism. On the one hand, there may be a residual Christian frame of reference in some, particularly Western, societies, but the relevance of theology is often no longer self-evident in these societies. On the other hand, in other parts of the world, particularly in Asia, Africa and Latin America, the interactions between Christianity and culture is often quite vibrant.

Public and contextual theologies have arisen partly in protest to the privatisation of Christianity and the dominance of Western culture. They are concerned with how biblical and theological disciplines can both engage particularity and speak to the contemporary world. These forms of theology recognise that theology competes in a public domain in which there are a range of ideologies and philosophies. Public and contextual theologies must be willing to interact with, and respond to, insights from other disciplines. Such theologies are designed to explore the relevance of fundamental Christian beliefs.

We believe that public and contextual theologies are central to the expression of the gospel. The ways in which the Good News transforms our social life and enhances civic trust is the burden of our work. This activity is undertaken in close collaboration with similar centres in South Africa, Western Europe and North America, and with scholars in other parts of the world.

This volume of essays originated at an important conference, *Validating Violence–Violating Faith?*, held at United Theological College, North Parramatta, Sydney, in May 2006. It focuses on the issues of public and contextual theology in relation to religious violence and reconciliation, and as such deals with an issue fundamental to the PACT research area. This volume contains twelve chapters, an introduction, and a concluding chapter on hermeneutical strategies involved in reading the violent elements found in texts of scripture. It contains contributions from Christian, Jewish and Muslim writers of a high standard of scholarship.

The chapters address the difficulties and challenges of dealing with violent stories, laws and images in the scriptures of a number of faiths. Most attention is given to Christianity, Judaism, and Islam. Half of the chapters contain detailed exegetical examination of scripture texts from these faiths, while the remaining chapters offer theological explorations and history-of-religions discussions of the issues. One chapter offers a creative reconstruction of a first century scenario; another treats the views of Mahatma Gandhi with critical acumen. Professor Christopher Stanley offers a comparative survey of the three 'religions of the book' in a thorough fashion, and Professor Garry Trompf provides a masterly overview of the issue across a wide span of human history, covering an exhaustive range of religious traditions. We believe that this volume makes a significant contribution to the consideration of Public Theology in the contemporary context.

James Haire
> Professor of Theology and Director, Public and Contextual Theology (PACT) Strategic Research Centre, Charles Sturt University

William W Emilsen
> Senior Academic Associate, School of Theology, and Principal Researcher, Public and Contextual Theology (PACT) Strategic Research Centre, Charles Sturt University

John T Squires
> Senior Academic Associate, School of Theology, and Principal Researcher, Public and Contextual Theology (PACT) Strategic Research Centre, Charles Sturt University

Contributors

Anastasia Boniface-Malle is from the Evangelical Lutheran Church in Tanzania. She currently works as a Translation Consultant for the United Bible Societies, and is in charge of the translation projects for the Bible Society of Uganda. She has lectured widely on many topics including the Psalms, the Hebrew lament tradition, the burdens of women and children, and the challenges upon African Christianity.

Chris Budden is a Uniting Church Minister serving in the North Lake Macquarie congregation in New South Wales. He is the past General Secretary of the New South Wales Synod of the Uniting Church in Australia, and past Chair of the Doctrine Working Group of the Uniting Church National Assembly. He is an Adjunct Faculty member of United Theological College, Academic Associate in the School of Theology, Associate Researcher within the Public and Contextual Theology Strategic Research Centre of Charles Sturt University. He has a particular concern for the way theology can be done on Indigenous land, and for the relationship between discipleship and citizenship in the modern nation state.

William W Emilsen is Lecturer in Church History and World Religions at United Theological College, Sydney, Senior Academic Associate in the School of Theology, a Principal Researcher within the Public and Contextual Theology Strategic Research Centre of Charles Sturt University, and Associate Professor of Church History in the Sydney College of Divinity. He edits the journal *Uniting Church Studies* and has written extensively on the history of the Uniting Church, including co-editing *Marking Twenty Years: The Uniting Church in Australia 1977–1997* (UTC, 1997) and *The Uniting Church in Australia: The First 25 Years* (2003). He has long been interested in the life and thought of Mahatma Gandhi, particularly Gandhi's intersection with Christian missions and missionaries. Among his writings on Gandhi are, *Violence and Atonement* (Peter Lang, 1994), *The India of My Dreams* (ISPCK, 1995), and *Gandhi's Bible* (ISPCK, 2001).

Jione Havea is Lecturer in Biblical Studies at United Theological College and Academic Associate in the School of Theology at Charles

Sturt University. He is also an ordained minister from the Methodist Church of Tonga, and a Principal Researcher with the Public and Contextual Theology Strategic Research Centre of Charles Sturt University. His interests are in biblical narratives, cultural studies, with leanings toward resistance and liberation movements.

Rachael Kohn is the author of *Learning from History: Pre–War Germany and Now* (Council of Christians and Jews in Victoria, 2007). Her recent books are *Curious Obsessions in the History of Science and Spirituality* (ABC Books, 2007) and *The New Believers: Re-imagining God* (HarperCollins, 2003). She has an MA and PhD in Religious Studies (1985) from McMaster University, Canada and in 2005 was awarded a Doctor of Letters Honoris Causa from the University of New South Wales for fostering religious understanding in Australia, through her books and radio programs, 'The Spirit of Things' and 'The Ark' on ABC Radio National.

David Neville is Senior Lecturer in Theology at St Mark's National Theological Centre (Canberra), Senior Academic Associate in the School of Theology and a Researcher within the Public and Contextual Theology Strategic Research Centre of Charles Sturt University. He lectures in New Testament Studies and his research interests include gospel studies, hermeneutics and social ethics. He has written two books on the relations between the synoptic gospels and edited a number of essay collections relating to Christian social ethics. David is married to Sonia.

Mehmet Ozalp has been involved in social, cultural and religious work since 1991. He has been focusing on the intercultural and interfaith area since 2000. He is one of the founding directors and the President of Affinity Intercultural Foundation. He has established and written material for a suite of short courses on Islam and personal leadership. He was a member of the Community Harmony Reference Group with the Community Relations Commission in Sydney Australia established by the Premier of New South Wales during the Iraq war of 2003. He has appeared on the ABC 'Compass' program and the ABC Radio 'The Spirit of Things' programme. He is the author of two books, *101 Questions You Asked about Islam* and *Islam in the Modern World*. He is currently doing a combined Masters/PhD in Islamic Theology and is an occasional lecturer on Islamic Studies in the University of Sydney.

Elizabeth Raine teaches Biblical Studies at Coolamon College and United Theological College and is Academic Associate in the School of Theology at Charles Sturt University. She is a Minister of the Word in the Uniting Church in Australia who has been a congregational minister, a school chaplain, a parish administrator, and a tenants' rights advocate. Her research encompasses the Gospel of Matthew, the wisdom literature of the Hebrew Bible, and questions relating to evil and theodicy in the Bible. She enjoys performing different styles of music and writing 'creative dialogues' with her husband, John Squires.

John T Squires is Senior Lecturer in Biblical Studies at United Theological College, Senior Academic Associate in the School of Theology and Associate Researcher within the Public and Contextual Theology Strategic Research Centre of Charles Sturt University. He is a Minister of the Word in the Uniting Church in Australia, having served in parish ministries in semi-rural and urban settings. John is the author *of The Plan of God in Luke-Acts* (Cambridge University Press, 1993) and the Commentary on Acts in the *Eerdmans Commentary on the Bible* (Eerdmans, 2003). His publications also include a number of journal articles and book chapters, most recently, the chapter on Luke's Gospel in the *Cambridge Companion to the Gospels* (Cambridge University Press, 2006). Amongst his interests, he includes writing 'creative dialogues' with his wife, Elizabeth Raine.

Christopher D Stanley is Professor of Theology at St Bonaventure University in western New York, where he teaches courses in Biblical Studies as well as courses that explore the role of religion in contemporary social conflicts. Dr Stanley earned his MCS degree in Biblical Studies from Regent College (Vancouver, Canada) in 1983 and his PhD in New Testament from Duke University in 1990. He has published widely in the field of New Testament studies, including two books and numerous articles in leading international journals. Much of his research has centred on Paul's use of Scripture, as seen in the titles of his two books, *Paul and the Language of Scripture: Citation Technique in the Pauline Epistles and Contemporary Literature* (Cambridge University Press, 1992), and *Arguing With Scripture: The Rhetoric of Quotations in the Letters of Paul* (T&T Clark, 2004). His most recent book, *The Hebrew Bible: A Comparative Approach,* will be published by Prentice Hall in 2008. He is currently working on a book entitled *Neither Jew Nor Greek: Ethnic Conflict in the Churches of Paul*.

Heather Thomson is Lecturer in Theology and Academic Dean at St Mark's National Theological Centre, Academic Associate within the School of Theology and a Researcher within the Public and Contextual Theology Strategic Research Centre of Charles Sturt University. Her theological interests include critiques of the Christian tradition for its sanctioning of violence, sexism and other forms of injustice, and the development of constructive theology that promotes peace-making and justice. Her more recent publications include: 'Dangerous Memory for an Incarnational church' in *Wonderful and Confessedly Strange: Australian Essays in Anglican Ecclesiology*, edited by B Kaye, S Macneil & H Thomson (Adelaide: ATF Press, 2006), and '"(I can't get no) Satisfaction": Eschatology, Theodicy and Our Sacred Power', in *Theodicy and Eschatology*, edited by B Barber and D Neville (Adelaide: ATF Press, 2005).

Garry W Trompf is Professor in the Department of Studies in Religion and Visiting Academic to the Centre for Peace and Conflict at the University of Sydney. He was formerly Professor in the History of Ideas at the same university, and Professor of History at the University of Papua New Guinea. He has held visiting professorships at the universities of California, Utrecht, Edinburgh, and at the Jung Institute, Zürich. During 2007, he was Visiting Professor in Anthropology at the University of Warsaw. His books include *The Idea of Historical Recurrence in Western Thought*, *Melanesian Religion*, *Payback*, and *Early Christian Historiography*.

Introduction

It is not easy to accept that violence lies at the heart of scripture. Violent images in the narrative; at times, these are present. Violent words, spoken by characters in the story; these are certainly evident. Violent actions in the text; quite clearly, these are to be found. Violence as a quality espoused by a great religious figure; this becomes problematic for believers. Violence at the centre of God's being, manifested in what God does and who God is; this raises profound theological dilemmas.

Perhaps, we may think, it is in the scriptures of 'other' religions, but surely not in 'ours', not those scriptures that have nourished us since childhood and shaped who we are. Yet, we cannot ignore this plain fact—no matter whether we are Christians, Hindus, Jews, Muslims or Sikhs, our sacred scriptures contain disturbing and violent texts.

Often these texts are ignored. They are not seen. They are omitted from lectionaries. They are glossed over. They are rarely preached or studied. And if they are, they are distorted beyond recognition or literally observed without understanding.

Ignoring violent texts is like camping on the bank of a crocodile-infested river. It is dangerous. It is naive in the extreme. These Leviathan-like texts should be treated with the utmost respect and caution. They can erupt with violent force when it is least expected.

Validating Violence–Violating Faith? might be thought of as a different journey along crocodile-infested rivers. Scholars from Jewish, Christian and Muslim traditions—nine Australians, one African, one American and a Tongan—train their spotlight on these texts, these 'reptiles' of violence. They know the terrain. They understand the habitus. They appreciate the dangers. Jione Havea, for example, an Old Testament/Hebrew Scripture scholar of Tongan origins, is like an experienced park ranger. He takes the reader along the river, or in his case the sea or a lagoon, on a journey of discovery. The texts of violence are simply there. They are neither approved nor avoided. They are to be understood, and part of that understanding is exploring the curious interrelation between violence, pleasure and grief. Havea argues that our general blindness to the violence in scripture is tantamount to ignoring the cries of the suffering. He is particularly sensitive to those texts in holy scripture that express violence against women, foreigners, youth, widows, the disabled and the poor. Following Jacques Derrida's and Judith Butler's observation that societies that have rituals of grief and mourning are less violent, Havea advances the challenging idea that texts of violence, interpreted and expressed within ritual, may play an important role in the moderation of violence.

Chris Stanley studies the river from an aerial perspective. Like a bush pilot, he flies low over the river—indeed, the three great rivers of Christianity, Judaism and Islam—observing, mapping, noting dangerous sections along the way. His two chapters provide the reader with a overview of the particular texts that have been used to justify violence as well as those texts that have been used to promote non-violence in the three Abrahamic religions. Stanley draws up a map—five models—to help the reader interpret the violent texts of scripture: (i) the 'theocratic model' which literally accepts the texts in all their detail; (ii) the 'cultural conditioning model' that interprets violent texts as a product of a particular time; (iii) the 'just war model' that accepts violence as a last resort and, then, only under strictly defined conditions; (iv) the 'progressive revelation model' which asserts that passages that endorse violence reflect an earlier stage in the religious awareness of a community—an awareness that is superseded by a move towards non-violence; and finally (v), the 'personalist model' that gives priority to verses pertaining to conduct for individual believers.

John Squires and Elizabeth Raine pitch their tent safely back from the river and tell us a kind of dreamtime story around the campfire. Drawing on the Markan account of Jesus' entry into Jerusalem (Mark 11:1–19), the reader enters into an imaginative dialogue between Gaius Scipio, a Roman centurion, and Amon, a Jewish priest concerning Yehoshua ben Joseph (Jesus). The story is both humorous and provocative. As the fire fades and the darkness spreads like ink, the reader is left with disturbing questions such as, Does God will violence? and, Did Jesus canvass the use of political action through violent means?

Anastasia Boniface-Malle takes the reader into the river: one shares her pain, feels the senseless violence perpetuated upon African women and children, hears the anguished cry, 'Violence is everywhere', and almost despairs of the Church's culpability. Yet, like the wildebeest fording the dangerous Limpopo River, she is drawn forward by an inexorable vision of God's shalom—a state of harmony existing among God, humanity and creation.

David Neville takes us to the river's mouth, the end of the river where it slowly meanders through mangroves and over mudflats before pouring into the sea. Here the river is most beguiling. Not all is what it seems. In these estaurine shallows, texts of violence present a disturbing reality. Neville asks the perplexing question, what are we to make of these texts that sanction violence at the end times? In particular, he asks, how are we to respond to the violent eschatology in Matthew's gospel when contrasted with his depiction of Jesus' nonviolent moral teachings?

In the Western media 'Islam' and 'violence' are almost synonymous. Daily suicide attacks, threats of jihad, and the epithet 'Muslim terrorist' all reinforce the view that Islam is a violent religion. Yet, if we follow Mehmet Ozalp to the source of that great river of faith, to the Qur'an and the teachings of the Prophet Muhammad, we discover a softer, kinder world. Although the Prophet never embraced non-violence as an absolute moral imperative, nonetheless, for Ozalp and many Muslims, the Prophet is the exemplar of the proper use of force in a world that is considered intrinsically violent. Ozalp explains to us that the Prophet laid down principles to curb violence and to ameliorate warfare that were far in advance of his time.

William Emilsen departs from a particular focus on the Abrahamic religions and, with Gandhi as his guide, travels the great rivers of the world, across all religions. It is a transformative journey. He records how texts of violence are confronted by Gandhi with absolute fearlessness. Scripture, tradition and religious authority are respected by Gandhi but never allowed to countenance violence. Gandhi tests the world scriptures on 'the anvil of truth with the hammer of compassion' — his twin principles of reason and non-violence. Faced with the absolute futility of violence, Emilsen argues that Gandhi's 'gospel of non-violence' is critical for a world bent on self-destruction.

Heather Thomson also employs a guide. With the assistance of James Gilligan, the American psychiatrist and criminologist, she explores a particular part of the river that is landlocked, polluted and threatened. Drawing on Gilligan's long experience of the destructive effects of violence on male prisoners — violence only generates more violence — Thomson shows how ill-conceived and misguided a punitive mentality is. Her plea to the Church is actively to create alternative cultures of non-violence by discerning those elements within scripture and tradition that promote peace.

Periodically rivers breach their banks causing great destruction and loss of life. Consequently, Chris Budden approaches the river with the eyes of a civil engineer. He thinks, how can he regulate the river's destructive forces? Where is a suitable location for a weir or a dam? He is particularly anxious to check the myth of redemptive violence that undergirds one of the more popular theories of the atonement — the penal substitutionary theory. He is also disturbed by the way that the myth of redemptive violence underlies American and, by association, Australian foreign policy resulting in the doctrine of pre-emptive strikes and propaganda justifying torture. Myths, however, are not easily checked. They are a collective response to people's hopes and desires developed over millennia. So while it is true that building the huge Aswan Dam across the Nile in Upper Egypt may have eliminated crocodiles downstream, checking the myth of redemptive violence presents a far greater challenge.

Rachael Kohn stakes a warning sign along the river's edge. She rehearses the history of non-violence and neighbourly co-operation that runs through Judaism. The central texts of this religion are not driven by the urge to convert—a factor which in other religious traditions has provided a stimulus to aggression, or worse. By contrast, the Jews have witnessed too many of their people taken by the horrors of the deep. The systematic slaughter of nearly six million Jews is almost too much to bear. And yet the fear remains; texts of violence, once employed to validate violence towards Jews in the past, now threaten the state of Israel. Crocodiles still lurk in the river.

Garry Trompf, with panoptic vision, gazes into the unfathomable depths of the river. He sees there the origins of humanity's propensity for violence stemming from an animal past and, like John Gray in *Straw Dogs* (2002), seriously questions the Christian belief that humans are radically different from all other animals. Trompf's central theme is that '[R]eligion in its basic, fundamental, perennial guises is deeply implicated in violence.' This fundamental religion, he argues, appeals to humanity's most basic instincts: it is colourful, festive and celebratory in expression; it is physically less restraining and more tolerant of what is considered 'right action' and places a high value on military valour. More disturbing, is Trompf's observation that this basic, fundamental and perennial religion, by its very syncretic nature, has the capacity not only to subvert salvation religions but also to transform them into something they were never intended to be.

This volume ends by revisiting each of the chapters with a view to identifying the main hermeneutical model employed by the authors. What strategies do we use to deal with violence in scripture? How does grappling with these texts inform and reshape our faith?

Part 1
Approaching the Scriptures

Pleasure and Grief, in Violence

Jione Havea

Without the capacity to mourn, we lose that keener
sense of life we need in order to oppose violence.[1]

Speaking is impossible, but so too would be silence
or absence or a refusal to share one's sadness.[2]

As interpreters of holy scriptures at homes, prisons, mosques,
synagogues, churches, shrines and beyond, we can no longer step over
the tremors and spills of violence in our sacred literatures, and in our
contexts and interpretive practices.

Split a sacred text, violence is there.[3] Take the Judeo–Christian
bibles, for instance. From the garden story in *Genesis* to the longing
for home in *2 Chronicles,* the last book in the Hebrew Bible, to the last
warnings in *Revelation,* the final book in the Christian Bible, multiple
manifestations of violence (physical, imagined, ideological, religious,
cultural and so forth) hold up the structures of the Bible. The *Varna*
system established by Hindu *Vedas,* which segregates society in four
privileged castes plus the Dalits, formerly known as the Untouchables,
who are not included in the caste system, is also violating. Into this
niche would fit the primarily degrading attitudes toward women in
the sacred texts of the world's major religions,[4] including the vast and
varied canon of Buddhist scriptures.

Lift a stone from your path, violence is there too, in its many
forms. From the racially loaded police chases at Redfern (New South
Wales, Australia) to the faces of refugees turned away from first world
borders, to the victims (crops, animals, humans, earth) of natural
disasters, to the strike of machetes and the thunder of bullets and bombs,
often waged under religious motivations, to the hidden beatings and
verbal abuses in domestic spaces, violence is there. Insofar as location
(concrete and ideological) and experience (personal and communal)
steer our biblical interpretations and constructions, and in order for
our interpretations to have public relevance, the escalation of violence
in human societies demands our attention.[5] Violence is all around us,
in biblical texts and on our paths.

Step back if you can from the act of interpretation, and you
might be surprised to find manifestations of violence in what we do

as interpreters. I have in mind here both the uprooting effect of the interpretive process, insofar as we analyse and unpack texts from different times and places so that they make sense in our placements, and the capacity of the interpretations that we produce to inspire violence. We often take refuge under the shadows of contextualisation, but we don't always account for the tears of relocation (to the text, and to the people and cultures from and through which the text has journeyed) that are required in order for contextualisation to happen. Many have argued that the interpretive task is a political task and interpreters often butt heads and cry, 'that's wrong' or 'that's silly' at each other's imagination and reconstruction. I would argue that those are also manifestations of violence, at a nonphysical level.

Violence abounds, overflows and intermingles, around and in the act of interpretation. In light of the foregoing, how then may we, as interpreters, proceed? With caution, for sure, and being mindful of the web on which violence tangles. In this chapter, I want to move beyond identifying and explaining the presence and the kinds of violence there are in the Bible,[6] toward *coming to terms with the web on which violence tangles,* or to use more Pacific Island images, *the mat on which violence sits,* and *the sea that carries violence across.* My aim is to make violence understandable without making biblical violence, whether in the name of God or in the name of God's chosen people or otherwise, acceptable. I propose to do this by sketching the *interrelation between violence, pleasure and grief.* But first, I shall briefly identify three of the currents in the sea of presuppositions that launch me into this study.

Sea of presuppositions
Firstly, I presume that sacred texts, from the West, East, and in-between, contain and disguise violence and so I feel that I do not need to argue or prove that there is violence in the Bible.[7] But for the ones who are in doubt, any children's storybook with pictures of brave young David defeating the giant, or Jesus hanging from the cross, should do the job. Artworks that are more graphic will also be helpful. The nineteenth-century Bible illustrator Gustave Doré has two illustrations of the Deluge that expose the senseless violence in that story.[8] In one, the viewer is confronted with a naked couple, with water rising up to their groins, holding up a child onto a crowded rock, maybe the top of a mountain, on which sits a tiger with a cub in her mouth. In this work Doré portrays the child reaching down to the couple, as if s/he is about to fall from the safety of the rock. Paradoxically, safety for the falling

child is on the side of a tiger with a cub. In the second image, bodies of humans and animals climb out of the water and Doré captures the tree breaking from the weight of the people, and as they fall back to the deadly water, Doré draws the attention of the viewer to Noah's Ark floating at a distance. The plight of the victims of the deluge becomes more visible and more piercing because of the safety represented by the distant ark in the background. One can't help seeing violence in these images, violence often overlooked when one only reads the biblical text.

Interpreters are blinded to the presence of violence in the Bible for a variety of reasons, including the refusal to see the bloodiness in the *acts of God* for the sake of God. Such blinding attitudes of piety depart from the form of piety in the story of Job, the innocent sufferer who questioned God and debated with religious traditions; a critical attitude that can also be heard in the lamenting voices in the Psalter. In other words, to be blinded to the violence in the Bible is to shut up cries such as:

> My God, my God,
> why have you abandoned me;
> why so far from delivering me
> and from my anguished roaring?
> My God,
> I cry by day—You answer not;
> By night, and have no respite (Ps 22:2–3).

Secondly, I presuppose that violence in holy scriptures contributes to the violence that takes place in contemporary societies. In other words, I want to believe that holy scriptures do influence the way people live, and the way things are.[9] This presupposition would be difficult to defend in my current location: When I moved to Australia in 2000, I was surprised by how eager my new friends and colleagues tried to convince me that Australia, compared to the United States, was a secular society. Why did they, mostly church folks, find it necessary to tell me that this was the case? Why did they assume that their perception of Australian societies is actually the way Australian societies are? What were they trying to say? What were they trying to hide? What did they gain by driving a wedge between the secular and the sacred? Were they hiding the influence of religion upon contemporary Australia? Were they disguising the place of religion in the settlement, or should I say invasion, of Australia? Were they telling me that my work is irrelevant because I deal with a religious text but their society is not religious? Does secularity equal to un-religiousness? Were they simply reacting to the fact that I am Tongan, a native of religious cultures whose population is almost all Christian? God forbids that a Tongan should teach, as I have been told, much less teach anything about the Bible.

The irony is that the same people also told me that Australia is a multicultural society, and for six years now, I have been wondering if these friends say that *Australia is secular because it is multicultural*. Do they see Australia as secular because it is multicultural and multifaith? If so, then Australia must be secular because of its non-Christian people, even though non-Christians are people of other faiths. I stand to be corrected. And at this time, I also wish to say that if we come to terms with our religious biases, which are racially motivated, we might realize that multicultural Australia is a religious society. That would enable us to understand how multicultural and multifaith scriptures contribute to the violence in our contemporary society. Let me add that I find the separation of the sacred from the secular most unhelpful and unrealistic.

Thirdly, I presuppose that acts of violence in the scriptures have to do with the exercise of and/or threats to one's power and honour. I see a link between violence and the exercise of power, and I suspect that subjects are more violent when their power/honour is challenged or threatened. The story of Elisha and the group of youth in 2 Kings 2 is an example of violence taking place when the honour of a bald prophet is threatened. In response, he calls forth two she-bears to mangle forty-two youth, for behaving as one expects of them: it is not strange that a group of youth would make fun of older/bald men.[10] When power is threatened, violence escalates; this suggests that violent subjects are not stable or secure because, if they were secure with their shortfalls, and with themselves, they would not have responded with violence.

These presuppositions hover around the issues that I will now address.

Web of biblical violence

At this juncture, I seek to make sense of the structure in which violence is contained and promoted in and by the Bible. I do not intend to justify violence, biblical or otherwise, but to explore how we might come to terms with the place of violence in the Bible and in the name of God. And also, to set a platform for imagining why accounts of violence, or *texts of terror* as Trible calls them, were included and sanctified in the Bible.[11] Trible focused on texts of terror for women, but we must acknowledge that subjects who suffer acts of violence in the Bible have many faces, such as the poor, the foreigners, the strangers, the young, the disabled, the widow, the orphan and so forth.[12]

Let me come to the issue from another angle: Who benefits from texts of terror? For whose interests were texts of terror included in the memories preserved in the Bible? These questions go to show that scriptural texts are written with particular interests in mind. Scriptural texts have agendas—we cannot claim that biblical texts do not have ideologies, as if it is only in their interpretation and application that they become political and violent. If the Bible did not have ideologies and/or the power to construct ideologies, it would not have survived its journey over centuries across many cultures and locations. The Bible is like a hurricane that gathers and grows in strength as it crosses bodies of water and cultures; it is a power-book whose 'power' contributes to its appeal for abuse and violence.

The Bible is political and loaded, hence a potential tool and weapon of violence. By acknowledging that the Bible has particular interests, and realising that readers too are interested, we are urged to read against the grains of texts of terror. To read against the grains of texts of terror is an ethical responsibility. This is the gist of David Clines's call for 'reading from left to right'.[13] Since the two main languages used in the Hebrew Bible, Hebrew and Aramaic, are written from right to left, to 'read from right to left' is to buy into the agenda of the text. But to 'read from left to right' is to read against the grains of the text; this metaphor materialises the call to read 'from the left' in the ideological plane. To read from left to right requires that one shifts one's sympathies, for instance, from Abel to Cain, from Sarai to Hagar, from Jacob to Esau, from Judah to Tamar and Dinah, from Moses and Aaron to Miriam, from Joshua to Rahab, from the Israelites to the Canaanites and the Egyptians, and so forth. The call to read from left to right, against the grains of the text, is therefore an ethical call. It is a call to read on behalf of subjects rejected from the favour of the biblical narrator.

To read from left to right is to undermine the violent agenda of the text, which is not an easy task because 'violence' is one strand woven with many others. I alluded to one of those strands earlier—namely, power and honour—and in the remainder of this chapter I will address the intersection between violence and pleasure, and violence and grief.

Violence and pleasure

There is something pleasurable and obsessive about violence.[14] Violence continues and develops because it gives some kind of pleasure to violent and violating subjects. There are several bridges under this link between violence and pleasure.

Firstly, on a personal level, I am intrigued with the way some of my friends, especially current inmates and ex-convicts, talk with pleasure about their strings of crimes. They know that their crimes are violent, hurtful and wrong, but they recall with fondness the rush of excitement in their violent actions, which blind them to their good conscience, and make them want to do more. Violence is addictive because it is pleasurable. These friends often speak of the itch to 'do one more job' so that they can feel the excitement again. This is not such a strange attitude, for one could easily argue that it is the same kind of bearing that set explorers and colonisers upon the high seas, and those dedicated to extreme sports on their course. There is a rush in doing edgy and dangerous activities; and acts of violence pop one's heart into one's throat. When one does not get the expected rush at one level, one moves to the next, and thus violence develops and accelerates.

Secondly, in sporting events, it is not uncommon for fans to get into fights and brawls sparking violence in relation and response to those events. Boxing and wrestling, for instance, attract many fans, some of whom react with violence, juiced by alcohol and the energy of the crowd of rowdy spectators. Sporting events survive because of the rivalry between fans. These fans see their sport as entertainment, rather than contact sports with violence. Wrestling and boxing are violent but they attract many fans who also see those events as forms of entertainment. The captivating appeal of wrestling and boxing is that fans find them pleasurable, bringing violence and pleasure into the same ring.

Thirdly, leading from the foregoing, is the irruption of *jouissance* which is how Jacques Lacan signifies the condition of bliss, arrival, fulfillment, which can be associated with sexual orgasm but also the attainment of a desired object or condition (for example arriving at a distant land for a voyager, or reaching the top of [to conquer!] a peak for a climber).[15] *Jouissance* (a French term meaning 'enjoyment') is not a purely pleasurable experience but arises through augmenting sensation to a point of discomfort (as in the sexual act, where the cry of passion is indistinguishable from the cry of pain), or as in running a race (which is at once exhausting and pleasurable). To yield to such activities and experiences, another might argue, is to give oneself to the allure of returning to the inorganic primal state that preceded life (so Freudian). As if it is a return to the beginning, which is close to death, bearing the marks of self-sacrifice, or death-drive. *Jouissance,* on the other hand, is a desire to transcend the present condition of lack. It is not about regressing, but transcending, and transgressing, the current state of lack, which an Augustinian might characterise as a fallen state to which we are condemned. *Jouissance* is where enjoyment and agony overlap, penetration merges the cry of passion with the cry of pain, as one breaks through from, transcends, the trapping arms of the present condition of lack. In the light of the foregoing, *jouissance* represents the stage at which violence and pleasure interpenetrate.

While there was tension, encouraged by an evil spirit of Yahweh (*ruah yhwh ra'ah*),[16] between King Saul and King David, two persons anointed to occupy one throne, David had opportunities to kill Saul but he, showing signs of someone basking in *jouissance,* claimed to be extending respect and loyalty to Yahweh's anointed. In the cave where Saul went to relieve himself (MT: 'cover his feet'), when David cut off the corner of Saul's cloak (1 Sam 24), and in the Wilderness of Ziph, when David took the spear and water jar from Saul's head as he was sleeping (1 Sam 26), David did not touch Yahweh's anointed. After both instances, David proclaimed at the hearing of Saul's men that they failed to protect their king but fortunately, he spared him in honour of Yahweh. These are moments of *jouissance,* where David glares in the faces of his enemies!

Fourthly, I briefly turn to Job, the upright person who experienced gratuitous suffering because Yahweh and Ha-Satan agreed on a wager. Ha-Satan had just returned from going back and forth on earth and Yahweh asked him if he noticed how upright Job was. Yahweh's bragging about his devotee sets a cycle of tests into motion, resulting in the destruction of Job's family, for the sake of a wager. Was this [lousy] wager necessary?[17] What did it try to prove? That Job would worship God regardless of the consequences? That Ha-Satan may have failed to notice Job, the kind of person for whom he was supposed to be searching? Most readers would accept Yahweh's evaluation that Job was an upright man. In whose interest, therefore, were the wager and tests conducted? The acceleration of violence from the destruction of properties to the killing of children is narrated as if it was a game in which God did not want to accept the counter-challenge by Ha-Satan, a game that God initiated.

Violence and pleasure intersect and critics hesitate to touch the victimisation of Job. It is less problematic to speak of suffering, whether innocent or otherwise, rather than victimisation—hence suffering becomes the distraction from the violence in the story world—for to do so would expose an abusive God.[18] It is easier to read from the end of the story where Job gets a new family as if to say that his suffering was not for nothing and as if the new family can take the place, and erase the memory, of the one lost earlier. It is also easier to delight in the pleasurable aspects of the story and the wager, and of the debates between Job and his three friends, blinding critics to their violent aspects. To account for these, reading against the grain, might lead one to embrace the solution suggested by Job's wife, 'Curse God, and die!' This is not because death is preferred to suffering, as if Job should submit to the death-drive, but because God deserves cursing, even if this means death. Her willingness to approach death is the point of transgression at the foundation of *jouissance*.

A similar instance in the Hebrew Bible is the account of the plagues in Exodus, where a succession of plagues occur as if they were the works of a malevolent and abusive god. Unlike the story of Job, the plagues have to do with a group of people (Israel) and it involves people from another culture (Egypt). At first, the more hardship the plagues bring upon Egypt the more difficult the oppression of Israel becomes. Egypt was not the only one plagued; Israel was violated as a consequence. Violence has many tentacles, grabbing more than one victim each time.

Whenever I read the account of the plagues in Egypt, I often ask myself: When will the violence stop? When will Yahweh stop hardening Pharaoh's heart so that he may allow Israel to go? It feels as if Yahweh is just fooling around, pulling the strings and enjoying it also, at the expense of Egypt. The outcome is that, so to speak, the screws tighten harder and harder on Israel. According to this view, the violence that fell on Egypt and Israel were pleasurable to Yahweh and Pharaoh; this is the kind of pleasure that draws people to wrestling and boxing matches. Yahweh and Pharaoh were aware of the violence involved, but they were also pleased with the experience!

The pleasure in and of violence is absurd. And if we wish to untangle and overcome violence we need to explore how violence and pleasure might be the effects of the same experience *and* expose the absurdity of that gory kind of pleasure. If we wish to read against the grain of texts of terror, we need also to name and challenge the forms of pleasure that fund them: in the story of Job, this pleasure is in the realisation that God is worshipped for nothing; in the plagues of Egypt, this pleasure is in the fear of the God of Israel.

Violence and grief

I grab in this section the line that Jacques Derrida and Judith Butler tow:[19] Societies that have opportunities and rituals to address and express their grief and mourning are not too violent,[20] and if they are violent, their violence is not extreme. Those societies have channels through which they embrace and unload their pain. Mourning becomes a way of giving relief to grief before it erupts in one's face in various forms of violence. Moreover, when in response to the departure or passing of another, mourning is a way of continuing to be connected, to be in touch with, to speak to, the other who has departed or passed, even though the other is gone, and precisely because that other is gone. Mourning is an opportunity to break through the limits of life, to reach beyond to the one who has departed. On the other hand, societies that discourage mourning also bar the embrace and expression of their grief, and this often bubbles to the point where they burst into extreme forms of violence. Both of these attitudes, the expression and the suppression of grief, are evident in the Bible.

First of all, regarding the expression of grief, voices of lamentation in the Psalter and beyond are windows for people to express their grief and sense of despair:

> How long, O LORD, shall I cry out
> And You not listen,
> Shall I shout to You, 'Violence!'
> And You not save? (Hab 1:2, JPS)

Voices of lamentation break through the barrier between humans and their God, calling the latter into accountability. Unfortunately, some of the voices of lamentation call for extreme actions:

> Fair Babylon, you predator,
> a blessing on him who repays you in kind
> what you have inflicted on us;
> a blessing on him who seizes your babies
> and dashes them against the rocks! (Ps 137:8–9,
> JPS).

One of the challenges therefore is how to confine such severe drives to the realms of grief and mourning so that they do not break through into violent actions. Biblical rules and regulations operate in this groove: in principle, rules and regulations bring into words actions and behaviors that are destructive so if people are mindful of those they can transfer their pain through the laws. When we read laws, unfortunately, we are easily bored and feel restricted, and rightly so. But laws can be openings for unloading ones pain, especially for complainants and the abused, who need to unload pain the most. Ironically, to feel restricted by the laws is to reveal where one stands and what one's privileges are; in other words, laws are restrictive to people with privileges. The sacrificial system operates along the same line: it provides opportunities for worshippers to channel and transfer their guilt and grief to the sacrificed elements.[21]

Secondly, regarding the suppression of grief, I consider the outbreaks of violence as the consequence of suppressed grief. When the Levite, back at his home, dismembered his concubine then sent a limb to each of the tribes of Israel, after having gone to woo her back and end up spending extra nights with his persistent father-in-law, then diverted on the way home, I wonder if his action was the bursting of grief (Jdg 19). He went to bring back his wife, and returned with the body of a fallen woman. We can't determine from the text if she was already dead when he picked her up and placed her on his donkey,[22] so we can't be sure if she was dead or alive when he dismembered her, or when she died, but his excessive behavior suggests a bitter and grieving soul. He was bitter and grieving because of his failure in his mission, he did not return with what he set out to gain, and by the ravaged state of his concubine's body when he reached home. Between Gibeah and home, his bitterness and grief boiled, and then burst upon arrival. If his bloody violent behavior is due to excessive bitterness and grieving, then I can understand it, even though I do not accept it.

The story of Absalom contains another example of the bursting of grief. Amnon, his half-brother, raped Tamar, Absalom's full-sister, and when Absalom heard about it, he suppressed his grief and Tamar's pain and wailing: 'Was it your brother Amnon who did this to you? For the present, sister, keep quiet about it; he is your brother. Don't brood over the matter' (2 Sam 13:20).[23] How can a raped victim, or any other victim, *not* brood over the violence committed? To do what Absalom suggests requires the suppression of a lot of grief. Two years later, excessive violence broke through. Absalom urged his father, who did not accept his invitation, to send Amnon and the other princes to the shearing of his flocks. Absalom organised a party for his brothers, and ordered his attendants to strike and kill Amnon when they see that he is merry with wine. This brought the feud between Absalom and David to a boil, leading to open rebellion, to Absalom laying with his father's concubines 'before the eyes of all Israel' (2 Sam 16:22), and eventually to the tangling death of Absalom in the hands of David's men (see 2 Sam 13:1 – 19:1). There are probably other personal and political reasons why Absalom killed Amnon, but what draws me to this story in this reading is the violence which results from the suppression of grief.

I highlighted in this section the links between violence and grief, in life and in religious texts, and suggest that if we want to uproot violence we must also deal with the grief that gave birth to it *as well as* the grief it causes. There is an interesting example of this in Exodus 22:2–3:

> You shall not ill-treat any widow or orphan. If you do mistreat them, I will heed their outcry as soon as they cry out to Me, and My anger shall blaze forth and I will put you to the sword, and your own wives shall become widows and your children orphans. (JPS)

On the surface, this law protects the widow or orphan, who has already suffered the grief of having lost a husband or parent. But this law has potential to bring about more grief, for the one who breaks it shall be killed and his wives will become widows and his children will be orphans. Grief feeds violence. Violence feeds grief.

In extreme cases such as these, as suggested earlier, one of our challenges is to name, express and contain grief so that excessive violence does not happen. This chapter, if it is not evident yet, has attempted to show that *sacred texts, and their interpretations, play a role in the suppression, expression and restitution of violence*.

Violence does not sit alone

Imagine, if you will, violence as a disfiguring body sitting on a mat, and imagine that we want to throw it out.[24] That will of course involve energy and skill, and our action will be seen as an expression of violence!

Nonetheless, continue imagining: as we approach the mat, we see other bodies sitting alongside, in conversation with, joyfully and irritatingly, laughing and crying with, and against, violence; they have formed a circle, and bonded relationships, so to throw one of them out requires that we face those other bodies.[25] I identified some of these bodies above: sacred texts, interpreters, power, status, gender, security, ritual, religion, pleasure and grief. There are other bodies I have not taken into account, such as the body (who is human? what constitutes life?), the matter of relationality (who is? who belongs?), the issue of cruelty (what gives? what violates?), and so forth.

Imagine then, as we reach down to grab violence in order to throw it out, we hear the other bodies saying, in fact, crying out, 'Wait. Sit. Talk to us first!'

End Notes

1. Judith Butler, *Precarious Life: Powers of Mourning and Violence* (New York: Verso, 2004), xviii–xix.

2. Jacques Derrida, *The Work of Mourning*, edited by Pascale–Anne Brault and Michael Naas (Chicago: University of Chicago Press, 2001), 72.

3. See *The Destructive Power of Religion*, edited by J Harold Ellens, 4 volumes (London: Praeger, 2004); Jack Nelson–Pallmeyer, *Is Religion Killing Us? Violence in the Bible and the Quran* (Harrisburg: Trinity, 2003); John D'Arcy May, *Transcendence and Violence: The Encounter of Buddhist, Christian, and Primal Traditions* (New York: Continuum, 2003).

4. See *Violence Against Women* (Maryknoll, NY: Orbis, 1994), edited by Elisabeth Schüssler Fiorenza and M Shawn Copeland; Marie M Fortune, *Sexual Violence: The Sin Revisited* (Cleveland: Pilgrim, 2005); Aruna Gnanadason, *No Longer a Secret: The Church and Violence Against Women* (Geneva: WCC, 1993).

5. Of course, there are various ways and degrees in which *we may allow contexts to condition* our theological constructions and biblical interpretations!

6. See James G Williams, *The Bible, Violence and the Sacred: Liberation from the Myth of Sanctioned Violence* (San Francisco: Harper, 1992); *Sanctified Aggression: Legacies of Biblical and Postbiblical Vocabularies of Violence*, edited by Jonneke Bekkenkamp and Yvonne Sherwood (London: T&T Clark International, 2003); Phyllis Trible, *Texts of Terror: Literary-feminist Readings of Biblical Narratives* (Philadelphia: Fortress, 1984); Renita J Weems, *Battered Love: Marriage, Sex and Violence in the Hebrew Prophets* (Minneapolis: Fortress, 1995); Cheryl Kirk–Duggan, *Pregnant Passion: Gender, Sex, and Violence in the Bible* (Atlanta: SBL, 2003); Cheryl B Anderson,

Women, Ideology, and Violence: Critical Theory and the Construction of Gender in the Book of the Covenant and the Deuteronomic Law (London: T&T Clark International, 2004); Shelly Matthews, *Violence in the New Testament* (New York: T&T Clark, 2005); René Girard, *Violence and the Sacred*, translated by Patrick Gregory (Baltimore: John Hopkins University, 1977); *Violence Renounced: René Girard, Biblical Studies, and Peacemaking*, edited by Willard M Swartley, (Telford, PA: Pandora, 2000).

7. For a short reading see John J Collins, *Does the Bible Justify Violence?* (Minneapolis: Fortress, 2004).

8. One may view these images at *Biblical Art on the WWW* (http://www.biblical-art.com/index.htm) and *The Gustave Doré Art Collection* (http://dore.artpassions.net/). The images were accessed on these websites on 16 November 2006.

9. See also Patricia M McDonald, *God and Violence: Biblical Resources for Living in a Small World* (Scottdale, Pennsylvania and Waterloo, Ontario: Herald, 2004).

10. See my 'Boring reading, forgotten readers,' *Uniting Church Studies* 10/2 (2004): 22–36.

11. Trible, *Texts of Terror*, *op cit*.

12. We should acknowledge, also, that there are other kinds of texts in the Bible; the Bible is more than its texts of terror.

13. David JA Clines, 'The Ten Commandments, Reading from Left to Right,' in *Words Remembered, Texts Renewed: Essays in Honour of John FA Sawyer*, edited by Jon Davies, Graham Harvey and Wilfred GE Watson (Sheffield: Academic, 1995), 97–112.

14. Another might also argue that pleasure and obsessions ride on the shoulders of violence, but that is the subject for another occasion.

15. See Jacques Lacan, *Ethics of Psychoanalysis, 1959–1960. The Seminar of Jacques Lacan*, edited by Jacques Alain–Miller, translated by Dennis Porter (New York: WW Norton, 1992).

16. The Massoretic Text of 1 Samuel 18:10 and 1 Samuel 19:9 is open for translation. Most translations follow the lead of 1 Sam 16:14 thus rendering these two verses as 'evil spirit of/from Yhwh/Elohim' but they might also be translated as 'spirit of Yhwh/Elohim [is] evil upon Saul'. This alternative translation gives the impression that Yhwh/Elohim is, truly, a jealous God!

17. There are interesting parallels between God's wager with Ha-Satan and the vow that Jephthah makes to God in Judges 10–11, the need for which is also questionable.

18. See David Penchansky, *The Betrayal of God: Ideological Conflict in Job* (Minneapolis: Westminster John Knox, 1991).

19. See especially Derrida, *The Work of Mourning*, *op cit*; Butler, *Precarious Life*, *op cit*.

20. I do not limit grief and mourning to the responses given to the death of another human. I see grief and mourning in responses to other losses in life also, such as departure (to another land) and abuse (in which case one loses 'face' through verbal, psychological and physical insult). Grief and mourning are the stuff of relationality, so they may not be as evident or as valued in cultures of individualism.

21. There are other effects of the legal and sacrificial systems, and the violent and rigid implications of the sacrificial system are absurd, but those are subjects for another place!

22. See Mieke Bal, 'A Body of Writing,' in *A Feminist Companion to Judges*, edited by Athalya Brenner (Sheffield: Sheffield Academic Press, 1993), 208–30.

23. There are other places in the Bible where grief and mourning are discouraged: One way of reading Jesus's comment 'let the dead bury their dead' (Matt 8:22) is to say that Jesus was moving the living away from the dead. Jesus, however, from familial and communal points of view, is insulting to the dead and the departed. Similarly, is the instance when Jesus refuses to receive a visit from his family but responds that his mother and siblings are those that do the will of his father (Matt 12, Mk 3, Lk 8). These comments are insulting especially since Jesus announced them in the hearing of the public.

24. See also *Nurturing Peace: Theological Reflections on Overcoming Violence*, edited by Deenabandhu Manchala (Geneva: WCC, 2005).

25. As practitioners of intertextuality and transtextuality affirm, no text sits alone so the sea of texts and stories needs to be addressed in their intertwining structures.

Words of Death: Scriptures and Violence in Judaism, Christianity and Islam

Christopher D Stanley

In the aftermath of 9/11,[1] many people in the United States embraced the idea that Islam is a violent religion whose holy book, the Qur'an, impels Muslims to use violence to take over the world and impose their beliefs on others. This view of Islam was especially common on the radio programs and Web pages of Protestant Fundamentalists, but it also made its way onto the editorial pages of many American newspapers. Most non-Muslims in the United States know very little about either Islam or the Qur'an, so statements like these from sources that they trust played a key role in shaping American opinion about Islam in the post-9/11 era.

It is therefore understandable that many American Muslims would have felt threatened and defensive about their religion during the last few years. Immediately after 9/11, numerous local and national Muslim leaders condemned the actions of the hijackers, arguing that such acts of violence were inconsistent with the tenets of Islam and the teachings of the Qur'an. Most drew a sharp distinction between 'true Islam', which they described as a religion of peace, and the misuse of Islam by radical Islamists like Osama bin Laden, whom they accused of twisting the words of the Qur'an to justify acts of political violence. This interpretation of the hijackers' actions was embraced by many in the news media and the political arena who, to their credit, wished to defuse the knee-jerk anti-Muslim sentiment that flared up in many sectors of American society after 9/11.

At the same time there were many Americans—mostly political conservatives, but some on the left as well—who found it difficult to accept this view of the situation. Some were driven by religious prejudice. In the eyes of many conservative Protestants, for example, Islam is a 'bad religion' because it rejects the central Christian doctrine that Jesus is the divine Son of God who brought salvation to all humanity (including Muslims) through his atoning death on the cross. Many in this group believe that Muslims are plotting to take over the world and stamp out Christianity. People like this see no reason to investigate what the Qur'an says about violence—Islam is a demonic religion, so no one should be surprised when its followers engage in violent acts.

Others who reject this narrow-minded view of Islam have found reason to question the oft-repeated claim that the acts of the 9/11 hijackers and other violent Islamists represent a distortion of the 'peaceful' religion of Islam. Some have pointed to verses in the Qur'an that appear to sanction or even encourage acts of violence, while others have noted how violence was used to establish, extend, and protect the Islamic empire during the centuries that it dominated the Middle East and to resist and overthrow colonial rulers in more recent times. In reply, Muslims have often claimed that the Qur'an approves of violence only when it is used to defend fellow Muslims or the Muslim community. But this view fails on two counts: it cannot explain the use of violence by Muslim states against one another during the era of the caliphate, and it overlooks the claims of violent Islamists like Osama bin Laden that they are in fact fighting in defence of the Muslim people in Palestine, in Iraq, and around the globe.

While I understand the desire of Muslims and their defenders (among whom I count myself) to minimise the violent aspects of their tradition and to highlight verses from the Qur'an that call for peace and non-violence, I question the long-term wisdom of this strategy. As non-Muslims learn more about Islam and the Qur'an, they cannot avoid noticing the many verses in the Qur'an that call for the followers of Allah to take up arms against non-Muslims, nor can they overlook the important role that Arab warriors played in the early expansion of Islam. In the face of these realities, the claim that Islam is a 'religion of peace' comes across as one-sided at best. Some even see it as a conscious attempt at deception, a ploy that reinforces their negative impressions of Islam.

A more fruitful approach would be to point out that religious violence is not a distinctively Muslim phenomenon. Virtually all sacred texts include verses that directly or indirectly justify certain expressions of violence, often by relating them to the will of a deity. Such ideas are usually grounded in the central tenets of the religion. In other words, violence in the name of God is not an abuse of religion; violence lies close to the heart of virtually all religious traditions.

Of course, this is not the whole story. Most religions also call on their followers to act lovingly toward others, to bear abuse with patience, to forgive when they are wronged, and to repay evil with good. Some even encourage their members to work for world peace, though not as many as we might suppose. But none of this changes the cold, hard reality that religious people have historically used sacred texts to incite or justify acts of violence.

Today, most religious leaders prefer to downplay the violent side of their tradition and emphasise their support for peace. As a result, their followers often develop a one-sided view of their own tradition that makes them quick to judge people from other religions who claim to have divine support for acts of violence. Many suspect that something must be wrong with a religion whose followers could engage in such dreadful acts. Yet these same people are often among the first to offer religious justifications for violence when they are convinced that their own religion, people, or nation is under attack.

In our ever-shrinking global village, it is vitally important that the followers of different religions should labour to understand one another rather than papering over their differences with shallow assertions of commonality if there is to be any hope of humans living together in peace. This includes trying to understand how and why people use sacred texts to justify acts of violence. Until we face this problem head-on, the world will continue to be locked in an endless cycle of misunderstanding, suspicion, prejudice, hatred, and retaliation. A village cannot long endure if its inhabitants cannot find a way to live together despite their differences.

In this chapter, I will offer a frank examination of the various ways in which Jews, Christians, and Muslims have used the words of scripture to justify and even encourage acts of violence. For the most part I will limit myself to highlighting key verses that have been used for this purpose and commenting on how these texts have influenced the beliefs and actions of Jews, Christians, and Muslims over the centuries. In a second chapter, I will explore some of the ways in which the followers of all three religions have sought to neutralise the violent passages in their scriptures and to promote peaceful, or at least non-violent, interactions with people outside their community.

I do not pretend to be an expert on moral theology, nor do I plan to offer any specific guidance to Jews, Christians, or Muslims about how they should handle the violent elements of their scriptural traditions. But I do hope that the material that I will be presenting in this chapter and the next will prove useful to Jews, Christians, and Muslims who are seeking to follow the path of non-violence in a world where violence is far too often justified by religious claims.

Violence in the Jewish scriptures

Since Judaism is the oldest of the three religions to be studied here, I will turn first to the Jewish scriptures. This analysis is complicated by the fact that Christians, along with Jews, honour the Jewish scriptures as a vital resource for moral reflection. As early as the fourth century CE, Christian leaders were quoting from the 'Old Testament' (the Christian term for the Jewish scriptures) to justify the use of violence by the newly Christianised Roman Empire, including the forcible suppression of non-Christian religions. Since that time, texts from the Old Testament have played a vital role in Christian debates over the moral status and limits of individual and corporate violence.

Jewish interpreters, by contrast, had no formal access to state power from the first century CE until the creation of the state of Israel in the mid-twentieth century. As a result, most of their debates over the morality of violence have centred on questions of personal conduct. Since the early twentieth century, however, Jewish religious and political leaders in the land of Israel have been forced to grapple with many of the same moral problems that challenged Christian leaders over the centuries. Following the lead of their ancestors, they turned to scripture for guidance.

Jews and Christians have not always agreed about which texts are relevant to the problem of violence or how these texts should be interpreted. But since both groups were reading the same materials, it was inevitable that they would come up with many of the same answers to the questions that troubled them. The following pages highlight some of the key biblical verses and motifs that have influenced Jewish and Christian thinking about the moral validity of violence. The presentation will follow the order in which the texts appear in the canon rather than the order in which they were composed.

The creation narratives

The first act of violence in the Hebrew Bible/Old Testament is performed not by humans, but by God. In Genesis 3:21–24, God kills some unidentified animals in order to make clothing for Adam and Eve, then drives the couple out of the garden and sets an angel with a sword at its entrance to kill them if they try to enter. Two themes concerning the use of violence are introduced here: violence toward animals and the violence of God.

Violence toward animals

Nowhere in the Hebrew Bible (or in the Christian scriptures, for that matter) do we find any indication that the killing of animals was regarded as a moral problem. While it is true that the deity offers the first humans only plants to eat (Gen 1:30), nothing is ever made of this limitation, and the post-flood generation is explicitly told that they may kill and eat the flesh of animals (Gen 9:1–4). The practice of sacrificing animals to the deity is also said to have begun at this time (Gen 8:20–21), though it is not until the Exodus era that Yahweh actually commands the ritual killing of animals (Exod 12:3–13). The Torah not only includes regulations for the conduct of animal sacrifices but also mandates that animals should be killed if they cause serious harm to humans (for example Exod 21:28–32). Such texts imply that the lives of humans are more valuable than those of animals. Not until the last few decades have Jewish and Christian animal rights activists begun to raise questions about the moral propriety of using violence against animals, with some quoting verses from the Torah that require the humane treatment of animals (Exod 23:12; Deut 22:6–7, 22:10, 25:4). The cessation of animal sacrifices in Judaism and Christianity resulted not from any moral reticence about the killing of animals but rather from shifts in ideology that occurred with the destruction of the Temple (Judaism) and the death of Jesus (Christianity). Muslims still perform ritual sacrifices at certain festivals.

The violence of God

A second important theme that emerges for the first time in Genesis 3 and continues throughout the Hebrew Bible is the violence of God. Again and again the God of Israel is portrayed as an instigator of violence, whether directly (acting on his own behalf) or indirectly (commanding humans to perform violent acts in his name). Examples of direct violence by the deity include the Genesis flood, which wiped out every living thing on earth; the destruction of Sodom and Gomorrah; the plagues on the land of Egypt; the repeated punishments of the Exodus generation in the desert; and various famines and droughts that the biblical prophets attributed to the hand of the deity. Indirect divine violence can be seen in the numerous laws that require the imposition of the death penalty for various offenses as well as stories in which God is said to have ordered the armies of Israel (or their enemies) to go to war and leave no survivors.

To be sure, the Hebrew Bible also contains passages that question the moral propriety of divine violence, as when Abram tries to talk

God out of destroying the cities of Sodom and Gomorrah (Gen 19:22–33; cf Moses in Exod 32:11–14) or when the psalmist complains of God's apparent injustice in allowing Israel's enemies to run roughshod over his people (Pss 44, 74, 80; cf Job 23:1–17, 30:16 – 31:40). For the most part, however, the biblical authors seem to regard violence as an essential feature of the deity's administration of the universe, comparable to the violence used by police officers and judges in their efforts to maintain order and justice in human societies. Unlike human authorities, however, the God of the Bible is a sovereign ruler who can do whatever he pleases with the created order, including humans. Since he is also a righteous deity, humans are left with no legitimate grounds for questioning the violence of God.

The ancestral narratives

The next major story cycle in the Hebrew Bible centres on the patriarchs and matriarchs of ancient Israel. For the most part these ancestors of Israel are portrayed as non-violent shepherds who reside on the margins of Canaanite society. The only instance of armed violence occurs when Abraham musters his servants to rescue his nephew Lot after Lot is taken captive by invading armies (Gen 14:13–16). This episode is not often cited by either Jewish or Christian authorities when discussing the legitimacy of violence, but it offers the first example of a moral principle that is taken for granted elsewhere in the Hebrew Bible—the validity of violence that is carried out to protect others from harm (Exod 17:8–16; Josh 10:1–15). The biblical narratives are filled with stories of kings and other leaders who use force to defend the people of Israel from attack, and no moral reservations are ever voiced about such actions. Stories like these were cited by Augustine and other Christian theologians to justify the use of defensive violence by Christian states in the face of centuries of Christian teaching that insisted that violence must be met with non-violence. Similar lines of reasoning led to the development of the Christian 'just war' tradition.

Jews have theoretically accepted the right of self-defence since biblical times. In practice they have usually relied on non-violent strategies when attacked, since the Jewish people have lived under foreign rule for much of their history and encountered stern repression on the few occasions when they tried to use violence to defend themselves. Matters changed in the twentieth century as Jewish immigrants who had taken up residence in Palestine began to form self-defence forces to protect them from attacks by the local Arab population. From 1948 onward, the newly formed state of Israel was compelled to fight to defend its existence. Jewish rabbis gave their blessings to these actions with rulings that cited biblical justifications for self-defence. Since the 1967 war, the Israeli government has consistently depicted its repression of the Palestinians as a form of self-defence against actual or potential attackers.

Additional justification for the use of violence by Israeli leaders was found in several biblical passages that described the entire territory of Israel as God's gift to Abraham's descendants (Gen 12, 15, 22). Many contemporary Jews have argued that this gift carries with it a duty to use violence if necessary to protect the land from anyone who seeks to interfere with Jewish control over the historic territory of Israel. Included in their number are many religious Zionists (both Jews and conservative Christians) who regard the creation of the state of Israel as the literal fulfillment of biblical prophecies that speak of the return of the Jewish people to their homeland prior to the coming of the Messiah. Both arguments can be heard within the Israeli settler movement, some of whose members have also called for the forcible removal of all non-Jews from the land of Israel. Christian Zionists have also cited these arguments to support their calls for massive US military aid to the Israeli government and unquestioning US support for Israeli actions against the Palestinians.

The Exodus narrative

The Exodus narrative is the most important story in the Hebrew Bible, as evidenced not only by its central position within the books of Torah but also by the dozens of times that the story is mentioned outside the four books in which it is recounted. The Exodus narrative has been paradigmatic for Jewish self-understanding since ancient times, providing authoritative guidance for both individual and social conduct. Much later, the story was taken over by Christians who viewed it as a prototype of the salvation that God would bring to humanity through Jesus Christ. In both communities the story has been used to justify various forms of violence in the name of God.

Violence toward outsiders

The Exodus narrative draws a sharp distinction between the people of God and outsiders. Outsiders are consistently depicted as a threat to the political and religious survival of Israel. Several texts warn against making treaties or alliances with them, and some call for outsiders to be destroyed (Exod 23:23–33; Num 33:50–56; Deut 7:1–6, 7:21–26, 12:1–3, 13:16–18). Texts such as these have helped to

foster xenophobic attitudes among both Jews and Christians over the
centuries, encouraging suspicion, fear, and hatred of other peoples and
thus contributing to the likelihood of violence.

Further support for such attitudes can be found in the fact that
the Exodus story never questions the propriety of violence toward
outsiders. In fact, most of the violence against other groups is performed
or aided by the deity. Examples include the ten plagues against Egypt
(which culminate in the God of Israel drowning Pharaoh's armies in
the sea) and the assistance that Yahweh gives to the armies of Israel
in their wars with foreign peoples on the way to the 'Promised Land'
of Canaan (Num 21:21–35, 31:1 – 32:42; Deut 2:26 – 3:22). Stories
such as these exercised a powerful influence on the imaginations of
black slaves in the American South, leading some to engage in violent
rebellions in the hope that God would intervene and rescue them from
their oppressors. More recently, the story of Yahweh delivering his
people from bondage has been cited by Christian leaders in Latin
America, and elsewhere, to motivate their followers to participate
in insurrections and wars of liberation under the banner of liberation
theology. Moreover, Jews and Christians alike have made frequent use
of the many Torah passages in which God promises to give military
victories to his people as long as they faithfully obey his laws (Lev
26:3–8; Deut 7:16, 11:22–25, 28:7–10).

Violence toward insiders
The Exodus narrative also contains many stories and laws that support
the use of violence against individuals who do not faithfully adhere to
Yahweh's decrees. Some speak of Yahweh acting on his own to punish
the offender (Num 11:33–34, 14:20–32, 16:23–50; Deut 28:15–46),
while others call for societal leaders, or the community as a whole,
to impose violent forms of discipline (Exod 32:25–29; Num 25:6–8;
Deut 13:1–11). Included in the latter category are a host of offenses for
which capital punishment is mandated—not only assault and murder,
but also adultery, practising foreign religions, working on Saturday,
and cursing one's parents. All of these acts of disciplinary violence are
linked to the holy and righteous character of Yahweh, who requires a
morally and ritually pure people to serve as his covenant partners.

Over the centuries, these stories and laws have been cited again
and again to justify the infliction of violent punishments upon people
who had failed or refused to follow the rules of societies that used
the Bible as a guide, including the torture and execution of heretics,
witches, homosexuals, and other notorious offenders. Women, too,

have suffered violent abuse for resisting male efforts to control their sexuality on the basis of these laws (cf Num 5:11–31; Deut 22:13–30). Such legalised forms of violence have been performed more often by Christians than by Jews, since Jewish communities have lacked the legal authority to impose violent punishments since the first century CE, though they were free to use informal forms of violence against violators of the Torah. More recently, the biblical system of justice played a role in shaping the criminal laws of the renewed state of Israel, including the imposition of capital punishment for certain offenses.

Conquest narratives

The story of the conquest of Canaan, as narrated in the book of Joshua, can be viewed as a continuation of the Exodus narrative, since it tells how the people of Israel ended up in the 'Promised Land' of Palestine after Yahweh had condemned their parents' generation to wander and die in the desert (Num 14:20–35). The conquest story extends the violence of the Exodus narrative into a new era, recounting battle after battle in which the Israelites emerge victorious because Yahweh is fighting on their side, punishing the previous inhabitants of the land for their repeated violations of his will. (How these people were supposed to have known the will of the God of Israel is never explained). Again and again the narrator reports that the Israelites slaughtered all of the inhabitants of the cities that they conquered, following the commands that Yahweh had given to their parents in the desert (Josh 6:20–21, 8:24–29, 10:20–21, 10:28–43, 11:1–23).

These stories of divinely ordered genocide, reinforced by similar verses in the Exodus narrative (especially the book of Deuteronomy), have been cited again and again by Christian warriors and colonists to legitimise the often hideous forms of violence that they inflicted upon the inhabitants of the lands that they wished to conquer, including murder, rape, forced removal, and enslavement. Identifying themselves as God's 'chosen people' and the local natives as 'Canaanites' allowed them to behave in ways that they would never have dreamed of doing under other circumstances. Similar reasoning led them to create repressive programs to stamp out non-Christian religious practices among the peoples whom they had conquered, following Yahweh's commands to destroy all of the Canaanites' objects of worship so that they would not pollute or corrupt the people of God (Exod 34:11–16; Num 33:50–56; Deut 7:1–6, 7:21–26, 12:1–3). Ironically, some

Christians cited these same verses as justification for purging their 'Christian nations' of Jewish influences.

For Jews, by contrast, the only practical value of these stories lay in their call for God's people to remain separate from their pagan neighbours, since for most of their history they lacked the power to engage in the violent repression of other groups. As Jews began migrating to Palestine in large numbers during the early decades of the twentieth century some of the members of the religious Zionist movement began to refer to Arabs and Palestinians as 'Canaanites' and to call for their forced removal or destruction. This kind of thinking helped to pave the way for a series of violent attacks against Palestinian villages that forced hundreds of thousands of civilians to flee the land of Israel during the 1948 war. Today, similar language can be heard from members of the Israeli settler movement who dream of removing all Palestinians from the Israeli-controlled West Bank area of Palestine, which they see as a vital part of 'biblical Israel'. So far, the Israeli government has not embraced these radical proposals, but the very presence of such modes of thinking has helped to increase the level of suspicion, fear, and violence between Israeli Jews and Palestinians over the last few decades.

Historical books
The rest of the so-called 'historical books' of the Hebrew Bible add little to the ideas that we have encountered thus far, though the matter-of-fact tone in which they report acts of murder, rape, assault, and military conquest helps to reinforce the impression that violence is a normal part of human life. Some of the violence in these books is performed by the deity (2 Sam 24:15–17; 1 Kgs 13:20–24; 2 Kgs 2:23–25, 17:24–25), but most of it is carried out by humans. Here and there we read about acts of violence that rebound negatively on the perpetrators (Jdg 20:1–48; 2 Sam 4:1–12; 1 Kgs 2:5–9, 21:17–24), but in nearly every case, the negative outcome reflects a divine judgment upon the moral or religious conduct of the actors, not a criticism of violence itself. In fact, more often than not, the violent act is punished by another act of violence.

Like the other books that we have examined, the 'historical books' contain narratives in which Yahweh guides the armies of Israel to victory, and stories in which violence is used to suppress religious practices, that run counter to the will of Yahweh. For the first time we read about the deity using foreign armies to punish his people for their sins (cf 2 Kgs 17:1–23, 21:10–15; 2 Chr 36:15–21), but this outcome had already been 'predicted' in the Exodus narrative (for example Lev 26:14–33; Deut 4:25–27, 8:19–20, 28:25–26, 28:49–57, 32:19–25). For the most part, these books simply offer additional examples of the kinds of divinely sanctioned violence that we have seen elsewhere in the Hebrew Bible, lending yet more credence to the arguments of Jews and Christians who wish to use the Bible to justify violence and warfare in the name of God.

Prophetic books
The idea of God using violence to punish people for their sins reaches its zenith in the prophetic books of the Hebrew Bible. In the earlier books, Yahweh threatens to send foreign armies to inflict painful sufferings upon his people; in the later books he promises to do the same to their enemies. Most of the prophets speak of human armies serving as the instruments of God's wrath, though some envision Yahweh acting on his own to fulfill his violent purposes. Now and then we hear a voice asking how these actions might affect the innocent citizens of the nations that are destined to suffer, but most of the time the prophets speak as though everyone is guilty and worthy of judgment. Military violence is the deity's weapon of choice, but we also hear of Yahweh manipulating the dark forces of nature (famines, sickness, etc.) in order to motivate his people to repent (Is 13:6–13; Jer 24:1–13; Hos 2:9–13; Amos 5:9–12).

Passages such as these have been cited repeatedly by Jews and Christians in their efforts to explain wartime losses, natural disasters, and other unexpected forms of suffering. In the last few years, conservative Christian leaders have interpreted the AIDS epidemic, the 9/11 attacks, the Pacific tsunami, and the flooding of New Orleans by hurricane Katrina as divine judgments against people who were not properly serving God. At least one Jewish rabbi has claimed that Ariel Sharon's debilitating stroke was a sign of divine displeasure with his decision to withdraw Israeli settlers from the Gaza Strip in 2005. Many Jews and Christians have come to view the Israeli army as an instrument of divine judgment when it engages in violent actions against Palestinians and others who are suspected of causing harm to Israel. Claims such as these add further fuel to the fires of violence that threaten to consume the Middle East.

Book of Psalms
The Book of Psalms is viewed by many Jews and Christians as a peaceful book because it elicits feelings of peace and comfort when

they read it. In reality, the book is saturated with violence. Much of the violence is similar to what we have observed thus far, including repeated claims that Yahweh will assist the king (or occasionally his enemies) in battle or send violent judgments upon his people. But the Book of Psalms also includes many passages that speak of violence between individuals, with the psalmists describing the physical and emotional sufferings that they have endured from others and calling on Yahweh to inflict gruesome punishments upon their tormentors in return (Ps 10:12–16, 28:3–5, 35:1–6, 58:6–11, 69:22–28, 137:7–9). Several of these psalms include vivid descriptions of the joy that the sufferers will feel when they witness Yahweh taking vengeance upon their enemies. In a similar way, many of the psalms of praise celebrate Yahweh's mighty victories over his enemies, both natural and supernatural (Ps 2:4–11, 9:3–6, 21:8–12, 29:3–9, 68:7–23, 110:5–7). Invariably these 'enemies of Yahweh' turn out to be people or forces that are thought to pose a threat to the psalmist and/or his people and are therefore worthy of divine punishment.

All of these texts presuppose the common biblical image of a violent deity who inflicts pain and suffering upon those who fail to do his will or who threaten the peace or survival of his people. In the context of the psalms, these images serve to legitimise and even intensify the violent thoughts and feelings that most people have toward those whom they view as personal or national threats. This potent mixture of religious devotion and violence has made the Book of Psalms a powerful source of inspiration for Jews and Christians who wish to justify their participation in war and other forms of violence, since they can claim that their actions are part of a divine plan to inflict punishment upon the enemies of God. Framing the situation in this way also makes it easier for them to convince others that God is on their side and will guide their forces to victory and provide for the faithful who fall in battle.

Apocalyptic texts
Undoubtedly the most violent materials in the Hebrew Bible are the texts that scholars call 'apocalyptic', a term derived from the Greek word *apocalupsis*, which means 'uncovering' or 'revealing' (Dan 7–12; Is 24–27; Zech 9–14, etc). The authors of apocalyptic texts claim to be revealing special insights that Yahweh has given them to deliver to his people, who are usually portrayed as suffering oppression from other nations that are more powerful than they are. Unlike the books of the prophets, apocalyptic texts insist that behind the human oppressors

of God's people stand invisible demonic forces that are engaged in a cosmic battle against Yahweh and his angels. Using vivid imagery and complex symbolism, apocalyptic writings seek to assure God's people that Yahweh will soon intervene with devastating violence to punish their oppressors (and the evil forces that assist them) and reward his people for their faithfulness under trial (cf Dan 7:11–12; Is 24:1–3; Zech 14:12–15). Until then, they are to wait patiently for God to act.

Apocalyptic texts do not encourage their audiences to take up arms against their oppressors, but they do assume that violence must eventually be repaid with (divine) violence. The image of Yahweh as a warrior and judge appears frequently in the Hebrew Bible, but the apocalyptic concept that the earth is a battleground between supernatural forces of good and evil is a new development in Israelite reflection on the nature of the universe. Implicit in this pattern of thinking is the conviction that God's enemies must be crushed in order for justice to prevail; negotiation and compromise have no place in a conflict with the personified forces of evil.

The apocalyptic view of reality has exercised a profound influence on the attitudes and imaginations of Jews and Christians across the centuries. Especially troubling is the subtle manner in which it grants divine legitimacy to the natural human tendency to demonise and dehumanise one's enemies. Examples of such attitudes can be multiplied, ranging from Adolph Hitler's successful efforts to portray the Jews as the demonic enemies of Germany to Ronald Reagan's identification of the Soviet Union as the 'evil empire' to George W Bush's labeling of Iran, Libya, and North Korea as the 'Axis of Evil'. Identifying a people or nation as the earthly embodiment of evil is one of the most effective ways for religious and political leaders to garner public support for the use of violence against their enemies. Some Jews and Christians have even gone so far as to stockpile weapons and make other plans for the great battle that they believe will take place at the time when God acts to bring justice to the earth. Most of these activities have proved to be harmless, but some have ended in violent conflicts with local authorities. Included with the Jews and Christians are the Essenes, whose community centre near the Dead Sea was destroyed by the invading Romans in 68 CE; the Peasant's Revolt, which left thousands of people dead across Germany at the time of the Reformation; and the Branch Davidians of Waco, Texas, whose members died in a fiery attack by American law enforcement authorities in the mid-1990s.

Violence in the Christian scriptures

Since Christianity originated as a sect of Judaism, it was inevitable that the Jewish scriptures (under the Christian rubric of 'Old Testament') would play an important role in shaping the beliefs and attitudes of Christians toward the use of violence. Christians have struggled over the centuries to figure out the best way to integrate the teachings of the two sets of texts, with some placing more emphasis on the older books, others on the newer collection, and still others trying to strike some kind of balance between the two. Since we have already examined how the Jewish scriptures influenced Christian thinking about violence, this section will be limited to verses in the Christian 'New Testament' that have been or could be used to justify acts of violence.

Jesus and violence

In recent years, Jesus has gained a reputation as a preacher of peace, love, and non-violence. This is a significant shift from earlier centuries, when Christians routinely cited the name of Jesus to justify the use of violence. Those who adopted this position were not ignoring the portrait of Jesus in the Gospels; they simply chose to emphasise those passages in which Jesus used violent imagery to describe what God was doing in his ministry. The parables in particular are filled with language that assigns a positive moral value to the use of violence, both divine and human. Other verses from the Gospels have also been used by Christians to support their calls for violence.

The violence of God

Many of Jesus' 'Kingdom of God' parables describe an impending judgment in which God will reward the followers of Jesus and punish the wicked with dreadful torments (for example, Matt 11:20–24, 13:41–42, 25:41–46). Nowhere in these parables does Jesus suggest that his followers should engage in violence to aid God in the task of judgment, but his language does imply a radical division of humanity into 'good guys' and 'bad guys'. Twenty centuries of Christian history have shown how easily this dehumanising mindset can be used to justify violence against people who are deemed 'evil' and therefore worthy of divine punishment. Some of the parables also show the deity (in the guise of one of the main characters) engaging in vengeful actions towards characters who have offended him (cf Mk 12:1–9; Matt 18:32–35, 22:7; Lk 19:20–24). No great imagination is required to see how such stories could be used to justify violent acts of vengeance by Christians against those who have caused them harm.

The violence of Jesus

The Gospels also contain several passages in which Jesus himself acts in a violent or threatening manner. In back-to-back episodes, Jesus drove a group of money-changers and animal vendors out of the temple courts (Matt 21:12–13; cf Jn 2:15, where he used a whip) and then cursed and killed a fig tree (Matt 21:18–22). Soon afterwards, he verbally abused the Pharisees and legal experts, condemning them all to hell (Matt 23:13–36). Earlier in the narrative he stated that he has come to bring not peace, but a sword (Matt 10:34–36), and according to Luke's Gospel, he told his followers to buy swords a few hours before he was arrested (Lk 22:35–38). Whether these narratives are historically reliable is beside the point; all that matters is that Christians across the centuries have taken them as valid images of Jesus. Passages such as these have made it easier for Christians to argue that they were following the example of Jesus when they use violence to support a cause that they regard as 'righteous'.

Divine violence outside the Gospels

Outside the Gospels, the New Testament contains numerous images of a violent deity giving vent to his wrath against his enemies. Several of the sermons in the Book of Acts speak of a coming judgment in which God will violently punish humans who fail to acknowledge him (for example Acts 10:42, 13:40–41, 17:30–31). This judgment is exemplified in the story of a man named Ananias and his wife Sapphira, who are struck dead when they lie to the apostles about what they did with the proceeds of a property sale (Acts 5:1–6). Paul's letters, too, speak repeatedly about the coming judgment of God (for example Rom 2:5–11; 1 Cor 3:10–17; 1 Th 5:1–3; 2 Th 1:6–10), as do most of the other books of the New Testament (Heb 10:26–31; 2 Pet 3:8–10, etc). Images of divine violence are especially common in the book of Revelation, which anticipates a time when God will inflict untold pain and suffering upon those who refuse to acknowledge him. The same book depicts Jesus as a mighty warrior who will conquer all of God's enemies, either destroying them or casting them into a lake of fire to be tormented (Rev 6:1–17, 8:6–12, 9:13–21, 16:1–21, 19:11–21, 20:7–15). Like the apocalyptic texts of the Jewish Bible, none of these passages call on humans to engage in violence; judgment is left in the hands of the deity. But this has not stopped Christians over the centuries from identifying their enemies as God's enemies and their armies as the tools of God's judgment against sinful and wicked humanity.

Paul and violence

In addition to images of divine violence, Paul's letters contain several
verses in which the apostle voices threats against people in his churches
who are not properly adhering to his teachings and outsiders whom he
thinks are misleading them. As a rule, he refrains from stating what
kinds of actions he might take against them (1 Cor 4:18–21; 2 Cor
10:1–6, 13:1–4), though in a couple of instances, he mentions the
possibility of throwing people out of the church (1 Cor 5:1–5; 2 Th
3:14–15). Most likely, Paul did not intend to use physical violence,
but his language certainly helped to lay the ideological foundation
for later Christians who laid violent punishments upon people who
refused to accept the teachings of the church, including imprisonment,
torture, and painful execution.

Christians and Jews

Finally, the New Testament contains a number of passages that depict
Jews who reject the Christian message in a negative light and either
declare or imply that they will be judged by God at some point in the
future (Matt 27:25; Jn 5:15–18, 8:39–59; Acts 13:44–47; 1 Th 2:14–16;
Rev 2:9–10). As early as the second century CE, Christians were using
these texts to demonise the Jewish people as enemies of God who stand
under God's curse. By the end of the fourth century, Christians were
wielding the power of the Roman state to limit the rights of Jews, and
by the Middle Ages they were actively persecuting Jews in a series of
violent pogroms that waxed and waned for centuries in the countries of
Europe. Christians also created and embraced a variety of anti-Jewish
slanders that added fuel to the fires of religious persecution. The
violence of the Holocaust, though not explicitly linked to Christianity,
was the natural outgrowth of centuries of anti-Jewish propaganda that
had its roots in the sacred texts of Christianity.

Violence in the Muslim scriptures

As we noted earlier, many non-Muslims seem to think that the Qur'an
is filled with verses that call for Muslims to wage an unremitting 'holy
war' against the non-Muslim world in an effort to forcibly convert or
eliminate all non-Muslims from the planet and set up a worldwide
Muslim empire. This view of Islam is commonly derided as ludicrous
by people who are familiar with the teachings of Muslim scholars.
Yet the fact remains that there are Muslim leaders today whose
public pronouncements lend credence to this stereotype of Islam, and
many ordinary Muslims appear to sympathise with their views. It is

not uncommon to hear such people citing verses from the Qur'an in support of their ideas.

Is this a valid reading of the Qur'an? The Qur'an does contain many verses in which the deity either commands or permits acts of violence, along with many others that depict God as a violent judge, as in the Jewish and Christian scriptures. Yet violence is no more central to the Qur'an than to the sacred texts of Judaism or Christianity. The illusion of difference arises from the fact that the Qur'an lacks the kind of narrative framework that ties together the Jewish and Christian scriptures. Verses pertaining to violence are scattered throughout the Qur'an with little or no indication of the circumstances in which they arose, making it difficult to judge whether particular statements should be taken as timeless expressions of God's will or as limited messages for specific historical situations. The fact that the Qur'an is framed as first-person speech also gives its pronouncements a timeless quality that distinguishes it from the Jewish and Christian texts. This first-person mode of address has led many non-Muslims (and some Muslims) to conclude that every verse in the Qur'an is meant to be applied universally and without limitation, including its calls for violence.

This approach to the Qur'an ignores the centuries-long scholarly tradition of Islam. Islamic tradition insists that the Qur'an was revealed verbally to Muhammad, but Muslim scholars have a long history of linking the various sayings of the Qur'an to specific 'occasions of revelation' and interpreting them in light of their original setting. This is especially true for the verses that call for violence. Muslim scholars disagree about how and when this interpretive principle should be applied, but its validity is widely accepted. Scholars also disagree about how particular passages should be interpreted in relation to other texts in the Qur'an. As a result, there is no single Muslim interpretation of the Qur'an, including its verses on violence. The best that we can hope to do here is to identify some of the major themes and sayings that have led Muslims over the centuries to endorse the use of violence.

Divine violence
Like the Jewish and Christian scriptures, the Qur'an is replete with verses that depict the deity as a divine judge who inflicts painful punishments upon humans (primarily Muslims) who refuse to follow his commands (1:3, 2:7, 2:39, 2:104, 4:10, 4:30, 4:56, 4:140, 6:6, 6:47–49, 7:4–5, 10:4, 45:7–11). As with the other texts, the Qur'an characterises these violent judgments as the deeds of a righteous God

who is committed to upholding the moral order of the universe, not the random and arbitrary actions of a violent deity. Most of the verses in question pertain to a final judgment that will take place at some unspecified date in the future when the wicked will suffer painful torments in hell, though there are also verses that claim that sinners will suffer while on earth, whether at the hands of God or his people. As in the Jewish and Christian texts, these sayings do not actively encourage humans to engage in violence, but they do predispose Muslims to divide humanity into 'good guys' (those who serve Allah) and 'bad guys' (everyone else) and to view non-Muslims (and more 'liberal' Muslims) through a lens of suspicion, fear, and judgment. As we observed earlier, this kind of dehumanising mindset helps to make violence more palatable to the members of any religion.

Defensive violence

The Qur'an also contains many verses that allow for or even command the use of violence in self-defence, whether individually or collectively (for example 2:216–18, 2:190–94, 9:12–15, 9:36, 22:39–40). Muslim scholars relate these verses to the days when the followers of Muhammad were few in number and faced persecutions and attacks from other Arabs that threatened their survival. Once the community was established, verses such as these were used to justify more aggressive forms of violence, including warfare, on the grounds that such acts were meant to defend the Muslim community from real or potential threats. Similar arguments can be heard today from many violent Islamists who insist that they are acting to defend a particular group of Muslims from attack (as in the statements of Hamas and Islamic Jihad concerning the Palestinians), or else to defend the broader Muslim world from the corrupting influence of Western values (as in many pro-*sharia* movements).

Aggressive violence

Also present, though less common, are verses in which God commands his people to engage in aggressive acts of violence. The targets of these actions are diverse. Some of the sayings are directed against polytheists, who are seen as standing under God's judgment (8:39, 9:5). Others target Jews and Christians, though more often the Qur'an grants these two groups special protection as 'People of the Book' (9:29, 33:26). Still others are directed against 'unbelievers' in general (4:84, 9:123). Over the centuries, many Muslim scholars have argued that these 'sword verses' abrogated earlier sayings that called

for peaceful responses to persecution or limited the use of violence
to self-defence. This 'abrogation' argument has allowed scholars to
blatantly justify aggressive wars of conquest by Muslim armies. The
same argument has been used in more recent times by violent Islamists
to justify attacks against non-Muslims.

The call to war

In several places, the Qur'an insists that participation in legitimate
acts of warfare is a religious duty incumbent upon all Muslims. Again
and again Muslims are told to fight and not hold back when they are
called to war, since God is on their side and will lead them to victory,
regardless of the odds against them. Those who fight are assured that
they will be rewarded by God, while those who refuse are threatened
with divine punishment (3:125–26, 3:172–75, 8:42–48, 8:65–67,
9:25–29, 33:25–27). The example of Muhammad is also cited here,
since both the Qur'an and the Hadith indicate that Muhammad served
as a military commander on several occasions and rallied his troops to
battle. Texts such as these have been cited repeatedly over the centuries
to motivate Muslims to participate in both offensive and defensive
wars. More recently, radical Islamists like Osama bin Laden have
quoted these verses as part of their effort to inspire other Muslims to
rally behind their cause, insisting that all Muslims have a religious
duty to fight against Western political and cultural oppression.

Violence as punishment

Finally, the Qur'an contains many verses that call for the use of
violence to punish those who violate specific provisions of the Qur'an,
including Muslims who turn away from the 'true faith' (4:89, 9:73–74).
Punishments for violations range from cutting off the hand of a thief to
execution (5:33, 5:39, 24:3). These verses served as the framework for
criminal laws in Muslim countries until their application was restricted
under colonial rule. In recent decades, many Muslims have called for
Muslim nations to throw out their Western legal and political systems
and return to Qur'anic systems of justice. These movements have met
with varying degrees of success. Some have resorted to violence in an
attempt to overthrow leaders who have rejected their demands, on the
grounds that these leaders have forfeited the deity's support by their
refusal to implement the provisions of the Qur'an. Muslim scholars
have repeatedly ruled against such actions as a violation of God's
appointed order, but the fact that the rebels claim to be upholding

the Qur'an has won them sympathy and support from many ordinary Muslims.

Conclusion

This cursory review of the scriptures of Judaism, Christianity, and Islam has highlighted some of the key images, stories, and injunctions that have been used over the centuries to motivate members of all three religions to endorse the use of violence. The close link between scriptures and violence is more obvious today in the case of Islam, since violent Islamists have repeatedly cited verses from the Qur'an to justify their highly visible attacks on Western societies and their Muslim supporters. But there have been many times in the past when an objective observer would have seen Muslims acting in a peaceful manner while Christians (and less often, Jews) were engaging in aggressive forms of violence that were justified by reference to scripture. Even today, one can hear Jewish rabbis quoting scripture to justify the use of violence against the Palestinian residents of the Occupied Territories and Christian leaders claiming biblical support for violent attacks on abortion clinics, homosexuals, and Muslim mosques. Actions such as these are less visible because they receive less media attention, but they are no less harmful to the people whom they target.

The bottom line is that all three sets of scriptures contain ample resources to justify the acts of Jews, Christians, and Muslims who believe that violence is necessary to achieve their ends. It is thus incorrect (or at least simplistic) to claim that Jews, Christians, or Muslims who justify acts of violence by reference to scripture are distorting or hijacking their sacred texts for illegitimate ends. The dark truth is that all three books of scripture have a violent dimension that most of their adherents would prefer to ignore, since it raises troubling questions about their conviction that their scriptures contain divine revelation and offer perfect guidance for moral conduct. But the evidence of history cannot be so easily dismissed.

Fortunately, this is not the whole story. Followers of Judaism, Christianity, and Islam have also found plenty of material in their scriptures to counter the arguments of their fellow religionists who quote scripture to justify acts of violence and to support their own calls for non-violence and peaceful relations with others. These people and their interpretations of scripture will be examined in the next chapter.

End Notes

1. The abbreviation 9/11 has come into common use since the events which took place on 11 September, 2001, when two planes crashed into the World Trade Center in New York City, another plane crashed into the Pentagon in Washington, DC, and a fourth plane crashed into a field in Pennsylvania. These events have often been taken to symbolise a change in the social order in the US and other western nations.

Words of Life: Scriptures and Non-violence in Judaism, Christianity and Islam

Christopher D Stanley

People who engage in violence invariably receive more media attention than people who labour quietly for peace, especially when they claim to be acting in the name of religion. It is therefore no surprise that many people today view religion as one of the leading causes of global violence, since that is what they see and hear on the evening news.

While it is true that religion is often associated with violence, this is only one side of the picture. Every survey of ordinary Jews, Christians, and Muslims reveals that those who promote the use of violence in the name of God are a minority within their own tradition. Most of the members of all three religions believe that their sacred texts teach the importance of love, peace, and forgiveness and allow for violence only under certain restricted circumstances. Most also have a negative view of people who use religion to justify acts of violence.

In this chapter we will review some of the verses of Scripture that have been cited by Jews, Christians, and Muslims to support their calls for nonviolent attitudes and actions on the part of their fellow religionists. From there we will move into a critical review of several models for interpreting scripture that the followers of all three religions have used at various times to formulate their responses to situations that might call for violent action.

Non-violence in the Jewish scriptures

Despite its popular reputation as a violent book, the Hebrew Bible contains many verses and ideas that can be used to counterbalance the more violent aspects of the text. Some are fairly obvious, while others are less so. Since the relevant materials are scattered throughout the collection, it makes more sense to pull together similar verses from different parts of the canon than to move through the texts in canonical order as in the previous chapter.

Critiques of divine violence

Alongside the many images of a violent deity stand a host of verses that portray Yahweh as a merciful, patient, compassionate God who refrains from punishing his people when they deserve it and uses violence only for positive ends. Most of Yahweh's acts of violence

are attributed to his righteous desire to discipline his people for their
sins, protect them from their enemies, or uphold the moral order of the
universe (Ps 30:4–5, 145:8–9; Ezek 20:1–22; Hos 11:8–11; Joel 2:18–
27; Mic 6:18–20; Zech 7:9–13). Even when his reasons are obscure,
the text presumes that Yahweh's violence has a righteous purpose (for
example Exod 4:24–26; 2 Sam 24:1–25; Job 34:10–30). Now and then
Yahweh is criticised for using violence, but the criticisms are invariably
rooted in the same ideal of divine justice that is used elsewhere to
justify Yahweh's violent acts (for example Job 7:11–21, 9:14–24,
30:16–31:4; Ps 44:1–26, 80:1–19). In other words, the Hebrew Bible
claims that Yahweh's violence always has a positive purpose, even
when it seems inexplicable to humans. In this respect it is qualitatively
different from human violence, which often springs from evil motives.
This qualitative difference suggests that the violence of God cannot be
used as a pattern for human actions.

Prescriptions for a peaceful and just society
The Torah contains a number of laws that call for the punishment
of people who engage in specific forms of violence (for example
Exod 21:12–27; Deut 19:11–13, 24:7). Similar ideas are implied
in several narratives that show Yahweh punishing people who use
violence against others (Gen 4:10–15, 6:11–13, 9:6, 49:5–6, etc). All
of these verses reveal a deity who holds a negative view of human
violence, as opposed to other passages where he seems to encourage
acts of violence. Elsewhere the Torah places limits on personal acts
of vengeance, calling for mercy and forgiveness instead (Lev 18:17–
18; Num 35:9–34; cf Exod 21:23). The Torah also enjoins Yahweh's
people to show kindness toward the weak and marginalised members
of Israelite society whose circumstances make them tempting targets
for violence and abuse (Exod 22:21–27, 23:6–9; Lev 19:13–16, 19:33–
34). Behind all of these laws lies a vision for a society in which every
member is treated with love and respect, a society in which no person
takes advantage of another nor harms another—in short, a society
characterised by peace, not violence.

Limits on the practice of war
The Torah also sets significant limits on the practice of war. According
to Deuteronomy 20, men who do not want to fight must be allowed
to return to their homes before a battle begins (cf Jdg 7:2–3), and
the residents of cities that surrender are to be spared, though their
possessions may be taken as plunder. Even kings were expected to

follow these provisions (Deut 17:14–20). Whether anyone in ancient Israel actually obeyed these laws is unclear (note the repeated references to the destruction of cities and their inhabitants in Judges), but they did play an important role in the later development of Christian just war theory. Christians who oppose the violence of war on other grounds have also quoted these verses when claiming exemption from participation in war. More recently, a number of Israeli soldiers have cited the provisions of Deuteronomy 20 to justify their refusal to participate in violent military actions against the Palestinian residents of the Occupied Territories, though their arguments have so far been rejected by the Israeli government.

Models of nonviolent action

Additional support for the practice of non-violence comes from a number of biblical narratives that show characters embracing nonviolent solutions to problems rather than resorting to violence. Many examples can be cited: Isaac's servants repeatedly move their flocks instead of fighting over wells that they have dug for their sheep (Gen 26:17–33); Jacob and Laban make a covenant and set a boundary between themselves rather than battling over their possessions (Gen 31:19–55); Esau forgives Jacob instead of exacting vengeance against his brother (Gen 33:1–15); Joseph similarly forgives his brothers and gives them a place to live when he had the power to punish or refuse to help them (Gen 45:4–15); the Israelites turn around when they are told not to cross Edomite territory rather than attacking the Edomites (Num 20:14–21); David overlooks the insults of Nabal at the request of his wife Abigail when David was prepared to exact revenge (1 Sam 25:2–35); and David resists his supporters' demands that he punish Shimei for mocking and cursing him (2 Sam 16:5–14, 19:16–23). In these and other stories, the nonviolent actions of the main characters serve as models for the conduct of readers who are faced with similar situations.

Visions of a future era of peace

Finally, the Hebrew Bible contains texts that anticipate a future era when wars and violence will end and everyone will live together in peace (Is 2:1–4/Mic 4:1–3; Is 11:6–9, 32:16–20; Ezek 28:25–26, 34:11–16, 37:24–28). The responsibility for inaugurating this new age of peace and plenty rests with Yahweh, not with his people. Nonetheless, the biblical vision of a peaceful world has motivated both Jews and Christians to work for the realisation of such a society here and now. Jews sometimes use the Hebrew word *tikkun* ('restoration') to describe this responsibility to work together with God to 'repair the world'. Elsewhere, the Jewish Bible speaks of humans praying or working for peace (Ps 29:10–11, 34:14, 120:7, 122:6–8) and celebrates the goodness of people living together in peace (Ps 133:1–3). Passages such as these offer a useful counterbalance to other verses that pronounce blessings on people who go to war.

Non-violence in the Christian scriptures

Most contemporary readers are familiar with the primary texts from the New Testament that call for non-violence and love for others. For this reason we can treat these texts in a more cursory fashion.

Visions of a nonviolent deity

As with the Hebrew Bible, the New Testament contains numerous passages in which God is described as patient, loving, merciful, kind, and forgiving (Rom 2:3–4, 5:5–10, 8:39, 9:22–24; Eph 3:18–19; 1 Jn 3:1, 4:16–19; 2 Pet 3:8–9). The deity's practice of doing good to those who reject him is even cited as a model for human conduct (Matt 5:43–48). Verses such as these serve to balance out the many other passages that speak of God as a violent judge who refuses to forgive and forget.

The call to make peace

Jesus calls for his followers to be peacemakers (Mt 5:9) and to live in peace with others (Mk 9:50). This includes not only resisting the urge to retaliate when one is physically attacked and abused (Matt 5:38:42) but also showing love and forgiveness toward the attacker (Matt 5:43–48, 18:21–22). Jesus himself exemplifies this kind of behaviour when he tells his followers not to use weapons to protect him as he is being arrested in Gethsemane (Matt 26:51–52). Similar ideas can be found in Paul's letters, where the apostle tells his audience to live in peace with others and not to retaliate if attacked. Instead, they should respond with kindness and leave vengeance to God (Rom 12:14–21; 1 Cor 4:12–13).

The life of love

Again and again the New Testament insists that the followers of Jesus will be known by the love that they show toward others. Jesus himself cites the biblical injunction to 'love your neighbor as yourself' (Lev 18:19) as the second most important of all God's commandments

(Matt 22:39). The authors of the New Testament letters likewise identify love and peace as the chief markers of a truly Christian life (Rom 8:6; 1 Cor 13:1–7; Gal 5:22; 2 Tim 2:22). Repeatedly they call on their audiences to love one another and to maintain peace and unity with other Christians (Rom 12:10, 13:8–10, 14:19–21; Eph 4:3, 4:32; 1 Th 5:13; Heb 12:14; Jas 3:18; 1 Pet 3:11; 2 Pet 3:14). Elsewhere they describe the deity as a God of peace (Rom 16:20; 1 Cor 14:33; 2 Cor 13:11; 1 Th 5:23; 2 Th 3:16; Heb 13:20) who gives peace to his faithful children (Jn 14:27, 16:33; Rom 2:10; Eph 2:14–18; Phil 4:7; Col 3:15). Many Christians have concluded that verses such as these undermine every attempt to defend the legitimacy of Christians using violence against others, particularly since several of the texts base their call for non-violence on the example of Jesus and of God's character of peace and love.

The call to endurance
Finally, the New Testament contains a number of passages in which the followers of Jesus are told to endure sufferings patiently, bearing witness for Christ in the midst of their troubles and entrusting their cause to God (Matt 10:16–23; Rom 5:3–5; 2 Tim 2:1–10; 1 Pet 2:18–25). Christians have long believed that such verses prohibit them from taking justice into their own hands or repaying violence with violence. Christians in the early centuries relied on these texts to carry them through experiences of persecution and martyrdom. Some even sought martyrdom in an effort to demonstrate their willingness to follow Jesus in the path of love and non-violence. Verses such as these have been challenged by some contemporary Christians who insist that it is psychologically harmful and morally indefensible to advise people to patiently endure abuse instead of seeking to free them from the yoke of oppression. Others, however, insist that these verses are consistent with the teaching and example of Jesus and should therefore be taken seriously and not dismissed.

Non-violence in the Muslim scriptures
Like the Hebrew Bible, the Qur'an has a reputation as a violent book. Yet the Qur'an contains numerous sayings that call for Muslims to devote themselves to lives of peace, love, and non-violence toward others.

The merciful deity
Like the Jewish and Christian scriptures, the Qur'an repeatedly

describes God as patient, merciful, kind, and forgiving toward his people, not simply as a violent judge (2:163, 3:16–17, 3:74, 3:129, 4:110–13, 9:102–6, 59:23). As with the other scriptures, these verses help to temper the many violent images of the deity that could be used to justify human violence.

Limits on the use of violence

The Qur'an also contains a number of verses that set limits on the use of violence. Some state that violence should only be used for defensive ends, not for aggression, while others say that even justifiable military violence should come to an end when the other party asks for peace (2:190, 2:193, 4:90, 8:61). Still other sayings indicate that there should be no killing except as authorised by Allah (4:92–93, 5:32, 17:33). Verses such as these leave room for violence and warfare within certain limits, but they prohibit the indiscriminate use of violence.

Endurance and peacemaking

Though the Qur'an allows for retaliatory violence, several passages insist that it is morally preferable to refrain from fighting. Rather than seeking revenge, Muslims should endure abuse with patience and repay evil with good (2:263, 5:45, 16:126, 41:34–5, 42:39, 42:43). The Qur'an also calls on Muslims to make peace between people who are fighting (49:9–10). Much of this language echoes verses from the New Testament. The fact that Muslims and Christians have often failed to live up to these ideals does not change the message of their sacred texts.

No compulsion in religion

Several times the Qur'an states that it is wrong to use force to compel people to believe (that is, conquest and forced conversion). Instead, Muslims are to peacefully invite others to embrace their faith and dispute with them only in the most courteous tones. If their appeal is rejected, Muslims are told to turn away and leave people in the hands of God (2:256, 7:87, 15:94–95, 16:125–27, 29:46). Contrary to popular mythology, Muslim nations have generally (though not always) attempted to follow these Qur'anic injunctions. During the Middle Ages, Jews and Christians were allowed to practise their religion freely under Muslim rule at the same time that Jews were being persecuted by Christians throughout much of Europe. Even today, only Saudi Arabia and Iran impose significant restrictions on the practice of Judaism and Christianity within their territories, though many Muslim nations enforce penalties against Muslims who join one of these religions. This is not the same as forced conversion, since these people are viewed as renegades who have abandoned the truth and must therefore be chastised for their own good and the good of others. What the Qur'an prohibits is the use of war and violence to compel non-Muslims to follow Islam.

The example of Muhammad

Finally, some Muslims have appealed to the example of Muhammad as recounted in the *hadith* to argue for avoiding or limiting the use of violence. According to the *hadith*, Muhammad engaged primarily in defensive battles to protect the nascent Muslim community from those who sought to destroy it, and he always stood ready to make peace on terms favourable to the other side. The *hadith* also recount several episodes in which Muhammad uses nonviolent means to avoid war and conflict, including flight, ruses, and negotiation. The *hadith* are not as binding on Muslims as the Qur'an, but they play an important role in guiding the community in cases where the Qur'an is silent or less than clear, since Muslims regard the example of Muhammad as a model for his followers. Unfortunately, the *hadith* are better known among scholars than among ordinary Muslims.

Interpretive models

As we have seen, the Jewish, Christian, and Muslim scriptures contain verses that can be used both to support and to restrict the use of violence by their followers. Over the centuries, the followers of all three religions have developed ways of handling these conflicting materials. At least five interpretive models can be discerned in the historical record. Some have been used by all three religions, while others have been more popular in one religious tradition or another. To avoid repetition, we will examine each model in turn and then discuss how it has been used (if at all) by Jews, Christians, and Muslims, rather than discussing each religion separately.

The theocratic model

The term 'theocratic' means 'rule by God'. Within all three traditions there have been people who have argued for the creation of a theocratic society in which all laws and social practices are based on the will of God as revealed in the scriptures. This model views the sacred text as a repository of divine revelation that should be literally obeyed in all of its details. Since there is no separation of religion and state in such a system, its supporters also look to scripture for guidance concerning the proper use of violence by both individuals and the state.

Theocratic models have held sway at various times in all three of the traditions under review here. Both the Jewish Torah and the Qur'an are filled with prescriptions for the operation of such a society. Scholars today debate the extent to which the laws of Torah were followed in ancient Israel, but the very existence and preservation of these laws indicates that there were Jews in antiquity who believed that the deity had a special blueprint for the social organisation of his people. Included in this blueprint were rules for divinely sanctioned uses of violence. For much of their history the Jewish people lacked the power to implement the broader social vision of the Torah, including its guidelines for violence. With the creation of the state of Israel in 1948, however, serious debates arose over how far the nation should go in using the Torah as a basis for national laws. The decision to create a parliamentary democracy represented a conscious rejection of the theocratic vision of the Torah. As a result of this decision, many ultra-Orthodox Jews refused to recognise the state of Israel, preferring to wait for a Messianic era when the laws of Torah would be properly implemented. Yet Jews of every stripe continue to use verses from the Hebrew Bible to justify the use of violence by the Israeli government.

The conversion of Constantine in 312 CE marked the ascension of the theocratic vision in Christianity. Prior to that time, Christians were a small minority group with no formal influence on the political system of the Roman Empire. Under Constantine and his successors, however, the idea of a 'Holy Roman Empire' directed by the Christian God became the dominant vision for society. In order for this vision to succeed, Christian theologians had to find a way to square the non-violence of the New Testament with the seemingly inevitable necessity for states to employ violence. St Augustine (354–430 CE) played a crucial role in this process. Most people know about Augustine's contributions to the development of 'just war theory', but few are aware of his highly influential arguments in favour of deploying violence against non-Christians and heretics. Both drew heavily on the social vision of the 'Old Testament'.

The arguments of Augustine, and others after him, placed the theocratic model squarely at the centre of Christian social thought in the Middle Ages. As a result, Christian thinking about violence came to be dominated by the stories and ideas of the 'Old Testament' rather than the teachings of the New Testament. The rise of the Enlightenment brought a shift to more secular modes of political analysis in the West, but Christian reflection on the legitimacy of violence continued to be heavily indebted to the theocratic model that was developed by Augustine and others. Even today, many conservative Protestants in the United States yearn to convert America into a society based on biblical laws, especially those associated with the movement called 'Christian Reconstructionism'.

Within Muslim circles, the theocratic model has dominated both scholarly and popular thinking about the manner in which society should be structured. Like the Torah, the Qur'an contains numerous prescriptions for the organisation and operation of society. The social vision of the Qur'an is heavily theocratic; all aspects of individual and social life are to be guided by the will of God. Because Muslims regard the Qur'an as the literal words of God, its vision for society has traditionally been regarded as normative. As a result, Muslim scholars have laboured since the early days of the Muslim movement to figure out how best to implement the provisions of the Qur'an within Muslim societies. Their judgments are embodied in the legal system known as *sharia*, which provided the foundation for Muslim social organisation from the earliest days of the caliphate (eighth century) until the imposition of Western legal systems during the era of colonial rule (nineteenth and twentieth centuries). Included under the *sharia* were extensive rules concerning the proper use of violence that resembled the Christian 'just war' model.

With the overthrow of colonial rule in the mid-twentieth century, Muslim nations were forced to grapple with the question of how far they should proceed in implementing the social vision of the Qur'an. Most adopted some kind of synthesis between Western legal systems and the *sharia*. Since the 1970s however, these compromise solutions have been challenged by Muslims who argue that Islamic nations should implement the full theocratic vision of the Qur'an. Some have turned to violence in their efforts to achieve what they regard as the will of God. This has led to bouts of violent repression that have served to reinforce the critics' conviction that their leaders have lost touch with the scriptural roots of their faith. In a few instances, such as in Iran and Afghanistan, theocratic groups have succeeded in taking power, but most have been outlawed and suppressed. In other places, supporters of *sharia* have created their own institutions, including *sharia* courts, within the legal framework of the existing Muslim state. In both cases, debates continue over how far the actions of the state (including its use of violence) should be shaped by the theocratic vision of the Qur'an.

Though theocratic models are favoured by many religious believers, the effort to put them into practice inevitably leads to an increase in the level of violence within a society. On the domestic side, violence (or the threat of violence) is invariably required to motivate people to conform to scriptural standards of conduct that are frequently at odds with contemporary notions of personal dignity and freedom. Violence is also needed to deal with the problems presented by dissidents and heretics. In the foreign policy arena, theocratic societies tend to be suspicious and fearful of outsiders who do not share their vision of the will of God. Sometimes this attitude can lead to an isolationist foreign policy, but in other cases it produces an aggressive and violent attitude toward other nations, including support for groups that use violence in an effort to extend the rule of God to other parts of the world.

Theocratic societies are difficult to create and maintain in a time when the world's social, economic, and political systems are becoming increasingly interconnected. Modern systems of communication, including satellite television and the internet, also make it harder for societal leaders to control the thinking and behaviour of their citizens. But these problems have not stopped many believers from working to create societies that are faithful to the will of God as revealed in their scriptures. Behind their efforts lies a firm belief that the deity will ultimately crown their activities with success, even granting them military victories if that is what is needed to reach their goal. People who are driven by a theocratic vision see little reason to engage in negotiation or compromise in order to achieve more realistic goals. Those who propose such policies are often derided as apostates who have turned from the way of truth and are tempting others to do the same.

The cultural conditioning model

Another approach to scripture that stands at the opposite end of the spectrum from the theocratic position is the 'cultural conditioning' model. Proponents of this view argue that scriptural passages that promote or endorse acts of violence are the product of particular social and political circumstances in the past and offer little or no guidance for handling contemporary societal problems. Compared with the theocratic model, this approach takes a more critical approach to scripture, either stating or implying that not everything in the sacred text should be taken as the eternally relevant will of the deity. Some would allow that God might have commanded his people to engage in violence at some time in the past but never meant for such instructions to be universally applied (that is, they were directed to a specific situation). Others argue that verses that endorse the use of violence were created by ancient followers of the religion in order to justify their desire to achieve social, economic, or political domination over others by claiming support for their plans from a deity who in reality would have been appalled by their actions. Both would agree that such passages should not be used today to guide moral reflection on social and political issues.

Within Judaism, two of the three major denominations (Conservative and Reform) incline toward this model, with the former taking a more conservative position (that is, such words may have been the will of God in the past, but they cannot be applied uncritically to today's world) and the latter a more critical stance (that is, God never intended for his people to engage in aggressive violence). The third major school, Orthodox Judaism, views the words of scripture as universally valid in principle, but they also believe that many biblical injunctions cannot be followed outside the land of Israel. Many would include texts that pertain to violence under this heading. Since the formation of the state of Israel, some Orthodox Jews have argued that the government should base its laws and policies (including its use of violence) on the laws of Torah, while others (the ultra-Orthodox) believe that this is impossible until the Messiah comes to establish God's perfect rule over the land of Israel.

Within Christianity, the cultural conditioning model is found primarily in more liberal Protestant churches where critical analysis of the Bible is routine. One common approach argues that Christians should use the non-violence of Jesus as their moral guide while rejecting the many Old Testament passages that place God on the side of violence. Such passages should be regarded as the faulty reflections of violent human communities, not the universally relevant words of God. People who follow this view also claim to reject all forms of theocracy as dangerous to the peaceful operation of modern secular and pluralistic societies. In practice, however, many still seek to influence the policies of government in directions that they regard as morally right, including lobbying for nonviolent approaches to social conflict that they derive from their reading of the Christian Bible.

Within Islam, a variant of the cultural conditioning model is used by more liberal Muslims who seek to make sense of the tensions within the divinely-revealed text by giving precedence to sayings that call for peaceful engagement with others and down-playing verses that support violence. Few Muslims would go as far as liberal Jews and Christians in acknowledging that the violent passages might not reflect the will of God, since Islam has traditionally insisted that every word of the Qur'an was revealed directly by God to Muhammad. This view of scripture limits the options of Muslims who wish to reconcile the apparent contradictions in their sacred text. On the other hand, Islam has a long scholarly tradition of linking verses of the Qur'an to specific events in the life of Muhammad and the early Muslim community. Some Muslim scholars have been willing to say that certain verses, including some that pertain to violence, were intended only for the era in which they originated, not for all time. Passages that call for peace and non-violence, by contrast, are commonly framed in more general terms that make them relevant to all eras.

The just war model
A third approach to the problem of scripture and violence, commonly designated the 'just war' model, originated within the framework of Christianity, but it has many parallels in Jewish and Muslim reflections on the validity of war and violence. In Christian circles, it was developed primarily by St Augustine as a response to the pressing question of whether it was morally acceptable for a Christian empire to use violence as an instrument of state policy. For Augustine, Christian reflection on the problem of violence must begin with Jesus' teachings about non-violence, which affirm non-violence as the norm for Christian conduct. Christians should consider violence only as a last resort, when no other solution is possible, and should engage in violence only under very strictly defined conditions. Even then, violence should be regarded not as a positive good but as a necessary evil, a temporary exception to the general Christian presumption against violence. Later Christian thinkers sought to refine various aspects of Augustine's model, but his overall approach to the problem has dominated Christian thinking on the morality of war and violence for the last 1500 years.

Unfortunately, the Christian just war model has been consistently misunderstood and abused over the centuries, with political leaders insisting that virtually any war they wish to fight is a 'just war'. Military leaders have also failed to abide by many of Augustine's strictures regarding the manner in which war is to be conducted. As a result, some Christians have argued that the just war model has outlived its usefulness. In fact, the whole idea that political leaders should have to justify their actions by reference to the Christian Bible or Christian theological traditions has become increasingly problematic as Western nations have grown more secular and pluralistic.

Within Jewish circles, there has been little need to reflect on the propriety of state violence until fairly recently, since the Jews as a people lacked the political power that would have motivated them to address the question. The fact that Jews were so often on the receiving end of violence at the hands of 'Christian' states made many Jews suspicious of all efforts to justify violence in the name of religion. With the formation of the state of Israel, however, Jewish thinkers were finally forced to reflect on the problem of state violence from a position of power. Even then the conversation was mostly muted, since the nation had to fight for its survival from the day it was created and therefore had little luxury to consider the abstract question of how to fight a 'just war'. Jewish religious authorities have long viewed self-defence as an acceptable justification for the use of violence.

Not until the 1967 war, when Israel came to rule over millions of unruly Palestinians, did the question of the legitimacy and limits of state violence come to be seriously discussed in Israel. In light of their history, most Israeli Jews have chosen to emphasise the abundant biblical evidence that supports the use of violence while downplaying verses that might point toward a nonviolent approach to social conflict. This attitude has given the Israeli government virtually free rein in employing violence against their Palestinian subjects, though such violence is still commonly justified as a form of self-defence. More recently, some Israeli Jews have begun raising the equivalent of 'just war' questions by calling attention to biblical verses that call for God's people to treat others (especially resident aliens) with love and respect, and to work with God to bring an era of peace to humanity. For the most part however, their arguments have fallen on deaf ears.

Since the earliest days of Islam, Muslim leaders have sought to define what qualifies as a legitimate war and how such wars should be conducted. Like the Christians before them, Muslim scholars were faced with a sacred text containing verses that called on believers to 'fight in the path of God' as well as sayings that enjoined them to forgive others and work for peace. Scholarly reflection on these texts produced a moral and legal system that resembled the Christian just war model, including the requirement for a formal declaration of war by a legitimate authority and the prohibition on causing harm to non-combatants. Muslim scholars also debated what constituted a defensive war, since such wars were clearly sanctioned by the Qur'an. Eventually they concluded that offensive warfare was also acceptable when performed in the service of God. As with Jews and Christians, the rulings of Muslim scholars have been used repeatedly to justify wars that were initiated for other reasons, though Muslim armies have usually made an effort to abide by Qur'anic provisions that regulate the actual conduct of war. In recent years, even these rules have been reinterpreted or ignored by violent Islamists who use indiscriminate violence against non-combatants and violate other aspects of the Muslim 'just war' tradition.

The progressive revelation model

A fourth approach, the 'progressive revelation' model, is similar to the cultural conditioning model in arguing that violent passages should not be allowed to shape modern reflections on the appropriateness of violence, but it follows a different path to reach that conclusion. Instead of denying the divine origins of these texts, the progressive revelation model asserts that passages that endorse violence reflect an earlier stage in the religious awareness of the community, an awareness that was subsequently qualified or superseded by a move toward non-violence. This mode of interpreting scripture originated in Christian circles, but all three traditions include people whose views resemble the model identified here as 'progressive revelation'.

Within a Christian theological context, the progressive revelation model is grounded in the belief that Jesus represents the pinnacle of divine revelation. Some Christians take this to mean that the nonviolent teachings and example of Jesus in the New Testament supersede earlier verses from the 'Old Testament' that permit or encourage violence. This is not to say that the Old Testament is bad and the New Testament is good, but rather that God revealed to each generation only as much truth as they were capable of understanding. The events narrated in the Old Testament represent an earlier stage in God's ongoing efforts to prepare humanity for the coming of Jesus, who fully revealed the character and will of God. This implies that verses in the Old Testament that pertain to violence have little bearing on Christian moral reflection, since they belong to an earlier era of divine revelation. Such an approach invariably leads to a more or less pacifistic theology and praxis with regard to violence.

In Jewish circles, the progressive revelation model is less useful, since Jews have traditionally maintained that the books of Torah are the most important part of the Bible and are not superseded by anything revealed later by God, even by an audible divine voice. The sayings of the biblical prophets are viewed not as fresh revelations but as interpretations and applications of the Torah. This is self-evidently true with regard to the prophets' attitudes toward divine and human violence—the prophetic books contain all of the same affirmations and criticisms of violence that one finds in the Torah. The closest that one gets to a progressive revelation model in Judaism is the traditional expectation of a future Messianic era when wars and violence will cease and all of humanity will live together in peace. Unfortunately, these texts say little or nothing about the proper use of violence in the present era, though some Jews have argued that they imply that God's people should work to establish a peaceful world here and now.

Within the Muslim community, a version of the progressive revelation model is implied in the scholarly theory of 'abrogation', which claims that some verses that were revealed to Muhammad later than others were intended to supersede the earlier sayings (cf 2:106, 16:101, 87:6–7). Since Muslims believe that every word of the Qur'an was revealed by God, the abrogation model is applied only in cases of apparent conflict between verses in the Qur'an. It has often been used to reconcile sayings that endorse violence with verses that call for peace and non-violence. The traditional view of Muslim scholars is that the more 'peace-oriented' sayings in the Qur'an were revealed by God early in the history of the community when Muhammad and his followers were a small minority and therefore would have been crushed if they had resorted to violence. By contrast, the 'sword verses' (that is, the more violent passages) were revealed at a later time when Muhammad and his followers were settled in Medina and had courts and armies at their disposal to establish a Muslim social order and to extend Islam to other areas. Since these verses came later, they take precedence over the earlier ones. Of course, this model presupposes that scholars are able to reconstruct accurately the chronology of the sayings, though Muslim tradition claims that the early scholars had access to sources that indicated the occasions when many of the sayings were revealed. Yet it is hard to avoid the impression that these scholarly rulings were also influenced by a need to justify the kinds of aggressive military actions that produced Arab victories over the Persian and Byzantine empires within a few years of Muhammad's death. Today, many ordinary Muslims employ a reverse form of the abrogation theory, arguing that the violent texts of the Qur'an relate to specific circumstances in the days of Muhammad while the peace-oriented sayings are more timeless and universal in their implications. This is the interpretive move that allows many contemporary Muslims to claim that Islam is a 'religion of peace'.

The personalist model

Like the other approaches that we have examined, the 'personalist' model is commonly associated with Christianity, but it can be applied in a limited way to Judaism and Islam as well. The basic idea is that verses that were intended for individual believers should be given precedence over verses directed toward societies, since the social prescriptions of scripture were designed for a societal order that no longer exists, if it ever did (that is, there are no divinely ruled theocracies today). Instead of labouring to figure out how to apply the theocratic provisions of ancient texts to modern societies, believers should devote themselves to following those verses that pertain to the conduct of individuals. Such a model requires believers to search their scriptures to uncover ethical norms and instructions that can be used to guide the conduct of individuals in any societal context.

Interestingly, all three sets of scriptures offer similar prescriptions concerning the way in which individuals should behave towards fellow group members. Believers are to treat one another with love, respect, kindness, patience, and forgiveness. None of the texts approves of believers using violence against one another as individuals, though there are passages in all three sets of scriptures that call for believers to exercise collective discipline against wayward members, including in some cases the use of violence.

The results are more ambiguous when we ask about proper conduct toward outsiders, since it is harder in the case of Judaism and Islam to differentiate what the texts say about the operation of society from their prescriptions for individuals. The documents that make up the Christian New Testament were written at a time when the followers of Jesus were a minority group living under Roman domination with no formal mechanism for influencing the broader society. As a result, they have little to say about how society should operate. The Jewish and Muslim scriptures, by contrast, were designed to provide guidance for a group of people who possessed the authority to direct their own affairs and the desire to order their collective existence in a way that reflects the will of God for human social relations. This explains why Christians invariably turn to the Old Testament when seeking guidance for the handling of social issues.

In practice, the experience of the Jews has not been markedly different from that of the early Christians, since the Jewish people had no state and thus no formal authority over societal structures for nearly two thousand years until the establishment of the state of Israel in 1948. As a result, many of the biblical guidelines for social organisation had no practical relevance for their lives. In their place, Judaism developed a strong ethical orientation that focused on how people should behave as individuals, an approach that is similar to the personalist model. With the creation of the state of Israel, the possibility arose that the biblical social laws would once again be used to define the structures and operation of an entire society. But this vision was stillborn, since Israeli society included not only religious Jews but also secular Jews who were unwilling to live under the strictures of Torah. As a result, the decision was made to create a secular democratic state that was influenced by biblical principles but not formally tied to the laws of Torah. Some Israeli Jews have lamented this development, looking ahead to a day when the social vision of their scriptures will be embodied in a Torah-observant Jewish state, but most seem to prefer the 'personalist' approach that views Judaism as a matter of individual practice.

Within the Islamic world, Muslim authorities held the reins of social and political power from the earliest days of the movement and made a serious effort to organise their societies according to the provisions of the Qur'an, including its sayings concerning the use of violence. Not until the coming of Western colonial rule did Muslims face pressure to downplay the social vision of the Qur'an and adopt a more 'personalist' view of their religion. Much of the organised Muslim resistance to Western colonialism was rooted in a concern to counter this suppression of the social dimension of their sacred text. The success of these independence movements once again raised the question of how the social provisions of the Qur'an should be realised in Muslim societies, leading to the internal conflicts that were discussed earlier. Today, the personalist approach to scripture is relevant only for Muslims living outside of Muslim countries, where they have no opportunity to shape their society along Qur'anic lines. It is not surprising that Muslims in these countries tend to stress the peaceful and nonviolent aspects of Islam, since much of the Qur'anic guidance for individuals emphasises the importance of peaceful relations with others.

This last observation highlights the complications that arise whenever religion is allied with political power and charged with shaping society. States inevitably have to use violence to maintain order within their borders and to protect their people against external threats. The fact that the Christian scriptures contain fewer injunctions to violence than the Jewish or Muslim texts can be attributed largely to the fact that Christianity arose in a context where the followers of the religion had neither the authority nor the necessity to provide guidance for the operation of the state. The Jewish and Muslim scriptures, by contrast, originated in communities with a shared religious vision in which societal leaders looked to religion to help them understand how to order their collective existence in accordance with the will of God. As a result, they could not avoid struggling with the thorny moral problems associated with the use of state violence. Christian leaders did not have to address this issue until the time of Constantine.

Conclusion

This overview of the sacred scriptures of Judaism, Christianity, and Islam has shown that all three texts contain passages that appear to legitimate the use of violence as well as verses that call for nonviolent forms of behaviour. Followers of all three religions have struggled long and hard to makes sense of this conflicting evidence. In the process, they have produced a variety of interpretive models that yield different understandings of the moral propriety of violence.

Of course, few people engage in violence solely out of a desire to be faithful to the words of scripture. Most are driven by social, economic, or political concerns. Yet there have been occasions in the history of all three religions when believers were convinced that their circumstances required the use of sacred violence. The fact that they could cite verses of scripture in support of their cause was a powerful tool for convincing others to go along with their proposals.

On the other hand, there have also been times when followers of all three religions have argued forcefully for nonviolent approaches to social problems. Many believers have trouble understanding why anyone in their community would choose this path when their tradition includes arguments that appear to reconcile their sacred texts with the judicious use of violence. Some attribute such attitudes to a peaceful (or cowardly) disposition, while others point to excessive idealism or naiveté. These explanations seriously underestimate the level of commitment that is required to actually live a life of non-violence, especially when it involves personal suffering. History tells of people in all three religions who have chosen to endure terrible pain and abuse, even to the point of death, rather than engaging in acts of violence. Such actions reveal a deep commitment to the moral truth of their religion. Yet the historical record also shows how often religious zeal has motivated Jews, Christians, and Muslims to perform violent acts in the name of God. The relation between scriptures and violence is a double-edged sword.

Part 2
Case Studies from Scripture:
Dealing with Violence

Violent Discipleship in the Gospel Traditions

Elizabeth Raine and John T Squires

> Then they bought the colt to Jesus, and threw their
> cloaks on it, and he sat on it. Many people spread their
> cloaks on the road, and others spread leafy branches
> that they had cut in the fields. Then those who
> went ahead and those who followed were shouting,
> 'Hosanna! Blessed is the one who comes in the name
> of the Lord! Blessed is the coming kingdom of our
> ancestor David! Hosanna in the highest heaven!!'
>
> Then he entered Jerusalem and went into the
> temple . . . on the following day, they came to
> Jerusalem. And he entered the temple and began to
> drive out all those who were selling and those who
> were buying in the temple, and he overturned the
> tables of the money changers and the seats of those
> who sold doves; and he would not allow anyone to
> carry anything through the temple. He was teaching
> and saying, 'Is it not written, "My house shall be
> called a house of prayer for all the nations"?; but
> you have made it a den of robbers' (Mk 11:7–10,
> 15–17).

In this way, Mark tells the story of Jesus' entry into the city of
Jerusalem and the incident which took place soon afterwards in the
temple courtyard. The details of this acclamation of Jesus are well
known: Jesus, the humble king on a donkey, the innocent man of God,
intent on a peaceful enterprise, enters the holy city of Jerusalem and
approaches the temple where the holy God is to be worshipped. When
he discovers the travesty of worship which is taking place on this holy
site, he rightly seeks to rectify it by direct physical action. This is the
traditional Christian interpretation.

We may think we are on familiar territory with this story. It is
a part of the story of Jesus that has been told and re-told, and most
Christians hear it from their earliest days. It forms the beginning of the
end of the story of Jesus—from these scenes, the Gospels move on to

Gethsemane, where Jesus is arrested; then to the trials of Jesus before Jewish and Roman authorities; and then to Golgotha, where Jesus is crucified. We know who was to blame for Jesus' death; we know that Pilate was afraid of the Jews and thought Jesus was innocent; we know that it was the crowd that turned on Jesus after celebrating his arrival. We know that Jesus did not set himself up as an earthly king, that he was intentionally humble by riding a donkey, and that he died an innocent victim of an evil conspiracy which culminated in a violent death on the cross.

We think we know all this, but do we? Can we be sure this is the real story? Or are there other dimensions to this story? The Christian approach to this story has been to see any violence inherent in it as the fault of other characters in the story—the Romans and the Jews—and certainly not the fault of Jesus, nor of God.

In this chapter, we invite you to join us on an imaginative journey and to think about this story from different perspectives, with different assumptions, and leading to different conclusions. We are basing our considerations on the fact that the Roman governor had an extensive intelligence network, which he used to keep tabs on all activity within his jurisdiction. From that factual basis, we offer you an imaginative reconstruction of a conversation which might well have taken place soon after the occasion of Jesus' entry into Jerusalem and the temple.

So, let us imagine that Pilate's intelligence dossier on Yehoshua ben Joseph has just been discovered by some diligent archaeologists. It contains the full record of an interview between Gaius Scipio, a Roman centurion, and Amon, a Jewish priest. And so we invite you to listen to this interview . . .

GS: Thank you for agreeing to meet with me, Amon. We have received some quite alarming reports about Yehoshua ben Joseph, the alleged teacher who is now strongly suspected of terrorist activity. We have been keeping an eye on this man, but until recently saw him as just another one of the fanatics that you Jews seem so fond of producing. Sure, there were crowds following him around in Galilee; but while he confined his activity to the countryside, we were not too concerned.

        However, the incidents of the last week, here in Jerusalem, are of a serious nature. I need answers for Pilate, the procurator. He is concerned, since it is coming near to your festival of Passover which always causes problems for us Romans. As you know, the population of the city more than trebles in size, the zealots are always ready to stir up trouble, and as usual we have had to put the troops on high alert, and call in extra legions from Syria. The watchtower over the temple courtyard now has to be manned twenty-four hours a day.[1] So we want some answers. I particularly want to ask you about what happened some days ago on the roadway leading from Bethphage into Jerusalem. You know what happened, don't you? Yehoshua ben Joseph led some sort of triumphal march into the city.

A: I certainly have heard of it. Everyone has. The word spread quickly. It's been the talk of the Temple precincts ever since it happened.

GS: Well, what were the people calling out? Some reports say that they were calling out in prayer. Why were they doing this? It is clear this Yehoshua character has made a mark on the people, and he was recognised and hailed as 'the one who comes in the name of the Lord'. They were saying, 'Blessed is the one who comes in the name of the Lord'. What did they mean by that?

A: They were quoting one of our special festival hymns. We know it as Psalm 118, the last of our special set of Hallel psalms. We sing them every year at the special festivals. This psalm, we sing at the Festival of Tabernacles. But originally, it was used as a hymn to celebrate the arrival of the king in the temple. Long ago, the king used to ride up to the Temple on the top of Mount Zion, for a ceremony to re-enact his enthronement. The king used to do this every year. Yehoshua was wanting to remind the people about the good times in the past, how our people used to celebrate. But I don't think you should read too much into it, really.

GS: But why did they cry out these words, from this particular psalm? It sounds like it was a political psalm. Yehoshua was riding up to the Temple to be crowned as King, wasn't he?

A: Well, we haven't had a king for a long time, now; and the Herods don't count. After all, they are in your pay — and they are not really true Jews. We've been ruled by foreigners like you for such a long time. But I'm not so sure that Yehoshua was wanting to make any kind of political statement with the way that he entered the city. He didn't want to be King.

GS: How can you be so sure? Wasn't it his own followers who were stirring up the crowd to cry out these words? Didn't he plant people in the crowd to try to get them all to acknowledge him as someone special?

A: Well, it is true that it was some of his followers who started this chant. But others picked it up. They just liked the atmosphere of celebration and rejoicing. They were heading into the city for a festival, for goodness sake! It is coming near to Passover, you know. Lots of people come to the city for this Festival. It's a happy time.

GS: As far as we are concerned, your festival of Passover is not a happy time—it always causes headaches for us Romans. Do I have to remind you that all of the Caesars have been more than willing to punish any rebellious behaviour on the part of you Jews? Do you not recall the time at the end of the rule of King Herod the Great (a most worthy client king of Rome), when Roman soldiers massacred 3,000 Jews as they celebrated the Passover in the Temple in Jerusalem?[2] And this was just for pelting the soldiers with stones. So in recent days, the disruption of temple activities, and the claims that were made at the time by Yehoshua ben Joseph, were all seen and heard by the Roman guard in his tower. And our current emperor, Tiberius, is no friend of the Jews either. Remember that Tiberius had the Jews expelled from Rome some years ago, and 4 000 Jewish freedmen were deported to Sardinia.[3]

        I am not sure that Caesar would see this as just a fun time. From what you have said, 'Blessed is the one who comes in the name of the Lord' sounds like a challenge to our Roman rule, to me. Are you sure that the followers of Yehoshua weren't trying to claim that he was going to take on the role of this king, now?[4]

A: Well, to do that, he would have to try to provoke some kind of military action. And he didn't do that. All he did was ride into the city while people sang psalms of celebration.

GS: I've heard that the people were crying out 'Hosanna'. What does that mean, 'Hosanna'?

A: Look, that's just an old Hebrew word for praise. They were crying out to Adonai, to our Lord, to thank him for what he had done. It was a prayer of thanks.

GS: A prayer of thanks—I see. But what were they giving thanks for? What had he done, this invisible Adonai god of yours? He hadn't actually done anything, had he?

A: Well, no, not really, but the people were happy. They were calling out to our Lord, crying out their 'thank you', so that everyone could hear how happy they were.

GS: But I can't understand what they were thankful for. You lot are always complaining about being oppressed by Roman laws and taxes and our religious traditions. Did the crowd forget that this day? Come on, what does the word really mean? What are its origins? I can ask the scribes, you know, and they'll tell me the truth. You wouldn't be hiding anything from me, would you?

A: Oh, well, I suppose I have to tell you, it comes from the word *hosa*, to save. So 'hosanna' literally means something like, 'save us, now'.[5]

GS: Save us! Save us! That doesn't sound like it was just a prayer of thanks. It sounds like a call to arms! Save us—from those horrible Romans, no doubt.

A: Oh, no, I don't think that was what they meant at all. Save us from doing silly things. Or save us from doing the wrong thing. That's what they meant.

GS: Well, that doesn't sound like a very happy thing to be saying. Are you sure they were saying prayers of thanks? Weren't they really asking Yehoshua to save them from us Romans?

A: Scipio, I don't think I can help you any more on that question.

GS: I am not convinced by your explanations as yet. Well, what about his mode of transport. Why was he riding on a colt?

A: Oh, he had a long way to go. People often ride on animals when they are going long distances.

GS: But he wasn't really going very far, was he? Just from Jericho to Jerusalem—that's only seventeen miles, isn't it—not really a long distance.

A: Well no, I suppose not.

GS: So why was he riding on a colt? Why wasn't he walking like everyone else?

A: I guess it was just the first thing that his people were able to find for him. They wanted to make him comfortable.

GS: Are you sure? Wasn't there a reason for him to choose a colt to ride on?

A: Hmm, I'm not sure. I thought it was just by chance that he was riding an animal. But maybe there was something more to it. Hmm . . . Oh, no, it couldn't be.

GS: Couldn't be what? Out with it.

A: Well, in our scriptures, one of the prophets refers to riding on a donkey—Zechariah, I think it is—and says that it would be a humble person who would ride on a donkey. 'Humble and riding on a donkey', it says. Yes, you will find in it the Book of the Twelve—it was Zechariah the prophet.

GS: Listen, whether he was on a donkey, an ass or a colt, he is clearly making a statement. Humble people walk into the city. Humble people don't draw attention to themselves. People with an agenda ride in triumphantly on beasts, and let the 'happy' crowd sing political songs at them.

A: Well, I don't know about that. I think you are making a bigger thing of this incident than it is.

GS: Tell me more about what this prophet of yours says.

A: Well, it is part of another hymn of praise. 'Rejoice', it goes, 'rejoice greatly, O daughter of Zion! Shout aloud, O daughter, Jerusalem!'

GS: So, it is like your psalm, is it? A psalm of praise, which is really a call for political salvation!

A: Oh no, not at all. 'Rejoice', it goes, 'shout aloud, for lo, your king comes to you, triumphant and victorious is he, humble and riding on a donkey'.[6]

GS: Oh really; 'triumphant and victorious', indeed! Only a Jew would try to be simultaneously triumphant and humble! And what was that reference to a king?

A: A king? Oh yes, a king. Oh well, I suppose you could argue that there was some small hint about that in his decision to ride into Jerusalem, mounted on an animal.

GS: You must know how we Romans feel about kings. We do not have a king ourselves, you will note. History has shown that kings are always to be associated with arrogance and misuse of power. Look at Alexander the Great. Great general, dreadful king. He let power really go to his head and of course this leads to bad political decisions, and civil disobedience and unrest. And even the great Julius Caesar—as soon as he set himself up as a king he was assassinated. The only kings we Romans tolerate are our client kings, who do exactly as they are told. The governor will take a very dim view of anyone setting themselves up as a king, you know.

       So, onto another matter. The people that were watching your Yehoshua ride along the road—why did they take off their cloaks and throw them over the animal he was riding on?

A: Well, that was just a sign of respect, a sign that they were showing deference to the travelers.

GS: No, I don't believe it. Isn't there more to it that than this? If it was a common sign of respect, then we would witness it daily. And we don't! So I want to know where your scriptures refer to this particular sign of respect.

A: Oh, I think it is in the books of the history of the kings of Israel.

GS: I see, the books of the *Kings*— indeed this is a surprise!

A: Well, yes. But this was back in the days when we had our own kings, before your Caesar ruled over us, with all of his soldiers and tax-collectors and so on. Anyway, in the second book of the Kings, there is the story about when the prophet Elisha anointed the young commander, Jehu, as the new king of Israel. When he came back to his troops in their barracks and announced to them what had happened, all the men took their cloaks off and spread them on the bare steps.

GS: And what did they say to him, I wonder?

A: Why, the trumpeters blew their trumpets and all the people cried out, 'Jehu is king! Jehu is king!'[7]

GS: Well, isn't that interesting. And so I suppose you don't expect me to think that yesterday, the people were about to call out, 'Yehoshua is king! Yehoshua is king!'? Do you take me for a fool? I can see that their shouts were disguised cries acknowledging Yehoshua as king.

A: Oh no, not at all!

GS: We hear that some people were waving leafy branches as he rode into the city. Why was this? Was this another royal symbol?

A: Of course not. It had an entirely different meaning. The branches relate to the Temple. They are part of our celebration, each year, when we remember how the Temple was purified and restored so that we could worship our Lord once again.

GS: And when was this?

A: A long time ago, many years ago, when Antiochus brought the time of shame to our people, and burned our Torah scrolls and polluted our Temple, and we had to stop offering sacrifices at the altar. The time when the blessed Matthias and his seven sons were victorious over the foreigners and restored the Temple worship. That's when the people waved their branches and shouted in praise to our Lord. It was a glorious time in the history of our people. You can read about it in the second book of our Maccabean heroes.[8]

GS: Indeed—a time when armed insurrection took place, when brigands and scoundrels fought against the armed might of the emperor, when they sought to appoint another King!

A: No, no, no . . . it was a glorious time because we remember how wonderful it was that we could worship again in our Temple. And that is what we can do now—worship in our Temple, thanks to your wonderful ruler and your brave Roman troops.

GS: Enough—don't make me sick. I know that's not what you really think about us Romans. And anyway, since you bring up the topic of the Temple, tell me—what do you make of this? When Yehoshua ben Joseph arrived in Jerusalem, he went straight to the Temple and looked around at everything. Then he came back the next day and caused havoc in the courtyard of the Gentiles. What was he trying to do? It's a good thing that he settled down and disappeared before our soldiers got there, or else he would be gone by now.

         I tell you, Governor Pilate and the Herodians are not going to stand for any of this nonsense. The last time general unrest broke out in Palestine, the rebellions were easily put down. It is amazing how the crucifixion of 2,000 Jewish insurgents and the selling of thousands more into slavery can quieten a restless population—just look at how effective your King Herod was at this.[9] The zealot movement has been a right headache to us since then. And I did hear that one member of Yehoshua's movement is a zealot. There have been rumours also that Yehoshua's disciples carry swords.

A: Well, travel is dangerous, you know—and the road from Jericho to Jerusalem is particularly dangerous for travel, especially at this time of the year, when lots of people are making their way to Jerusalem for the Passover. With such large crowds moving along the road, it is easy for those robbers to hide behind rocks and under cliffs and spring out onto the road and take what they can from the pilgrims and businessmen on their way to Jerusalem. I reckon that if you stopped every traveler and checked them to see if they were carrying a dagger or a small sword, then most of them would be—or most of the adult males, at any rate. Self-protection is pretty important, you know—and making sure that you could protect your wife and daughters and sons, if you were traveling as a family, would be sensible, too.

GS: But Yehoshua and his friends weren't traveling as a family group, were they?

A: Well, no, but that didn't mean that they wouldn't be carrying arms. I mean, business people carry swords, too. It's just common sense. You just never know when some brigand might attack you. And you can't depend on other people coming to your aid if you do get attacked. It has been known for people to lie, injured, on the side of the road for some time before somebody stops to help them.

GS: Hmm . . . you make it sound so matter-of-fact and normal for people to be wandering along the road armed to the teeth with swords and daggers and weapons. Everyone knows that 'brigand' really means 'zealot'—these people are not just stealing people's goods and money, they are plotting to bring about full-scale change in the social order.

A: No, no, not at all—we are not talking about a full-blown armed rebellion, you know. We would not dare to contemplate such a treacherous activity against the wonderful rule of the Romans. But you have to realize that the Pax Romana doesn't guarantee full safety for everybody on all occasions. There is still an element of trouble-makers in our midst, you know.

GS: Precisely my point. And how do we tell if someone is a potential trouble-maker, a threat to public order, a secret terrorist? Why, we listen to what the crowds are saying about him, and we keep out ears open for news of political activity. Just like your Yehoshua was doing yesterday. And what about his companion, Simeon the Zealot?[10] Now he is a worry, isn't he?

A: Well, he is a bit of a wild card, I must admit. But I don't know that he is still stirring up trouble, like in the old days. I've heard it said that he has reformed—that he has changed, he's a different person, now.

GS: Well, at this point I'm not interested in Simeon, or in any of the others—until they show their hand in the same way as Yehoshua. For the moment, we have him in our sights, and we will be watching him carefully. And if anyone else steps out of line, we will go after them, too. But it is Yehoshua that we are most interested in. He's our main target. He's been acting far too suspiciously. And you know, anyone who claims to be a King is setting himself against the Emperor. Amon, tell me, in confidence, what do you make of him? Do you think that his friends really do believe that he is the King of the Jews, like some of them are saying?

A: Oh, I think that is stretching things just too far, Scipio. This man cannot be the Messiah, the Anointed One, the man chosen by God for the special task that is reserved for the Holy One of Israel. He doesn't have any of the qualities of the Messiah. I know that some of my fellow Jews think that he is a special person. But then again, we have a track record of making this kind of claim. I mean, there was that Egyptian some years ago, and Theudas, and the prophet called Ezekias who gathered quite a following, and there were others; [11] but none of them came to anything. Their movements just fizzled out. They weren't the Messiah, despite what their followers said.

GS: Yes, but none of them went into the temple courtyard and overturned the tables and caused such a commotion, did they? Most of them went out into the desert, much like that strange man, Johannan, the one who wants everyone to be baptised and to repent and follow him. [12] Yes, they were all strange figures — but they were not political threats. Yehoshua is different. There is something about him, something that worries us. You know, even some of your own race have seen this man for what he is. I have heard that there were moves afoot to have him stoned because he practises sorcery and is leading Israel astray.[13] If what you say about him merely celebrating an ancient custom is true, why have these rumours arisen?

A: I wouldn't want to comment on this. I think that it is up to Adonai to judge whether a person is a sorcerer or not. If he is dabbling in this kind of activity, he will get his punishment soon enough. What Yehoshua should be doing is coming to the Temple and making his sacrifices, like an obedient and pious Jew. Like so many of us are doing, even as we speak.

GS: But that is precisely the problem — when he came into the city, with people shouting out and waving branches and singing in praise of him, he wasn't acting in a humble way — he was acting like the King of the Jews! And when he went into the Temple, he didn't make his sacrifices like you require. He caused a commotion! And some of his friends carried swords! In fact, didn't he order his followers to sell their cloaks and buy some more swords? [14] And this is the man who says, again and again, that he is here to bring in the Kingdom of God. What does that mean? Surely a man who plans a kingdom plans to be King of it. It doesn't sound to me like he has an obedient attitude towards the Caesar of Rome, our exalted ruler.

A: Look, Scipio, calm down, will you. You are getting over-excited here. Don't make too much out of what is really nothing. I'm sure he is no threat to Caesar.

GS: Well, does he support Caesar? I don't see how you can believe that he does support Caesar. After all, this is the man who says, again and again, that he is here to bring in the Kingdom of God. What does that mean?

A: The Kingdom of God—here we are, back to the King once again. Well, 'the Kingdom of God' is an age-old idea amongst our people.[15] Yehoshua was probably just using it in a general, pious sense to mean that we know that God has given us abundant gifts and wonderful resources and rules over the earth from his throne in the heavens.

GS: So, why does he tell stories that refer to the ruler killing messengers that are sent to him? Or about banquets that include all sorts of disagreeable and undesirable sorts, sitting at table with people of wealth and prestige? This is starting to sound suspicious, you will have to agree.

A: I will?

GS: Yes, you will! And why is it that most of these stories seem to end up with some sort of alternative vision of reality? With a kingdom in which 'the first will be last and the last will be first'? Does he have no sense of propriety? And why does he speak about the humble being exalted and the powerful being overthrown? Can't you hear the problem with all of this rhetoric? And what is worse, Yehoshua makes some very specific suggestions about how this new kingdom should be instigated. 'Wars and rumours of wars . . . nation will rise against nation . . . brother will betray brother to death . . . children will rise against parents'[16] . . . and didn't he even call on people to take up their swords?

A: What? To act with violence?

GS: Yes—we are told that he said, 'I have not come to bring peace; I have come to bring a sword'.[17] It is clear that he is inciting revolution. Amon, can't you understand how Rome views all these reports? Failing to show due deference to Caesar, advocating an alternative way of living, breaking down the time-honoured markers of social order, calling people to use violence to bring about this radical new way of being—we just cannot stand for this any longer. He is clearly a threat to us.

A: I'm sure he is no threat to you, Scipio. I think his words are being exaggerated. Or they are being used as symbols; they're not literal. I can't believe that he is fomenting an uprising. I'm positive he's no threat . . . yes, I'm sure, Scipio.

GS: No, I'm not convinced, Amon. I am sure that he is more of a threat than you are making out. We have to do something. And if you don't help us to act, you will find yourself in trouble. Do I have to remind you, that you priests are appointed by us Romans? The members of your Jewish priestly aristocracy retain their powers only by Rome's grace. We can easily remove them. If you know what is good for you, you will co-operate with us, and you will find a way to silence him.

A: Well, just let me deal with it. I will ask around and see what we can do. I will take steps to have him silenced. We can work with you. Rest assured, we don't want to upset you. We are prepared to do whatever it takes to keep the peace with our Roman overlords. Leave it for the moment, and let me see what we can do. I promise. I'll work out some sort of plan. We can deal with him. Don't you worry.

GS: I am not worried—it is you that has to worry, my friend. And if you don't do something about Yehoshua, then we will make sure that he is dealt with. You well know that Pilate has a serious lack of sympathy for Jewish sensibilities. Don't you remember the incident of the ensigns in the temple? We had the images of the emperor painted onto the ensigns and we brought them in by night, but you lot soon discovered their presence. Though multitudes of you Jews hastened to Caesarea to petition Pilate for the removal of our so-called 'obnoxious' ensigns, for five days he refused even to listen to you. Then, on the sixth day, when he took his place on the judgment seat, he had all the Jews surrounded with soldiers and threatened with instant death unless they ceased to trouble

him with the matter. Do you seriously think that the governor
is going to give your terrorist compatriot a fair trial? With all
this evidence against him? [18]

A: Oh Scipio—you Romans always think that you can solve
problems by using violence. But you can't. It's not always
that simple. Do you honestly think that using more and
more force is the way to solve all the problems that you
encounter?

GS: Yes we do! And we have shown that this is so, again and
again. And don't you lecture me about not using violence.
You Jews can be just as ruthless about using violent means
to achieve your goals. Don't you remember those terrorists
under Mattathias? [19]

A: Oh yes—yes, indeed!

GS: They were the ones who went on a rampage for day after day,
slaughtering the troops and terrorising the peasants, weren't
they?

A: Well . . . um, ah . . . yes, I . . . um . . . I suppose so.

GS: They seem to be heroes to some of your people. And all that
they did was use violence and fear.

A: Well, as I said to you before, they are indeed heroes. But
not because they used force and happened to kill some
soldiers. They are heroes because they stood up for the truth
at a time when evil ruled. They acted to restore the temple
and to reinforce the Torah. They were doing what was right
and proper in the eyes of Adonai. [20] We don't honour them
because they were violent. But they had to use violence, to
press home their case. Their violence was simply the means
they had to use to achieve their goal. They had no choice.

GS: They were political terrorists.

A: No, they were heroes. They were religious heroes. They
rescued Israel from the hands of lawless men. That was quite
different from today; we would never act like this against the
peace-loving Romans!

GS: Well, I certainly hope so! Now, getting back to Pilate and
your problematic prophet, Jehoshua—I think it is likely that
our governor will act soon.

A: You do? So soon?

GS: Yes, soon! You should not forget that Pilate was the one who
appropriated funds from your Temple to build the Jerusalem
aqueduct—the aqueduct that brings you water for your daily

needs. Although the crowd protested against him, Pilate
had already planted soldiers dressed as civilians among the
multitude, and when he gave the signal, they fell upon the
rioters and beat them severely with clubs. It was only then that
the riot was quelled—thank goodness Pilate intervened![21]

And remember, there was another incident, much closer
to home for your Yehoshua—the time when Pilate, displeased
by the attitude of a number of Galileans, had them killed and
their blood mixed with the sacrifices.[22] So don't for a minute
think that we are going to sit back and let things get out of
hand!

A: Well, no, I suppose not . . .

GS: So just remember what I told you before—Pilate had no
        qualms about crucifying 2,000 Jewish insurgents on one day;
        he could easily order the same sort of intervention once more,
        you know. So don't think that we will give you much time to
        sort this out.

A: Oh, well, if you say so . . .

GS: Indeed I *do* say so! You need to move quickly, Amon; if you
        don't stop this man carrying out his rebellious intentions,
        then we will act against all of your people, to shut down the
        movement and remove the problem! How else do you expect
        us to be able to keep the peace? And when we do act, you can
        be sure of one thing—*you* will be sorry!!!

A: Alright, Scipio, I get the point. I'll get the other priests
        together and work on them. It might take a few days, but let
        me assure you that we will sort this out. You won't have to
        intervene. Consider it done. After all, it is surely better that
        one man die for the people than to have the whole of our
        nation destroyed.

As we return, now, to the twenty-first century, and leave behind
our imaginary interview concerning Yehoshua ben Joseph, we refocus
our attention on the matter of violence. Our dialogue has revealed two
very clear points of view in relation to the violence that runs through
the story of Jesus.

For the Roman centurion, Scipio, violence was integral to daily
life. As a soldier, he was charged with keeping the order of society;
at times, this could mean implementing violent actions in order to
suppress uprisings or subdue dissent. Violence was a tool of the state
which served a purely pragmatic end. There was no ideological baggage

wrapped up in violent actions; it was simply a means by which political power could be maintained and social cohesion could be guaranteed. Caesar validated Roman violence for pragmatic political purposes.

Amon, the Jewish priest, demonstrates a second point of view: that violence was unavoidable in that particular age, when Israel was occupied by a foreign power. Violence was part of daily life, but not all forms of violence could be justified. Indeed, under the dominance of the Romans, most Jewish expressions of violence were to be avoided. Amon tries valiantly to assure Scipio that he will act as a broker with the rebellious elements of Jewish society, and convince them to suppress their violent tendencies for the sake of good order in society.

There were, however, some particular expressions of violence that were actually honoured and celebrated. The actions of the Maccabean martyrs were regarded as demonstrating fidelity towards the Torah; their violence was a justifiable expression of piety which was accommodated and incorporated into the Jewish worldview. This ideology was perpetuated by the various figures and movements often grouped together under the 'Zealot' banner: direct violent action for political ends with a strong religious underpinning. It was what was believed about the promises made by the divine which provided validation for the violence that might be expressed by Jews.

Running through the story is the perspective of a third character—Jesus himself. Was Jesus an adherent of the Jewish point of view, that violence could, at times, be a valid form of action? This is a contentious claim, which scholars in past decades have debated extensively. The shadowy Jehoshua of our imaginary conversation, who lies beyond the words of Amon and Scipio, is a figure who used physical violence to implement his wishes in the 'incident in the temple' soon after his arrival in Jerusalem. Beyond that singular incident, he may well have contemplated the further use of violence. Indeed, the political impetus which Scipio sees in the words of Jesus (especially in his apocalyptic speeches) offers a plausible platform from which violent actions might legitimately be launched. If Jesus was political, did he canvass the use of political action through violent means?

As the story unfolded, Jesus was denied the opportunity to implement such violent strategies. So, the story demonstrates that violence involves not only perpetrators, but also victims. Indeed, Jesus is best remembered as the victim of violence—wearing the crown of thorns, hanging on the cross, buried in the tomb . . . even, raised from the dead, bearing the scars of physical punishment. The story of Jesus cannot be imagined, cannot be told, without violence as integral to the narrative plot. The movement which Jesus initiated gained impetus from the series of violent actions perpetrated on Jesus. From our place in human history, we must note that Christianity (as we call that movement) came to birth out of violent deeds. We cannot 'wash our hands' of this violent dimension.

Can we suggest that there is a fourth perspective which emerges from this story? We might call this the perspective of God, who, we might imagine, looks at this story with a particular interest, and approaches it with particular goals in mind. Although it is claiming far too much to be able to know the mind of God, we are given pointers towards this in the scriptural texts found in the Christian canon. The 'good news of Jesus, Messiah, Son of God', which we know as Mark's Gospel, portrays Jesus, before his death, wrestling with the fate that lies in store for him—a violent death. He accepts his fate as the will of God.

The 'orderly account of the events that have been fulfilled' which was dedicated to the most excellent Theophilus (by one Luke, according to later tradition) continues this approach and its sequel, the Acts of the Apostles, contains clear and unequivocal claims that the death of Jesus was an integral part of a larger sequence of events which, taken as a whole, took place as 'the definite plan and foreknowledge of God'. The book of the beloved disciple, which we name as John's Gospel, interprets these violent acts as expressions of the predestined intentions of the deity, who reveals his glory through the crucifixion of Jesus.

And the self-proclaimed apostle, Saul of Tarsus, regards the violent death of Jesus on the cross as the means of transformation for subsequent believers—the paradigmatic movement from life into death and then back into life. Such scriptural texts base their claims of religious insight firmly on the violent actions which ultimately eventuated, soon after the conversation between Scipio and Amon turned from intelligence collection to plotting and planning. They provide the ultimate validation for violent actions: God willed it.

The implications of these reflections are deeply disturbing. We offer no simple solution or glib conclusion. Instead, we are left with lots of questions. We assume that Jesus was the Messiah. Certainly, his followers came to see him in this light. But there were other ways he would have been seen by others of his time. Did he deliberately set out to become a target of the Romans, when he rode into the city? Did he deliberately set out to dismantle the temple cult—or at least to point to the need to reform it—when he overturned the tables in the temple courtyard? Could he have been seen to be a terrorist—another one of the Zealots, out to overturn the Romans? At what point would Jesus have been seen as a serious threat to the Roman Empire and the Jewish authorities, and their mutual interest in ensuring the stability and order of society?

Is it acceptable to employ limited and targeted violence to resolve a situation, in order to prevent the escalation and further spread of violence? Is it better that one man die rather than a whole nation be destroyed?

Endnotes

1. The effect of the influx of pilgrims into Jerusalem at the three annual festivals is discussed in great detail by J Jeremias, *Jerusalem in the Time of Jesus* (London: SCM, 1966), 58–84 (and see especially the Excursus on 'The number of pilgrims at the Passover', 77–84) and EP Sanders, *Judaism: Practice and Belief, 63BCE–66CE* (London: SCM, 1992), 119–45 (and see especially pages 132–38 on Passover).

2. This took place in 4 BCE; see Josephus, *Antiquities* 17.213–18.

3. Jews were expelled from Rome by Tiberius in 19 CE; see Josephus, *Antiquities* 18.81–84. Also under Tiberius, Jews were deported to Sardinia; see Tacitus, *Annals* 2.85; Suetonius, *Tiberius* 36.

4. For a survey of scholarly views regarding the messianic and political dimensions of this passage, see FJ Moloney, *The Gospel of Mark: A Commentary* (Peabody: Hendrickson, 2002), 220, especially notes 21 and 22.

5. See the discussion in W D Davies and D C Allison, *The Gospel According to Saint Matthew* (International Critical Commentary), (Edinburgh: T&T Clark, 1997), 3:124–25.

6. Zech 9:9.

7. 2 Kings 9:1–13.

8. 2 Maccabees 10:1–8.

9. The slaughter of 2 000 Jews by Varus, Governor of Syria, is reported by Josephus, *Antiquities* 17.286–298. He continues with a vehement polemic against Herod (*Antiquities* 17.299–314).

10. Luke 6:15; Acts 13. He is 'Simon the Cananaean' at Mark 3:18 and Matthew 10:4.

11. These individuals are each noted by Josephus. The Egyptian, when Felix was procurator: *Antiquities* 20.169–72; *Jewish War* 2.261–63; Acts 21:38. Theudas, when Fadus was procurator: *Antiquities* 20.97–99. Ezekias, at the start of the reign of King Herod: *Antiquities* 14.159–60,

167; *Jewish War* 1.204–06, 256. Josephus also refers to other unnamed 'deceivers and imposters' at *Antiquities* 20.188 and *Jewish War* 2.259.

12. Mark 1:2–8 and parallels; Josephus, *Antiquities* 18.116–19. The claim made in this passage of Josephus, that "Herod was afraid lest John's great influence over the people might lead to a revolt", is not reflected in any New Testament indication of the political threat potentially posed by John.

13. The Greek word for 'sorcerer' is applied to Jesus but given the softer translation of 'deceiver' in modern English versions; see Matthew 27:62–64; John 7:12,47. John's Gospel indicates that the growing disquiet about Jesus (John 5:18; 7:12,25–27,32,44) leads to attempts to stone him (John 8:59; 10:31).

14. The command is found at Luke 22:36; for evidence that followers of Jesus carried swords, see Mark 14:47 and parallels, and Luke 22:38.

15. The Psalmist affirms, 'The Lord has established his throne in the heavens, and his kingdom rules over all' (Ps 103:19) and declares to God, 'your kingdom is an everlasting kingdom' (Ps 145:8–13). Note also the frequent affirmation that 'the Lord is King': 1 Chronicle 16:31; Psalm 10:16; 29:10; 47:2,7,8; 93:1; 96:10; 97:1; 99:1; Isaiah 33:22.

16. Matthew 24:6,7; Luke 12:52.

17. Matthew 10:34.

18. The incident with the ensigns is reported by Josephus at *Jewish War* 2.169–74; *Antiquities* 18.55–59. (Scipio fails to report, however, that in this instance Pilate ultimately backed down from his threats against the Jews.) For the debate regarding Pilate's attitude towards the Jews, see RD Sullivan, 'Pontius Pilate', *Anchor Bible Dictionary* (New York: Doubleday, 1992) 5.395–401; HK Bond, *Pontius Pilate in history* (Cambridge: Cambridge University Press, 1998); and W Carter, *Pontius Pilate* (Collegeville: Michael Glazier, 2003), 1–20.

19. 1 Maccabees 2:1–70.

20. 1 Maccabees 4:36–61; 2 Maccabees 10:1–8.

21. Josephus, *Jewish War* 2.175–77; *Antiquities* 18.60–62.

22. Luke 13:1–5.

From Violence and War to *Shalom* in the Hebrew Bible

Anastasia Boniface-Malle

We live in a world of violence and wars. Terror is all around![1]

There is more violence in our societies than ever before, such as the recent outbreaks between Hezbollah and Israel, the conflict in Darfur, and the Lord Resistance Army killing and maiming, mostly children, in Uganda. Rape, child molestation, wife battering, child labour, female genital mutilation and the like are pervasive in our societies.

We witness daily senseless abuses of especially women, young girls and children. In July 2006, two heartbreaking incidences happened in the Maasai community. A twelve year-old girl was forced to marry a thirty-eight year-old man. She was too young to perform sexual intercourse, and for this 'failure' she was returned to her parents and was beaten to death by young men (Morani) in the community. The community killed this young girl, in the name of culture. A few days later, another young girl was forced to marry a sixty-five year-old man. The girl ran away and hid at an evangelist's house, but she was later taken out by force when the evangelist was away. This girl also was punished for running away from her so-called husband.

The Maasai community is not the only one that perpetrates domestic violence.[2] Everyday in Kenya and Tanzania we hear about child molestation, especially of young girls whose sexual parts are damaged by adult men, most of whom are relatives or trusted family friends. Terror is all around! Child molesters, rapists and batterers are everywhere, as are their victims, in all walks of life in our communities.

Along the streets of major cities in East Africa, one sees countless street children sniffing glue and petrol to 'get high'. Street children are considered a nuisance and a shame for the community. People shoo them away like unwanted birds. Birds are sometimes treated better than these children. But, who made them 'street children'? Where are their fathers? Violence is indeed everywhere and all around us!

Our faith traditions contain a legacy of war and violence, but we avoid this most exigent and odious issue of our faith. If we look at incidences of war and violence, we find both Christian perpetrators and victims. The church perpetrates violence through discrimination, embracing destructive culture and through silence, partly because we do not know how to respond theologically and partly because we are caught up in a culture that endorses violence. We need to be *shocked into action,* as in the horrible story in Judges 19, where the people, in shock, said, 'Such a thing has never been seen or done, not since the day the Israelites came up out of Egypt. Think about it! Consider it! Tell us what to do!' (Jdg 19:30).

Violence is all encompassing; it can be physical, social and economic, emotional and psychological, and it has implications on personal and communal levels. Violence is all over the world but its intensity is felt differently in each place. We live in a violent world. Think about it, consider it! And tell us what to do!

Crises of faith

How do we understand our contemporary situations of war and violence when we neglect our own traditions of war and violence? How do we come up with profound theological responses and reflections to such issues if we do not address the wars and violence in the Bible? How do we deal with the issue of rape which is so rampant in our societies today? Why is the Bible silent over the issues of rape? Why do laws get twisted when they favour land inheritance for women (Num 27, 36)? Is patriarchy so deeply rooted in our cultures that we endorse the patriarchal injustices maintained in the Bible?

Christian churches in Africa have multiple ways of dealing with war and violence in the Bible. They may highlight passages that speak of God as loving, peaceful, righteous and just; avoid passages on war and violence; spiritualise 'war' by interpreting all wars in the Bible as spiritual fights between God's people and the devil and blaming Satan/ devil for all crimes/evil because he can't be seen; or they may claim that all violent and war passages reflect the historical and cultural conditions of the author, and therefore, those passages can be ignored in good faith.

These strategies do not solve the problem of war and violence. The Bible contains hundreds of passages which talk about people doing violence to each other. And there are many passages that talk of God's violence or wrath, slaying someone, threatening people with violence and/or the image of God as warrior. To ignore violence and war in the Bible is tantamount to ignoring violent atrocities and accepting domestic violence as a pattern of life, with its consequent physical, emotional, social, economic and political scarring. The Bible is loaded with similar incidences, which show at their core the paternal rights of men over their children. The story of Lot's daughters is one such incident (Gen 19). Lot was willing to give his two virgin daughters to be sexually abused by local hoodlums instead of his male guests. He considered it better for his daughters to be assaulted by these men rather than his guests. The story of Jephthah's daughter (Jdg 11) is another story of violence. Tamar's rape by her step-brother Amnon and David's silence over it (2 Sam 13) is indicative of how rape is silenced in African societies. When Absalom killed Amnon as revenge for violating his sister, David grieved. But he didn't grieve for Tamar.

In patriarchal societies, gender inequality is an accepted norm. In such societies, both men and women are made to believe that men must exercise control over women and show their 'maleness' in aggressive ways. The use of double standards such as condoning male sexual perversion and condemning women's irresponsible sexual behaviour is another form of violence. In most African societies, wife beating is considered not a crime, but rather a 'discipline' for disobedience or for talking back to her husband. Even rape is often considered a woman/ girl's fault. Some of the excuses given by rapists and the community are: 'she should not have exposed herself', 'she made me do it', 'she asked for it and then when I was ready she changed her mind', etc. In general, sexual violence is considered the woman's fault. Both African culture and the biblical culture demean a woman's image. A woman must be submissive to her husband or father. Christianity and most major religions of the world concede and justify male supremacy and the submission of the woman.

War in the Hebrew Bible

The war legacy is pervasive in the Hebrew Bible (Deut 7:1–7; 1 Sam 15:2–3; Zeph 1; Ps 137:8; Job 16:11–14) and is most notable in the Book of Joshua where conquest involves killing the natives, occupation and division of the land under God's command. God is involved in the massacre of the people as God sides with and fights for Israel (invaders). The basis of all this is God's faithfulness to the promises made to the patriarchs. God ensures the fulfillment of the promise by directing and participating in Israel's battles. The savage dispossession of the people, ethnic cleansing and genocide of native inhabitants constitute much of the Book of Joshua. Yet, the Book of Joshua is one of the favourite books that people read, especially 'comfortable' passages like Joshua 1:8, 9:24 and so forth. Hymns of victory are based on this book and its 'heroism', for the miracle of the 'walls tumbling down'.

In Joshua 6:21 we read: 'They devoted the city to the Lord and destroyed with the sword every living thing in it—men and women, young and old, cattle, sheep and donkeys' (Deut 7:2–5, 20:16–18: Num 25:1–5, 31:14–17; Exod 23:33). Israel was to obey the ban or else they would find themselves under the punishment of God (Josh 6:18). In Joshua 7:6–9, Achan and his family disobeyed the ban and as a result Israel, lost the battle because Yahweh withdrew his help. This became a source of devastation for Joshua. The Book of Joshua mentions thirty-one kings defeated in bloody battles (Josh 12:24) and after every battle, *the city and everyone in it are put to the sword,* as ordered by the Lord (8:22; 10:28ff; 11:11ff; my emphasis).

When Israel was in Canaan they indulged in idolatry, appearing to have forgotten the commandment. God punished them by handing them to foreign rulers. The summary of the circle of sin, cry and deliverance is enumerated in Judges 2:11–3:6. In the Book of Judges, God used judges to deliver Israel; a total of thirteen wars were fought.

Scholars from different times have given different interpretations of the Holy Wars. According to von Rad, the concept of 'holy war' must be understood in the context of the covenant and cult. Holy war was a 'covenant affair situated in the specific cultic and political affairs of Israel'.[3] In this context, Yahweh was Israel's defender, a political leader, marking a difference between Israel and other religions: Yahweh is the God of Israel. Holy war presupposes collective liability of the confederacy and allegiance to covenant obligations.

Holy war for von Rad was particular; it presupposes the institution of the cult. Holy war later became a literary genre, and was rationalised and spiritualised when it was dissociated from the cult; it was used to serve theological ends, especially during the monarchy. There was divine intervention in the amphictyony, but in monarchical Israel, there was divine cooperation; the human agent (the king) was involved.

Von Rad's theory set the tone for later critics, two of whom are important for this chapter. Manfred Weippert suggested that holy war was an anachronism, for it has no basis in ancient texts.[4] He argued that none of the ritual and ideological components of von Rad's holy war were in any way unique to Israel; on the contrary, they were part of the practice and ideology of war common in the Ancient Near East and probably in all of antiquity. In Israel there was no distinction in principle between the charismatic leader of war in the period of confederacy and in that of the monarchy.

Fritz Stolz did a comprehensive survey of the holy war at the same time as Weippert. Stolz did not assume an amphictyony, and denied that Israel shared common experiences of war.[5] There was no homogeneous institution of holy war in the beginning of Israel's history. The tribes shared experiences of 'Yahweh's wars', crediting Yahweh with victory over military conquests, but these wars shared no common pattern, ritual or ideological, no common vocabulary, no common cultic or political setting. According to Stolz, 'holy war' was an invention of the Deuteronomistic theologians — a literary and theological fiction.

These theories address the problem of wars in the Hebrew Bible but they do not answer all of our questions.

Violating conquest–occupation stories

The idea of a 'conquest' of the land has become a traditional way of describing Israel's entry into the land in the books of Joshua and Judges. Without careful reading, the books of Joshua and Judges appear as sequential narratives of Israel's rise to power as a dominant force in Canaan. This is the traditional view of the books.

Internal evidence from the two books however reveals inconsistencies. At certain points the Book of Joshua indicates that conquest was swift and complete: 'So Joshua took the whole land, according to all that the Lord had spoken to Moses; and Joshua gave it for an inheritance to Israel according to their tribal allotments. And the land had rest from war' (Josh 11:23).

There is conflicting evidence which shows that there was no 'sweeping victory'. Other cities and kings remained unconquered. The list of conquered cities in Joshua 12 includes some that were not taken until the time of David and Solomon 200–250 years later (for example, Jerusalem, Gezer, Taanach, Megiddo, Dor). The Joshua tradition recalls that Israel did not take Jerusalem in the time of Joshua (Josh 15:63); this is confirmed in 1 Samuel where the capture of Jebus, the city that would become Jerusalem, is a key event in the account of David's reign as King (1 Sam 5:6–7).

Yet, the defeat of the king of Jerusalem and the incorporation of Jerusalem into the tribal territory is mentioned in Joshua both in the battle reports (Josh 10) and in the list of cities captured by all Israel under the leadership of Joshua (12:10; 18:28). Likewise, Joshua reports that the king of Gezer was defeated by all Israel (10:33; 12:12), his city incorporated into the territory of the tribe of Ephraim (16:3), and then given to the Levites as one of the Levitical cities (21:21). Yet the Joshua traditions also remember that the city of Gezer was never controlled by the Israelites under Joshua (16:10). This is confirmed in Judges 1:28–29 (see also 1 Kgs 9:16f).

The foregoing suggests that Israel did not annihilate the Canaanite inhabitants of the land (for example Josh 6:21). The account in Joshua is complex. The first half of the book describes complete and total control of the land under Joshua and 'all Israel', with the land divided between the tribes while the 'land had rest from war'. Yet accounts later in the book seem to describe a situation quite different in which the allotments were made to each tribe who were then responsible for taking the territory assigned to them (18:1–3).

Beyond the repeated emphasis on 'all Israel' in certain places in Joshua, there is little evidence that Israel was a united army of all the tribes. Joshua and Judges presume a group of loosely allied yet fiercely independent tribes that were quick to fight each other and some of the tribes were displaced from their original allotments because they could not conquer the cities given to them, as in the case of the tribe of Dan (19:40–46). The Danites simply could not take the Philistine strongholds, and were likely harassed by the Philistines who were not too happy about newcomers trying to occupy their territory. Driven from their assigned land the tribe of Dan moved to the far north and settled there. The Joshua traditions refer matter-of-factly to this reassignment of territory (Josh 19:47–48; cf Jdg 18):

> When the territory of the Danites was lost to them,
> the Danites went up and fought against Leshem, and
> after capturing it and putting it to the sword, they
> took possession of it and settled in it, calling Leshem,
> Dan, after the name of Dan their ancestor. This is the
> inheritance of the tribe of Dan, according to their
> families—these towns with their villages.

In a similar manner, the western half of the tribe of Manasseh was assigned the territory that lay along the eastern Megiddo Plain to the Jordan Valley, the site of one of the strongest Philistine fortresses in the area at Beth-shean (or Beth-shan). They complained to Joshua about their allotment under the guise that they had not been given enough land, when it seems apparent that they simply could not take the Philistine garrisons in the area (17:12, 16):

> Yet the Manassites could not take possession of those
> towns; but the Canaanites continued to live in that

> land . . . The tribe of Joseph said, 'The hill country
> is not enough for us; yet all the Canaanites who
> live in the plain have chariots of iron, both those in
> Beth-shean and its villages and those in the Valley
> of Jezreel.'

Joshua was not sympathetic to their plight and told them that they would have to defeat the Philistines in order to have their land (17:17–18). Later in the time of Saul, we learn that Beth-Shean was still a Philistine fortress on whose walls the mutilated body of Saul and his sons were hung as Philistine war trophies (1 Sam 31:12).

There are also hints that some of the tribes were forced to merge with other tribes, or perhaps were decimated in this period by the Philistines. For example, the tribe of Simeon was absorbed into the tribe of Judah (Josh 19:9; cf Jdg 1:17). Simeon's territory lies at the western and southern edges of Judah, the territory closest to the Philistine strongholds. The tribe of Simeon, even though portrayed as part of Judah, plays little role in Israel's history and is not mentioned again after the sixth century BCE.

Likewise, the tribe of Gad shared its territory with the tribe of Rueben on the eastern side of the Jordan (Deut 3:12). And the tribes that were assigned territory occupied by other Canaanite strongholds along the Megiddo Plains (Issachar and Western Manasseh) and along the Phoenician Coast (Asher) virtually disappear from Israel's history during the period of the Judges.

All this suggests that what appears on the surface of the Book of Joshua is not the whole story. What appears to be a 'clean' and simple conquest and subjugation of the Canaanites by a unified people under the leadership of Joshua may have been a much more protracted affair and had an exceedingly more complex history.

This raises questions that go deeper than the historical questions: If the Book of Joshua itself preserves the memory of a more difficult and more complicated version of Israel's entry to Canaan, why do present readings of the book simplify the story? Was the book constructed to focus on one aspect of the story, but unhesitatingly provided details of a different version of that history? If one aspect was emphasised, what was the purpose of doing so? And what was the purpose of providing details that would bring the historical aspects of that version into question?

We raise questions that cannot be answered by investigating just the historical problems of the book. There are more questions, of literary composition, of intent and purpose, which are finally theological questions. The Book of Joshua is a polemic and should be viewed for what it is, 'theology' (as barbaric as it is) rather than history, a kind of 'political theological' commentary.

Violating war stories: polemic against Baalism

Israel's settlement in the land of Canaan was a landmark of religious crisis. After the settlement, Israel's life was different from the nomadic life of the wilderness. Following the settlement, Israel engaged in agriculture as a way of life. Yahweh's provision ceased after they ate the first produce of the land (Jos 5:12). The occupation account implies that Israel settled among the inhabitants of the land, the Canaanites, who were agriculturalists and experts in raising the produce of the land. Their success was attributed to the god of fertility who was known as Baal. The Baal cult revolved around the cycles of nature. This worship was meant to ensure the survival and prosperity of people and nature. People engaged in the fertility cult for the sake of farming, livestock and even for the growth of human population. In order for the Israelites to harvest enough produce of the land, to have good livestock and to increase in number like the Canaanites, they had to learn the techniques and rituals associated with fertility. Consequently, they became worshippers of Baal. The Book of Judges tells us that they engaged in the worship of the gods of the land especially Baal, the head of the pantheon responsible for fertility of the land (cf Jdg 2:11–3:6). Baal was the God of the water and storm and posed a threat to the belief in Yahweh the God of Israel.

In many ancient religions, even in African traditional practices today, gods that are said to be directly involved with rain and fertility play a central role in the community. In pre-industrialised societies, farming and livestock become fundamentally a sole way of survival. Therefore, rain is crucial. From a theological point of view, the prophets of Israel criticised Baal worship as a reason for exile. Nevertheless, from a human point of view, the existence of Israel in the land depended on the rain. And since the Canaanites had rituals and worship associated with rain, it is not puzzling that Israel had to espouse this kind of worship. However, this became a threat to the monotheistic religion of the wilderness. 'The fact that the Israelites were settled among the Canaanites, for whom the worship of Baal was so important, and that Palestine was a land utterly dependent for its fertility upon rain, which was held to be Baal's realm of influence, accounts for the tempting nature of this cult as well as OT polemic against it.'[6]

The prophets of Israel and especially the Deuteronomists had to defend their faith in Yahweh. From the exodus and wilderness experiences, Yahweh was known and worshipped as liberator God. However, with the threat of Baal worship, the Deuteronomistic historians had to convince Israel that it was Yahweh, not Baal who controlled the course of nature. It is in the land of Canaan and especially during the Solomonic era that Yahweh was confessed as the Creator God. This was due to the threat of the worship of other gods who were considered false by Israel prophets. However, the greatest threat for Israel was Baal, also known as Baal-Hadad. Although the Hebrew Bible mentions foreign gods, Baal was the most frequently appearing deity who was widely worshipped out of the belief that he was the god who controlled the cosmos.[7] Baal was the fertility and weather god of Western Semites. Baal was often associated with the goddess Astoreth (Jdg 2:13), and in the areas of his altar there was often an Asherah (see Jdg 6:30; 1 Kgs 16:32–33). The bulk of Ugaritic mythological texts deal largely with Baal activities. While the Bible and Pritchard's *Ancient Near Eastern Texts relating to the Old Testament* mention various deities, Baal was the head of the pantheon. The fact that Israel was severely criticised for the worship of Baal, attests to the fact that the Baal cult was critical for the existence of the people.

At this point, it is pivotal to examine this Baal cult and why Israel was so strongly criticised by the prophets for the worship of this god.

The economy of Palestine depended on the adequacy of rain at regular intervals. Hence, the worship of Baal in Palestine was inextricably bound to the economy of the land. Even before they reached the Promised Land, Israel was already allured to the worship of Baal of Peor at Shittim where they ate sacrifices for the dead and indulged in whoredom (Num 25:1–1; Ps 106:28). In the time of Judges, there was a strong opposition to Baal worship and a call to worship Yahweh alone which confirms that Baal had many adherents even among the Israelites (see Jdg 2:11,13; 3:7; 6:25). This aspect of worship (fertility cult) was criticised by the prophets (see Is 57:3–13; Jer 19:5; Hosea 2:8–13, 13:2) but the polemic against Baalism comes to the fore especially in the Deuteronomistic literature.

The conflict of Yahwism and Baalism reached a climax with Elijah's challenge to Baal's prophets to settle the question whether it was Baal or Yahweh who really supplied the rain (1 Kgs 18). However, the spectacular victory for Yahwism did not have a lasting effect. There was a flourishing Baal cult at Samaria in the ninth and eighth centuries BCE. In Judah, the murder of the queen mother Athaliah, a Baal worshipper, and of Mattan, priest of Baal, along with the smashing of the altars and cult images in the Baal temple (2 Kgs 11:18), did not wipe out the cult (2 Kgs 12:3–4), nor did Hezekiah's efforts succeed against the cult of idol worshippers (see 2 Kgs 18:3–4, 23:4–10).

The cult of Baal was already prevalent even before and during the times of Elijah. However, Elijah attributed Baal worship to the breach of Yahweh's commandment. His message was a call to return to the worship of Yahweh, the creator of the universe. The people of Israel were reminded that the true worship of Yahweh will ensure their prosperity and bounty in the land, for Yahweh will give them rain (Deut 11:14). On the contrary, if they worship other gods, or disobey Yahweh's commandments, 'the Lord's anger will be kindled against them, and Yahweh will shut up the skies so that there will be no rain and the ground will not yield its produce; and they will soon perish from the good land' (Deut 11:16–17). Although they settled in the land, the climate of the land depended on rain, and without the rain there was no survival. In dry areas, where agriculture was crucial for sustenance, rain became the symbol of divine providence and a sign of Yahweh's control over nature. If the people showed that they were depending on other gods for rain, Yahweh became enraged and admonished the people, threatening that the land would vomit them up. But such theological truth was not so clear and sufficient for the newly agrarian Israelites. They had to learn from the settled and experienced inhabitants of the land.

Holy war and the complexities of Old Testament traditions

Given this challenging background, both the prophets and the Deuteronomists had to convince the people that Yahweh was more powerful than the gods of the land, especially more powerful than Baal-Hadad. The widespread use of war imagery and language in the Hebrew Bible can be attributed to the complex structural and cultural forms of violence so deeply embedded in many societies including that of the Ancient Near East. Anthropological studies of many societies attest to this reality. Human societies propagate cultural violence especially through myths, folk tales and legends of heroism and similar feats. Every religion has different ways of describing God/god depending on their particular worldview. Like many African societies, the Biblical worldview was mainly patriarchal, so most of the images of God were male and warlike. For example, in the *Song of*

Sea, we see images of God as a 'Man of War'. However, the Hebrew Bible also contains images of God that portray the tender care of God as a mother eagle. There are also other complex images in which God comes as a wind or a still voice. Fundamental to the understanding of the 'war' images and passages in the Hebrew Bible is the element of justice. The prophetic call was the call of justice, especially by the pre-exilic prophets. Because of the failure of judges and kings to render justice in the society, the prophetic interpretation focused on Yahweh as the guardian and promoter of justice. The aspect of justice was extended beyond the borders of Israel. Nations that tried to thwart Yahweh's plan had to be destroyed. Coupled to the idea of justice was the issue of holiness. Anything that obliterated holiness in Israel had to be destroyed.

The mythological stories are a major source of war-like language in the ancient literature. In most of this literature, contests between the gods are prominent. For example, in Babylonian mythology, Marduk, the lesser god, fights Tiamat, the goddess of the sea, and defeats her. As a result, Marduk ascends to power as creator god. Marduk was given fifty names by the lesser gods. In the Ugaritic Baal cycle, Baal-Hadad was given two weapons by Kothar-wa-Hasis (the builder/craftsman god) to beat back Sea (Yam) to its own realm. The Ugaritic text reads:

> Drive Sea from his throne, River from the seat of his dominion. You shall swoop in the hands of Baal, like an eagle in his fingers. Strike the head of Prince Sea, between the eyes of Judge River. Let Sea sink and fall to the earth. And the stick swoops in Baal's hands like an eagle in his fingers. It strikes the head of Prince [Sea], between the eyes of Judge River. Sea sinks, falls to the earth, his joints fail, his frame collapses. Baal pounces and drinks Sea, he destroys Judge River.
>
> (*KTU* 1.2.IV:19–27)

The Deuteronomistic literature has a language that resonates with this mythology, such as Joshua 2:9–11, where Yahweh is portrayed as one who has power over sea and controls heaven and earth. The Deuteronomistic historian put this confession in the mouth of Rahab, the Canaanite. Yahweh's terror is felt by the Canaanites because of the report that Yahweh divided the Sea. In Joshua 5:1 and 6:36–40 we read similar holy war language.

The Deuteronomistic historian felt the need to defend the expression of faith in Yahweh against the influence of these widespread mythologies by attempting to convince the people that Yahweh controlled all nature, even storms and wind (see Josh 10:10–11 and Jdg 5). A similar account is found in the Ugaritic mythological texts where Baal is confessed as the one who controls storms and is able to send hailstones:

> The word of a tree
> The whisper of a stone
> murmur of heaven with earth
> the deep with the stars
> stones of lightning which heaven does not know
> a matter which people do not know
> and the multitude of the earth do not understand
> I will execute, and I will reveal it
> in the midst of my mountain, the godly Zephon.
> (*KTU* 1.3.III:22–29)

The stories of Elijah and Elisha are centred around water miracles to remind Israel that it is Yahweh who is the one who controls nature, not Baal. For the Deuteronomistic historians, these polemics were literary techniques used to wage 'war' against the challenge of Baal worship.

Violence and war in the setting of *shalom*

Central to the Old Testament is the claim that God acts in human history. These were mostly the acts of salvation, but they have been interpreted by different theological voices over the centuries. These varied interpretations depended on the context, so to interpret the context, both political and social, they had to draw on the idea of salvation history. Events were also interpreted as acts of God. God was not projected entirely as a political God who was involved in savage wars; it was also noted that when God spoke, things happened (Gen 1; Is 40). This was a part of the exilic understanding of God. During the exile, after the downfall of the kingship, the power of God was seen to be at work through God's word, through the Torah, and through the people's keeping the commandments.

In the Old Testament we can learn much about God's grace in the midst of wars and rumours of wars, but, of equal importance, we can also be confronted by the nature of our own human sinfulness and the limits of trust in human power for our security.

Many discussions of the Old Testament foundations for peacemaking have narrowed too quickly to the accounts of Israel's wars, without attention to the wider context of the Old Testament understanding of the world, and people's relationship to God in the world. It is the Hebrew concept of *shalom* that will aid us most in identifying this wider context. *Shalom* is the Hebrew word most often translated as peace. Its basic meaning is wholeness—a state of harmony existing among God, humanity and all of creation.

A full understanding of *shalom* begins with creation. *Shalom* is God's intention for creation from the beginning. All elements of creation are interrelated. Each element participates in the whole of creation, and if any element is denied wholeness and well-being (*shalom*), all are thereby diminished. This relational character of creation is rooted in all creatures' common origin in a God who not only created all that is, but who continues to be active in the world, seeking our *shalom*. Several aspects of *shalom* are particularly important for addressing the issues of war and violence.

Firstly, the Hebrews, along with most of their contemporaries, saw the world as constantly poised between the possibilities of order and chaos. The point of Israel's distinctive understanding of creation was not that God had brought something out of nothing, but that in the face of chaos, with its power to destroy and render meaningless, God the Creator had brought order. God has brought chaos under control, and in so doing, has given us the gift of wholeness of life.

Any biblically-based search for peace must begin with the notion that *shalom* is far broader than the absence of war. Paul Hanson writes, 'Perhaps the best way to begin to understand *shalom* is to recognise that it describes the realm where chaos is not allowed to enter, and where life can be fostered free from the fear of all which diminishes and destroys.'[8] Since all that would bring order out of chaos originates in God's creation, *shalom* can never be regarded as solely a human product.

Secondly, the opposite of *shalom* is not war, but chaos. Thus, concern for peace must place our opposition to war alongside an equal concern for every enemy of well-being and wholeness: injustice, oppression, exploitation, disease, famine. Within this broad concern for the things that bring chaos and destroy *shalom*, war certainly has a special place. War is that form of chaos which results from the violent attack of one group of people on another.

In such a world of broken unity, any participation in war risks serving chaos rather than *shalom*. But since God involved the divine self in that broken world, our most faithful response is to seek to discern that divine involvement and to pattern our participation in the world after its witness of grace to us.

Thirdly, recent studies have stressed that *shalom* was seen by ancient Israel not as a far-off ideal but as the natural human state. Humanity was essentially peaceable. As W Sibley Towner states, 'Far from being an extraordinary ideal, *shalom* is the norm which is to be contrasted to the extraordinary out-of-orderness of warfare, disease, and the like.'[9] Peace comes naturally to human beings unless we are divided or corrupted by injustice and exploitation—which in our history have often erupted into the violence of war. As biblical people, we are to work out of the assumptions of peace as the basis for trust, not out of the assumptions of war as the foundation for never-ending mistrust.

Israel's call to be a covenant community is the call to be a community possessed of an alternative consciousness and pattern of life in the world. *Shalom* is the word used in covenantal contexts to describe the goal of Israel's mission as God's people. *Shalom* is what results when God's justice, compassion and righteousness, seen clearly in God's deliverance of Israel from the Egyptian oppressor, is echoed by Israel's justice, compassion and righteousness lived out as its vocation in the world. The prophets Deutero-Isaiah and Ezekiel term this relationship with Yahweh a 'covenant of peace' (Is 54:10; Ezek 37:26). In effect, the vocation of a faithful community is to witness to the possibilities of *shalom* in the world and to the source of such *shalom* possibilities in God.

The fortunes of Yahweh, unlike those of the gods of other ancient Near Eastern religions, do not rise and fall with the fortunes of kings. This God is properly understood as not tied to the fate of any nation or group. This God is free to manifest divine power where the world sees only powerlessness. It is from divine freedom that the gifts of grace come, not from claims of obligation or ownership laid on God. Even to those who have known God's grace, God warns, 'I will be merciful to whom I will be merciful' (Exod 33:19; Amos 9:7), and even perfect righteousness creates no special obligation on God's part (see Job). Such a God may appear as *shalom* active in the most surprising places, and is in no way limited to institutionally approved, socially acceptable or religiously orthodox manifestations (see Deutero-

Isaiah's understanding of Cyrus as God's messiah (45:1)—and, of course, Jesus himself).

God is not only free from, but free for, choosing freely to become vulnerable to the world's pain and suffering. God says to Moses. 'I know [experience] their suffering' (Exod 3:7). Thus, the God of *shalom* is especially present in the midst of human need and especially caring of the poor, the oppressed and the hurting. The quality of God frequently used to describe this divinely chosen vulnerability is compassion (*rehem*), a word derived from the Hebrew word for womb or uterus. God's compassion is a metaphor for the womb, expressive of the tender oneness yet separateness shared between a mother and the child she is carrying.

God's fidelity is expressed in a refrain from Psalm 136, 'For God's steadfast love endures forever.' God's commitment is to the covenant of *shalom* without reservation or limits. Steadfast love (*hesed*) is made present in the world by justice (*mishpat*) and righteousness (*tsadeqah*), exercised in their full integrity without compromise, with no loyalty to any authority save the vocation of bringing *shalom* into a broken world.

Communities of covenant faith are explicitly called by God to reflect these same qualities in their life. They are to be 'in the world but not of the world,' free from all claims to ultimate loyalty except the vocation of witness to God's *shalom*. This is not a freedom to manifest an aloof disregard for the world; it is a freedom to enable a constant and consistent predisposition on the part of the faithful for identifying with the world's needs—special care for the victims of injustice, oppression, poverty, war, hunger, disease and loss. Faithfulness in this task of being vulnerable to the world's suffering comes from the pursuit of justice and righteousness by the community in its own life, in its treatment of the stranger and the sojourner and in its relationship to the nations.

Central to Israel's story is the witness to God's defeat of Pharaoh and the Egyptians in order to bring about the liberation of the Hebrew slaves. In the Exodus tradition it becomes clear that God's presence in history entails an implacable opposition to oppression and injustice— forces that work toward chaos and against God's *shalom*. Such evil brings suffering on the powerless, and God's judgment is committed to vanquishing that evil. Thus, against such forces of chaos, 'Yahweh is a man of war' (Exod 15:3). Israel, however, must recognise that although such judgment is within God's power, it is not appropriate to Israel's own human power. In the face of Pharoah's armies, Israel is told, 'The Lord will fight for you, and you have only to be still'. (Exod 14:14).

It is true that some early traditions of Israel portray Yahweh as warrior God. This, of course, is a source of concern for many Christians. However, a closer look at the Old Testament implies that human participation in war is diminished. Given the fact that Israel had a weak and unprofessional army, the active participation of Yahweh in bringing wholeness was critical. God as warrior could be trusted to oppose those forces that destroy *shalom* and bring chaos.

Christians are called to peace and not war

In the Old Testament, there can be no *shalom* when there is no salvation or when a person is chained to some 'prison.' Apparently, due to Israel's need for political intervention, we have confused the Hebrew idea of *shalom* with their need for peace and tranquility from political aggression. This confusion has extended to the fact that political liberation or deliverance from political tyranny is often mixed with the idea of salvation. While this is true, we must understand that there is no demarcation line between the 'secular' and the 'religious' in Israel's understanding. Thus, the idea of political salvation in itself, is not a secular act. It is religious, because the political success in Israel is largely attributed to Yahweh's doing, and failure or loss in war is attributed to Israel's failure to obey, or as a consequence of their misdeeds, including the violation of justice, worship of idols, and so on.

Is there a relationship between *shalom*/wholeness and justice? As we have noted, the Hebrew mind did not make any distinction between *shalom* and justice. When social order is not executed in society or in the covenant community, there will be no *shalom*. 'Justice is deliverance, rectifying the gross social inequities of the disadvantaged' (Ps 76:9).[10] In other words, justice as deliverance is aimed at putting an end to conditions that produce the injustice (Ps 10:18). Injustice abrogates *shalom*/wholeness; hence, there is no wholeness in the midst of injustice. *Shalom* is a profound and all-encompassing concept. Justice is one aspect of *shalom*. 'In Zech 8:16–19 the notion of peace is joined with *mispat*, where the root *slm* again is used in its meaning of true or complete justice. And *shalom* is joined with *'emet*, "truth". Peace, truth and justice are parallel terms.'[11] Peace, like justice and truth, occurs in the context of relationships. 'Peace encompasses a relationship that is ordered, a relationship of equity.'[12] This relationship is informed and shaped by the covenant God. Hence, such wholeness is made manifest in the covenant community. In the eschatological passage of Isaiah 9:1–7, the coming rule of justice and rightness is brought by the 'Prince of *Shalom*', whose rule is characterised by wholeness, because the Prince upholds justice and rightness. In Isaiah 32:17–18 we read:

> The fruit of righteousness will be peace; the effect of righteousness will be quietness and confidence forever. My people will live in peaceful dwelling places, in secure homes, in undisturbed places of rest.

When all relationships are justly and fully lived, then people can speak of peace. These relationships include those of nature, social and political as well as the wellbeing of persons in the entire community. In contexts where terror is all around, the Hebrew Bible calls for return to *shalom*!

Endnotes

1. This chapter is taken from a longer paper entitled 'War, Violence and the Bible: Terror all around!' parts of which were presented as the Thatcher Lecture at United Theological College, North Parramatta (17 August, 2006).
2. Although Maasai culture endorses forced marriages, they do not molest children, however, as we see in our towns in Eastern Africa. Although the examples cited here are drawn from the Maasai, there is much violence done to women and children in Eastern Africa and the Maasai alone are not to be blamed.
3. Gerhad von Rad, *Holy War in Ancient Israel*, translated by Marva J Dawn (Grand Rapids: Eerdmans, 1991), 10.
4. Cited in von Rad, *Holy War in Ancient Israel*, 20.
5. Cited in von Rad, *Holy War in Ancient Israel*, 22.
6. J Day, 'Baal', *The Anchor Bible Dictionary*, edited by David Noel Freedman (New York: Doubleday, 1992), volume 1, 547.
7. See *Dictionary of Biblical Imagery*, edited by Leland Ryken *et al* (Leicester: Intervarsity Press, 1998), 339.
8. 'War and Peace in the Hebrew Bible', *Interpretation*, volume 38 (1984), 347.
9. 'Tribulations and Peace: The Fate of Shalom in Jewish Apocalyptic', *Horizons in Biblical Theology*, volume 6 (1984), 18.
10. SC Mott, 'Justice', *Harper's Bible Dictionary*, edited by PJ Achtemeir (San Francisco: Harper and Row, 1985), 519–20.

11. JP Healey, 'Peace', in *Anchor Bible Dictionary* volume 5, 206.
12. Healey, 'Peace', 206.

Violating Faith via Eschatological Violence: Reviewing Matthew's Eschatology

David Neville

Soon after the turn of the millennium, John Dominic Crossan wrote the following in response to Dale Allison's portrait of Jesus as a 'millenarian prophet':

> We are now finally out of a terrible century, a century of world-wide killing fields, a century worse by execution if not by intention than any in our past. At such a moment, our very humanity demands that we reject definitively the lure of a violent ultimacy, a violent transcendence, or a violent God. If, on the other hand, we sincerely believe in a violent God, we must surely follow openly the advice of Mrs Job: Curse God and die.[1]

If one takes seriously Crossan's appeal to reject 'the lure of a violent ultimacy, a violent transcendence, or a violent God', what is one to make of biblical texts that envisage eschatological scenarios involving divine violence? With this perplexing question in mind, this study probes Matthew's eschatology to ascertain its moral dimensions.[2]

In *The Moral Vision of the New Testament*, Richard Hays concludes his discussion of Matthew's eschatology with a subsection entitled 'Eschatology as Ethical Warrant'. His remarks are worth pondering:

> [I]n Matthew, eschatology becomes a powerful *warrant* for moral behavior. The motivation for obedience to God is repeatedly grounded in the rewards and punishments that await everyone at the final judgment . . . This is nowhere more evident than in Matthew 24:37 – 25:46, where he appends to the Markan apocalyptic discourse five units of additional material stressing in various ways the necessity of being prepared for the coming of the Son of Man . . . The aim of such stories is to instill godly fear in the

> hearers and to motivate them to do the will of God
> while they still have opportunity, before the judgment
> comes upon them.
>
> It would not be correct to say that these stories
> provide only *warrants* for obedience to God; they
> also define significant ethical *norms* having to do
> primarily with just and merciful treatment of others
> and with responsible use of property . . . The parable
> of the sheep and the goats, with its powerful portrayal
> of care for the needy as the basic criterion for God's
> eschatological judgment of human deeds, has had
> a powerful impact on the church's imagination;
> the story reinforces Matthew's earlier emphasis on
> mercy as the hallmark of the kingdom of God.[3]

In response, three points may be made briefly as an overture to the following discussion. Firstly, Hays correctly notes that 'in Matthew, eschatology becomes a powerful warrant for moral behavior'. Yet the particular moral warrant he identifies within Matthew's narrative is ethically problematic. Secondly, for Hays, the parables of judgment in Matthew 24–25 provide not only warrants for obedience to the will of God but also 'define significant ethical norms', including just and merciful treatment of others. Perhaps so, but what Hays does not detect (or confess to detecting), and which I do detect, is an ultimate validation of violence. And thirdly, there can be no doubt that the parable of sheep and goats in Matthew 25 has had a potent impact on the church's imagination, perhaps best exemplified in Michelangelo's 'Last judgment'. But I am less confident than Hays that this parable reinforces 'mercy as the hallmark of the kingdom of God'. Certainly that is not *all* it reinforces, as Michelangelo's painting attests.

Orientation and perspective

One of the most disquieting realities of our world is religious legitimation of violence, especially the scriptural sanction of violence in the three 'religions of the book' — Judaism, Christianity and Islam. One frequently hears adherents of these religions assert that Judaism or Christianity or Islam is a religion of peace. Yet in the case of all three, their respective scriptures and traditions suggest otherwise.

All three? Even if church history is littered with the broken bones of peoples and cultures victimised by church-authorised violence, surely one can appeal to the New Testament as a collection of authoritative writings that fosters peace. Yet even the New Testament contains violent texts, few more ethically disconcerting than those that look forward to eschatological vengeance. After all, such texts provoke the question whether—when all is said and done—God is violent.

Against this backdrop, I am in quest of biblical resources for a *teleology of peace*. I accept John Milbank's argument that, contrary to postmodern suspicions, the Christian metanarrative presupposes an ontology of peace—if not in evolutionary history, at least in the being and intention of the Creator.[4] In short, theologically understood, the pan-historical experience of violent conflict is not primal reality but a distortion and desecration of God's original—and originating—intention for the world. I also accept that Jesus' mission and message were non-violent; he repudiated violence himself and instructed his disciples to follow his example in this respect. So, with regard to the Christian metanarrative, both the formative beginning and decisive midpoint of the story that makes sense of the Christian life affirm *peace as the determinative reality*. Violence is a derivative distortion.

But what about the end or *telos* of our story—as envisioned in scripture and Christian tradition? All too often the God of original *shalom* and the prince of peace are depicted as having to resort to violence to bring history to its desired and destined dénouement. If Christian eschatology presupposes violent retribution as the means to God's rectification of all things, this implies that violence, not peace, ultimately prevails. Moreover, this implication has what might be called proleptic moral suasion, that is, the power to shape moral imagination, character and behaviour here and now.

To discard the concept of divine judgment would be to consign history to the rule of 'might makes right'. So Matthew's expectation of eschatological judgment *per se* is not ethically problematic; what is morally troubling is the kind of judgment he anticipated. Matthew's eschatology is dominated by the threat of violent retribution for those ultimately deemed unrighteous, wicked or evil. This is not simply a perturbing feature in the history of (Christian) ideas. As Günther Bornkamm noted, 'No other Gospel is so shaped by the thought of the Church as Matthew's, so constructed for use by the Church; for this reason it has exercised, as no other, a normative influence in the later Church.'[5] In many respects, Matthew's influence is cause for celebration, yet it must be recognised and dealt with—theologically, morally and pastorally—that violent eschatology is part of the legacy of this brilliant, and baffling, Jewish-Christian scribe (Matt 13:52).

In response, some might retort: If you do not like Matthew's depiction of eschatological vengeance, perhaps you do not fully appreciate the weight of resistance to God's will in the world; or, the Gospel of Matthew is authoritative sacred scripture, and you must simply accept the divinely inspired portrait of the future Matthew offers. Yet here is the rub: Matthew *himself* featured—indeed, placed in a prominent position within his narrative—Jesus' injunctions to non-violence, nonretaliation and respect for enemies. The moral vision of Jesus, as reflected in the beatitudes and so-called 'antitheses' of Matthew 5, is widely recognised as an ethical high-water mark.[6] Moreover, the mission of Jesus as depicted by Matthew embodies his non-violent teaching. Jesus is no hypocrite, according to Matthew; his words and his actions are 'in sync', we might say. On the other hand, Matthew's eschatological parables envisage either Jesus (as the returning Son of humanity), or the One who authorised Jesus' mission, as resorting ultimately to violent retribution.

Eschatological violence in Matthew's parables

The tension in Matthew's Gospel between Jesus' moral vision and eschatological violence is explored in Barbara Reid's study, 'Violent Endings in Matthew's Parables and Christian Non-violence'.[7] Reid not only recognises but also seeks to resolve the tension between the moral guidance of Jesus in Matthew's Sermon on the Mount and the image of God (or God's agents) ultimately dealing violently with various kinds of persons in several Matthean parables. To that end, her discussion proceeds as follows: firstly, she surveys references to various forms of violence in Matthew's Gospel; secondly she describes how Jesus and his disciples are depicted as victims of violence, but in this section she also devotes considerable space to the enigmatic sayings in Matt 11:12 and 10:34–36; in her third (and longest) section, Reid discusses responses to violence described by Matthew, focusing especially on Jesus' teaching concerned with non-retaliation and love for enemies in Matt 5:38–48; in a brief fourth section, she explores eight Matthean parables that feature eschatological violence; fifthly, she evaluates four possible solutions to the moral tension inherent in Matthew's Gospel; and finally, she identifies additional theological and hermeneutical questions arising from her discussion.

The eight parables discussed by Reid are the twin parables of the Tares and the Dragnet (Matt 13:24–30, 40–43; 49–50); the parable of an Unforgiving Slave (Matt 18:23–35); the parable of Tenants in a Vineyard (Matt 21:33–44); the parable of a Wedding Banquet (Matt 22:1–14); the parable of a Waiting Slave (Matt 24:45–51); and the final two parables of the Talents and Final Judgment in Matt 25:14–46. Of these eight parables, four are unique to Matthew (Tares; Dragnet; Unforgiving Slave; Final Judgment). The four other parables have parallels (or partial parallels) in Luke's Gospel, but only one, Tenants in a Vineyard, is also found in Mark's Gospel. The picture that emerges from these parables in Matthew's Gospel is that people determined to be wicked, unresponsive or irresponsible will ultimately experience God's retributive violence.

Beginning with those parables unique to Matthew's Gospel, the twin parables of the Tares and Dragnet are found in the collection of parables relating to the reign of heaven in Matthew 13. The first thing to note about the parable of the Tares is that it is one of only two parables in Matthew 13 to be given an interpretation; the other is the parable of the Sower. Moreover, the parable of the Tares is the only one about which the disciples request an explanation of its meaning. Clearly, Matthew did not want it to be misunderstood! In Matthew 13:37–43 this parable is given an allegorical interpretation, with the tares representing those who belong to the evil one and the harvest representing the end of the age. According to Matthew's end-time scenario, angels sent by the Son of humanity will first sort out from the righteous both what causes people to fall away and those persons who act contrary to Torah, then discard them into a fiery furnace, a place of 'wailing and teeth-grinding'. This is a favourite Matthean phrase, first used in Matthew 8:12 to warn that those who expect to join the patriarchs of Israel at the eschatological banquet may well have their places taken by outsiders from east and west and be thrown into darkness outside the reign of heaven. The phrase 'wailing and teeth-grinding' occurs nowhere else in the New Testament except Luke 13:28 (parallel to Matt 8:12). But Matthew delights in the phrase, using it a further five times in the parables of the Tares (13:42), Dragnet (13:50), Wedding Banquet (22:13), Waiting Slave (24:51) and Talents (25:30). This speaks volumes about his mindset.

The same end-time scenario depicted in the parable of the Tares is replayed in the briefer parable of the Dragnet. Repeated phrases include: 'This is how things are at the conclusion of the age' (13:40, 49); 'And they (angels) will cast them (the non-righteous) into the furnace of fire' (13:42, 50); and 'There, there will be wailing and teeth-grinding' (13:42, 50). For those with ears to hear (13:43b), Matthew goes to the trouble of repeating himself. No interpretation is needed this time.

The parable of the Unforgiving Slave in Matthew 18:23–35 is also a parable of the reign of heaven. Reid notes that this parable, which she names 'Forgiveness Aborted', concludes with the king or master handing over the unforgiving slave to be tortured.[8] But she ignores the force of the concluding exhortation in Matthew 18:35: 'So also my heavenly Father will do to you (plural) unless each of you forgives his/her brother from your (plural) hearts.' Here Jesus concludes his instruction on forgiving largesse, in response to Peter's question about how often he should forgive an offence-prone brother (18:21). This parable is intended to reinforce Jesus' instruction to forgive limitlessly—not seven times but seventy-seven (or seventy times seven) times. Yet the conclusion to the parable envisages God dealing with unforgiving persons in a most unforgiving way! Indeed, the image of Jesus' heavenly Father handing over unforgiving believers to torturers is obscene.

The 'parable' of Final Judgment (Matt 25:31–46) is the finale to Matthew's eschatological discourse, which itself is the fifth and final discourse marked by the refrain, 'When Jesus had concluded these sayings/instructions/parables . . . ' (Matt 7:28; 11:1; 13:53; 19:1; 26:1).[9] This 'parable' of Final Judgment of the nations reiterates the notion of separating the righteous from the unrighteous, this time according to the criterion of whether or not one has attended to the needs of 'the least significant'. Those deemed not to have attended to the needs of 'the least significant' (hence those of the judging king) are banished to 'eternal' fire and punishment. Many Christian advocates of justice see in this passage their *raison d'être* for activism on behalf of the poor and powerless, yet how much thought is given to the character of the judging king on whose behalf such activism is conducted?[10]

So much for the four parables that belong to Matthew's special tradition, commonly designated 'M'.[11] What of the other four shared with the Gospels of Luke and (in one instance) Mark? The parable of Tenants in a Vineyard not only appears in all three synoptic gospels, but it also occurs in the same context—following Jesus' arrival in Jerusalem, his symbolic disruption in the temple and the subsequent question about his authority to do 'these things'. However, Matthew interposes another of his unique parables, the parable of Two Sons (21:28–32), between the question regarding Jesus' authority and the parable of the Tenants (21:33–46). In other words, despite the shared context, Matthew's parable of the Tenants is the second of two parables told by Jesus in response to the request by chief priests and elders to disclose the source of his authority. Both feature work in a vineyard, which may explain their juxtaposition. Furthermore, both in Jesus' response to the question about the source of his authority and in the parable of Two Sons, he refers to the mission of John the Immerser. The parable concludes with Jesus' admonition that toll-collectors and prostitutes enter the reign of God (not 'heaven', despite belonging to 'M') ahead of chief priests and elders because, unlike the chief priests and elders, toll-collectors and prostitutes believed John (and presumably responded appropriately). In short, the parable of Two Sons is a parable of reversal.

A Matthean emphasis in the parable of the Tenants may be seen in Matthew 21:34a, 41d and 43, each of which is uniquely Matthean. Matthew 21:34a reads: 'But when the season for *fruit-bearing* drew near . . . '. Matthew 21:41 ends with Jesus' interlocutors asserting that other vine-dressers will give to the vineyard owner *fruits* in their appointed seasons. Finally, Matthew 21:43 has Jesus say, 'For this reason I tell you that the reign of God will be withdrawn from you and given to people-groups producing its *fruits*'. For Matthew, 'bearing fruit' is code for right conduct in accord with God's will (Matt 3:8–10; 7:16–20; 12:33).

As Reid notes, 'In the parable of the treacherous tenants (21:33–46), the response of the landowner to the murder of his servants and son is to put those evil ones . . . to a miserable death, and to lease the vineyard to other tenants who will give him the produce at the harvest time (21:41).'[12] Yet she does not note that 'they' (presumably the chief priests and elders of 21:23 or chief priests and Pharisees of 21:45) make this inference in response to Jesus' question, 'So, when the master of the vineyard should happen to arrive, what will he do to these vine-dressers?' (21:40). While their inference is reasonable, the way in which Jesus responds suggests they are off the mark. Moreover, while Jesus' statement in Matthew 21:43 seems to confirm the inference of leasing the vineyard to other vine-dressers, it does not reiterate the notion of ensuring that bad people will come to a bad end. Reid draws attention to the harshness of Matthew 21:44, which seemingly grants to the stone of 21:42 destructive prowess, but she ignores its textual uncertainty.[13] So perhaps Matthew's version of the parable of the Tenants is less vindictive than Reid makes out.

Reid seems to accept that the parable of the Wedding Banquet in Matthew 22:1–14 is the same as the parable of the Great Feast in Luke 14:15–24, despite the different literary context and relatively few verbal parallels. Certainly there are similarities, and Reid correctly

identifies violent and vindictive elements in Matthew's parable that
are absent from Luke's:

> In the parable of the wedding feast (22:1–14),
> Matthew adds the detail that the king's envoys were
> seized, treated shamefully, and killed (v 6). The
> king in anger sends his troops and destroys those
> murderers and burns their city (v 7). Another group
> of servants is dispatched to go into the streets and
> gather all whom they find, both evil . . . and good (v
> 10). The uniquely Matthean conclusion (vv 11–14)
> has the king confront an improperly attired guest,
> who is then bound hand and foot and cast into the
> outer darkness, where there is weeping and gnashing
> of teeth (v 13).[14]

Matthew 22:1–14 follows closely upon the parables of Two Sons
and Tenants in a Vineyard (Matt 21:28–44), and Matthew seems to
link this third parable to the previous two. As in Matthew 21:35–
36, Matthew 22:6 notes that slaves sent out are killed, a seemingly
gratuitous detail except that it prepares for the king's retribution in
Matthew 22:7. Moreover, as in the earlier parables of the Tares and
Dragnet, those gathered at the wedding feast include both the evil and
the good. Yet the parable does not end by separating out the righteous
from the unrighteous and consigning the unrighteous to outer darkness,
as in the earlier parables; rather, one guest without a wedding-garment
is silent when asked how he gained entry without suitable attire, so is
thrown out into the domain of wailing and teeth-grinding! The detail
that this guest remained silent when questioned (Matt 22:12b) might
prefigure Jesus' silence when questioned by the religious leadership
and Pilate (Matt 26:63; 27:14).[15] Perhaps the parable once functioned
as a parable of reversal (like the parable of Two Sons), making much
the same point as the warning in Matthew 8:11–12.

Although the parable of the Wedding Banquet in Matthew 22:1–14
is quite dissimilar from its (alleged) Lukan parallel, the same cannot be
said of the parable of a Waiting Slave in Matthew 24:45–51, which is
very similar in content to Luke 12:41–46, even if placed in a different
context. It is difficult to know whether Matthew envisaged one slave
only or two. The introduction of the term 'bad', 'evil' or perhaps
'irresponsible' in Matthew 24:48 suggests a second slave, but this may
simply be a description based on how he decides to treat fellow-slaves

after surmising that his master is delayed. In terms of violent endings, there is little to separate this Matthean parable from its Lukan parallel; in both, the slave is diced in two and shares the fate of undesirables ('hypocrites' in Matthew 24:51; 'the faithless' in Luke 12:46). The Matthean accent appears in the addition of the grisly phrase, 'There, there will be wailing and teeth-grinding' (24:51).

Like the parable of the Wedding Banquet, the parable of the Talents in Matthew 25:14–30 is significantly different from its alleged Lukan parallel, the seemingly conflated parable of the Minas located immediately prior to Jesus' entry into Jerusalem (Luke 19:11–28). Set within the context of the eschatological discourse of Matthew 24–25, the parable of the Talents is the third of four parables seemingly intended to drive home the point of Matthew 24:42 and 44: 'So be watchful, because you do not know on what day your Lord is arriving'; 'So you also be ready, because the Son of humanity is arriving when you do not expect it'. As Reid points out, the slave who did nothing with the talent entrusted to him is consigned to outer darkness where there is wailing and teeth-grinding,[16] like the irresponsible slave two parables earlier (Matt 24:45–51). Compared with its (alleged) Lukan parallel, one is hard-pressed to say that Matthew's version is more violent overall, since in Luke's parable the nobleman-king orders his opponents slaughtered. On the other hand, understood in context, the figure of the nobleman-king in Luke's parable is unlikely to represent the returning Son of humanity, as the master in Matthew's parable almost certainly does.

While one can agree with Reid that all of these Matthean parables end in violent punishment and therefore depict God or God's agent(s) meting out violent retribution at the end of the age, it is not entirely clear that 'in the parables that Matthew takes over from Mark or Q, he intensifies the violent punishments for those who do evil'.[17] In the parable Matthew shares with Mark, the parable of the Tenants, Matthew's version is more vindictive than Mark's, especially if Matthew 21:44 is genuinely Matthean. But in all four parables shared with Luke, there is not a great deal to separate Matthew from Luke, apart from Matthew's repeated phrase, 'There, there will be wailing and teeth-grinding'. However, this is not to gainsay Reid's main point, which concerns the discrepancy between, and moral implications of, contrasting images of God in Matthew's Gospel:

> Throwing evildoers into a fiery furnace, binding
> them hand and foot, casting them into outer darkness

> where there is weeping and gnashing of teeth, putting
> them to a miserable death, cutting and breaking
> them into pieces and crushing them, destroying
> murderers and burning their city, depriving them of
> the presence of God, putting them with hypocrites or
> with the devil and his angels for all eternity stand in
> clear contrast to the boundless, gratuitous divine love
> described in the Sermon on the Mount (5:44–48).
> The punishments meted out in the parabolic endings
> present a far different picture of how God acts. Is
> there inconsistency in God's actions? Which path are
> disciples to take as children of God who are supposed
> to imitate divine ways?[18]

Having set out to resolve the tension within Matthew's Gospel
caused by these contrasting depictions of God's character, Reid offers
four possible ways of doing so.[19] One is to acknowledge that in the
process of composition, the gospel writer may have incorporated
diverse strands of tradition without trying to reconcile contradictory
materials. Yet in the case of the stock phrase, 'There, there will be
wailing and teeth-grinding', this clearly represents the gospel writer's
perspective. Moreover, as Reid observes, even if this solution is
illuminating at a compositional level, the moral problem remains.

A second resolution is to view the gospel writer as a teacher
addressing disciples at different stages of moral development. In
other words, Matthew's parables with violent endings are instructive
for those who operate at the level of reward and punishment, while
the Sermon on the Mount is for those at a higher level of moral
development. Yet as Reid notes, this distinction must be imposed on
the narrative; it certainly does not emerge from the Gospel itself since
nowhere is there any indication which teachings of Jesus are directed
towards those at a lower or higher level of moral development. One
might add that in so far as Matthew's parables of judgment at the end
of the age depict the action of God or God's agent(s), one is entitled
to regard vindictive retribution as morally superior to love that seeks
to emulate the (supposed) indiscriminate goodness of God. In other
words, how God acts ultimately might be considered more morally
compelling than how God acts penultimately.

A third resolution is to deny that the principal characters in the
parables of retribution represent God. 'Rather, these parables unmask
the violence of these characters and the unjust systems they perpetuate.

Their purpose is to lead hearers toward action that confronts such injustice.'[20] Some of Matthew's parables are patient of such an interpretation, but as Reid points out, it is difficult to argue this case for the parables of the Tares and Unforgiving Slave. The same might be said of the parable of the Dragnet, which echoes the parable of the Tares, and the 'parable' of Final Judgment. The context of the parables of the Waiting Slave and the Talents also suggests an interpretation along the lines of eschatological retribution.

Reid's preferred resolution is to demarcate decisively between divine and human violence:

> Another explanation is that the kind of non-violent confrontation of evil that Jesus advocated in the Sermon on the Mount is not applicable to the kind of situation envisioned in these eight parables. All of them can be understood as portraying an end-time setting with a reckoning that is final.[21]

One can agree with Reid's assessment of the likely eschatological dimension of each of the parables she examines without accepting her view that 'this interpretation satisfactorily resolves the tension'.[22] Admittedly for Reid, this implies that disciples are not in a position to emulate eschatological retribution; rather, disciples of Jesus are bound by his instruction to confront evil, injustice and violence non-violently. Yet Reid makes an assertion that exacerbates the tension she claims to have resolved: 'Non-violent confrontation of evildoers is not pertinent to scenes of end-time judgment.'[23] If this is purely a descriptive assessment of Matthew's moral vision, it may be accurate, but in view of alternative perspectives, even within the New Testament, one is entitled to ask why this should be so. After all, if evil can only be undone by greater evil or if violence can only be vanquished by greater violence, has either been overcome? Reid is cognisant of the problem that followers of Jesus might well authorise violence against perceived evildoers by appealing to eschatological violence on God's part. This is a significant moral dilemma. Yet there is another, arguably more destructive, problem, which concerns our theology (in the sense of reasoning about God) and what flows ethically from it. For if one accepts that God's ways are our ways, only more forceful and potent, that is idolatry (understood theologically) or projection (understood psychologically).

In the final section of her essay, Reid raises the question of our understanding of the 'nature' or 'character' of God: 'Does God at the end-time set aside compassion and engage in vindictive violence?'[24] Her answer is that this question cannot be adequately answered exegetically but must be addressed within the context of systematic and constructive theology. With respect to Matthew's Gospel, she may be right, but I consider that the story of Jesus, even as told by Matthew, undoes the logic of eschatological violence. In other words, Matthew's story of Jesus is more determinative than the stories told by Jesus within his narrative, even the uniquely Matthean parable of Workers in a Vineyard (Matt 20:1–16), which is more consonant with Jesus' moral teaching in the Sermon on the Mount.[25]

The moral problem of eschatological violence in Matthew

There can be little doubt that Matthew's eschatology presumes that God or God's agent(s) will ultimately indulge in retributive violence against the unrighteous, irrespective of the criteria used to separate the righteous from the wicked (obedience to Torah interpreted by Jesus or compassion for 'the least significant'). It is also undeniable that in Jesus' moral teaching, especially in the Sermon on the Mount, as well as in his example, violence is eschewed as being incompatible with the 'character' of God. There is therefore an inherent tension between Matthew's violent eschatology and his depiction of the non-violent moral instruction of Jesus grounded in the indiscriminate love ('perfection') of God.

For Matthew, hypocrisy or incongruity between word and deed, teaching and action, was anathema. To label an opponent a hypocrite was, for Matthew, a severe insult. This is why he liberally applied the term to scribes and Pharisees (Matt 23:13, 16, 23, 25, 27, 29), who were more likely to have been his own than Jesus' opponents, but ensured that in many and varied ways Jesus acts as he teaches. In *Matthew: A Retrospect*, Davies and Allison detail many connections between Jesus' words and deeds before concluding: 'One could go on and on in this vein, citing instances of Jesus acting in accord with his speech.'[26] However, what Matthew anticipated on the part of the eschatological judge, the returning Son of humanity, is incongruent with what the self-same Son of humanity taught about responding to violence.

While this tension is troubling for some, though not all, today, Matthew may not have perceived it as inherently contradictory. He may even have failed to perceive the tension, as Allison avers:

. . . Matthew, understandably enough, did not share the modern aversion to hell. He was educated into the first-century Jewish and Christian traditions, in both of which the God of love is equally the God of judgment. Surely, then, if he could talk with us, the evangelist would be unsympathetic with our contemporary queasiness about transcendent wrath and punishment. There is no indication from first-century Jewish or Christian texts that anybody back then perceived divine love and judgment as necessary antitheses.[27]

Point taken. Yet it is one thing to grant that divine love and divine judgment are not antithetical, *quite another* to accept that vindictive and violent retribution is compatible with the calibre of divine love understood—even by Matthew—to be responsible for human redemption. In other words, judgment need not necessarily imply violent retribution.[28] Moreover, even if Matthew failed to perceive the theological-cum-moral problem of eschatological violence, that does not imply the absence of a problem, nor indeed that (all) his contemporaries failed to perceive it.

Reid seems to accept that the moral problem of violence within Matthew's Gospel is satisfactorily resolved by strictly demarcating between divine eschatological violence and non-violent conduct on the part of disciples of Jesus. At a theoretical level, she may be right; allowing that God is entitled to use violent retribution when all other means have been exhausted does not imply that violent retribution on the part of human beings, even if understood to be acting on God's behalf, is to be condoned. Yet theory is often undone in practice. For whatever reason, those enamoured of the idea of God's eschatological violence can as easily support violent means in the here and now as disavow them.[29] Attitudes and behaviours are shaped by what we hope for, and it is not so straightforward a matter to separate human morality from perceptions of divine reality. In other words, it is more difficult than Reid assumes to acknowledge the divine entitlement to violent retribution without arrogating the same prerogative to human beings, especially persons convinced that they are acting on God's behalf.

Matthew's pronounced theme of divine eschatological violence poses theological, moral and ontological problems for Christian disciples today: it encourages a sub-Christian conception of God; it fosters violent attitudes and behaviours that are antithetical to the moral instruction of Jesus; and it provokes the question whether violence might not be intrinsic to reality rather than a derivative distortion. In view of these problems, how might we respond?

Concluding reflections

In the Crossan citation with which this chapter opens, he asserts that '. . . our very humanity demands that we reject definitively the lure of a violent ultimacy, a violent transcendence, or a violent God'. Yet what is demanded by 'our very humanity' is open to multiple, even conflicting, interpretations. To my mind, Christology provides the key. Various New Testament writers and subsequent Christian thinkers perceived in Jesus the measure of God. Nowhere is this more clearly expressed than in the prologue to the fourth gospel, where the Logos incarnate in Jesus is affirmed as the exegete of God (John 1:14–18). Matthew's near-equivalent notion is Emmanuel, God present with humanity in the historical person of Jesus. Whatever the divine content is which we attribute to 'God with us', as displayed in the mission and message of Jesus, this surely should take priority over whatever residual knowledge of God remains to be disclosed eschatologically.

In the search for a resolution to the various problems arising from Matthew's violent eschatology, we can be grateful that we have four canonical gospels rather than one only. Had the early church decided that differences between the gospels implied that only one could be accepted as authoritative, that single Gospel might well have been Matthew's. Fortunately, Matthew's synoptic counterparts mute the theme of eschatological violence. Mark's Gospel, in particular, seems to display something much closer to a teleology of peace in line with his noncoercive Christology. In short, there are exegetical resources within scripture itself for combating (peacefully, of course!) a violent God-image.

Although exegesis is important, the interpretive imperative is more important still, especially since scripture contains more than one perspective on violence. In other words, interpretive choices can and must be made! Exegetical studies indicate that within the gospel tradition(s), eschatological violence is a *Matthean* emphasis, which can plausibly be explained as a response to specific socio-historical circumstances.[30]

This is not to say that Jesus did not believe in eschatological judgment, punishment or hell. Perhaps his mindset was similar to Matthew's. Yet even if his mindset were similar to Matthew's, the common story told by all four gospel writers of how Jesus responded to violence and of what he taught his disciples with respect to responding to violence is determinative. In other words, the story Matthew told contains within itself the wherewithal to deconstruct his own eschatological outlook, at least in part. Thus, the interpretive task involves desisting from prejudging—and thereby pre-empting—the form divine judgment might take.[31]

Endnotes

1. John Dominic Crossan, 'Eschatology, Apocalypticism, and the Historical Jesus', in *Jesus Then and Now: Images of Jesus in History and Christology*, edited by Marvin Meyer and Charles Hughes (Harrisburg, PA: Trinity Press International, 2001), 97–98. Crossan was responding to Dale Allison, *Jesus of Nazareth: Millenarian Prophet* (Minneapolis: Augsburg Fortress, 1998).
2. On Matthew's eschatology in relation to the Gospel's socio-historical context, see David Sim, *Apocalyptic Eschatology in the Gospel of Matthew* (Cambridge: Cambridge University Press, 1996); Vicky Balabanski, *Eschatology in the Making: Mark, Matthew and the Didache* (Cambridge: Cambridge University Press, 1997).
3. Richard Hays, *The Moral Vision of the New Testament: Community, Cross, New Creation: A Contemporary Introduction to New Testament Ethics* (Harper San Francisco, 1996), 106–107.
4. See John Milbank, *Theology and Social Theory: Beyond Secular Reason* (Oxford: Blackwell, 1990), Part IV, 'Theology and Difference'.
5. Günther Bornkamm, 'End-expectation and Church in Matthew', in *Tradition and Interpretation in Matthew*, edited by Günther Bornkamm, Gerhard Barth and Heinz Joachim Held, second edition, translated by Percy Scott (London: SCM Press, 1982), 38.
6. On the Beatitudes in particular, see Christopher Marshall, 'The Moral Vision of the Beatitudes: The Blessings of Revolution', in *Faith and Freedom: Christian Ethics in a Pluralist Culture*, edited by David Neville and Philip Matthews (Adelaide: ATF Press, 2003), 11–33.
7. Barbara E Reid, 'Violent Endings in Matthew's Parables and Christian Non-violence', *Catholic Biblical Quarterly* 66 (2004): 237–55. (My thanks to Elaine Wainwright for alerting me to this study.)
8. Reid, 'Violent Endings', 249.
9. Although partially parabolic, Matthew 25:31–46 is not a parable in the strict sense.
10. A (further) sting in the tail is that the 'sheep' are *unaware* that what was done for insignificant people in need was done also for the judging king. Will advocacy on behalf of those in need be judged as 'righteous'

if done *because one is aware* of the judging king's identification with such people?

11. Other uniquely Matthean parables are: Hidden Treasure and Priceless Pearl (13:44–45); Workers in the Vineyard (20:1–16); Two Sons (21:28–32); and Ten Bridesmaids (25:1–13), another eschatological parable with a disconcerting ending.

12. Reid, 'Violent Endings', 249.

13. Matthew 21:44 is closely paralleled by Luke 20:18, but there is no Markan parallel.

14. Reid, 'Violent Endings', 249.

15. WD Davies and Dale C Allison, *A Critical and Exegetical Commentary on the Gospel according to Saint Matthew*, 3 volumes (Edinburgh: T&T Clark, 1997), 3.205, draw attention to the silence of the Sadducees in Matthew 22:34.

16. Reid, 'Violent Endings', 250.

17. *Ibid*, 249.

18. *Ibid*, 250.

19. *Ibid*, 250–53.

20. *Ibid*, 251. (Here Reid summarises a view she considers inadequate.)

21. *Ibid*, 252.

22. *Ibid*, 253.

23. *Ibid*, 252.

24. *Ibid*, 253. This is only one of five considerations raised in Reid's final section, all of which merit reflection.

25. Framed as this parable is by mirror-image reversal sayings (Matt 19:30; 20:16), Matthew could not have emphasised more emphatically that justice in the reign of heaven is different from, but not less than, human conceptions of fairness.

26. Davies and Allison, *Gospel According to Saint Matthew*, 3.715–16.

27. Dale Allison, *Studies in Matthew: Interpretation Past and Present* (Grand Rapids: Baker Academic, 2005), 248–49.

28. For 'a nonretributive approach to eschatological judgment', see Christopher D Marshall, *Beyond Retribution: A New Testament Vision for Justice, Crime, and Punishment* (Grand Rapids: Eerdmans; Auckland and Sydney: Lime Grove House, 2001), 188–97.

29. See Marshall, *Beyond Retribution*, 178; also Robert Wall, 'The Eschatologies of the Peace Movement', *Biblical Theology Bulletin* 15/1 (1985): 3–11, who argues that 'Christian hawks' tend to share Matthew's eschatological outlook whereas 'Christian doves' tend to appeal to Luke's more realised eschatology.

30. See, for example, Sim, *Apocalyptic Eschatology*, 179–243.

31. For further elaboration of the perspective presented in this essay, see my more detailed study, 'Toward a Teleology of Peace: Contesting Matthew's Violent Eschatology', forthcoming in the *Journal for the Study of the New Testament*.

Peace and Military Engagement in the Qur'an and in the Actions of the Prophet Muhammad

Mehmet Ozalp

Global terrorism, suicide bombings and the identification of Muslims with terrorist activities have caused many to question the core teachings of Islam and the practices of the Prophet Muhammad[pbuh].[1] While a minority of Muslims respond in violence to what they perceive to be injustice done to them, other Muslims with extreme views seem to justify their violent actions with references to the Qur'an and the teachings of the Prophet Muhammad[pbuh]. Horrified by what they see in news coverage, many non-Muslims wonder about the peaceful nature of Islam. Some critics go even further to claim that 'violence is in the nature of Islam' as the Qur'an seems to allow and justify wars and killings and that the Prophet Muhammad[pbuh] engaged in warfare in his lifetime.

There is a need to analyse critically claims of both camps and examine how the Qur'an refers to warfare, what actions the Prophet Muhammad[pbuh] took, and behaviours he displayed in military engagement. Was violence and aggression part of the Prophet Muhammad's plan to advance Islam? Or did he find himself and Muslims under attack from a hostile world having to fight for survival and, in doing so, followed a humane and ethical standard of warfare? I will attempt to explore the answer to this question by looking at the following four areas: (i) General characteristics of Islam in the Qur'an; (ii) Military engagement in the Qur'an; (iii) Circumstances that lead to wars engaged by the Prophet Muhammad; and (iv) Warfare in the actions of the Prophet Muhammad[pbuh].

I will argue that the Prophet Muhammad[pbuh], who is accepted by Muslims as the embodiment of Qur'anic teachings, in fact, practised a deliberate strategy of peace and diplomacy to deal with the conflicts of his time. He practised active non-violence in the face of suffering persecution and economic embargo that he and his followers endured in Mecca. After having to migrate from his home town, he established a pluralistic and multifaith society in Medina. He took active steps to sign treaties with all neighbouring tribes. He even signed a disadvantageous ten-year treaty with the Meccan leadership, much to the discontent of his followers, to end the conflict. Despite this, there

was a hostile world which attacked Muslims in Medina. Engaging
these attackers in warfare was inevitable.

The fact that the Qur'an includes verses that discuss warfare and
that the Prophet Muhammad[pbuh] lead armies in a number of battles
may seem counterintuitive to a God-revealed religion. The historical
evidence suggest that this aspect of Islam is actually an advantage
rather than being a liability. Since warfare has been around since
time immemorial and that inevitably people will find themselves in
some defensive warfare and international conflict, a 'final religion'
like Islam would have to provide guidelines in this area as well. As
a result of these guidelines, we do not see any holocausts, holy wars,
inquisitions, systematic rape of women and mass murder of civilians in
Muslim history. Without the guidelines of the Qur'an and the example
set by the Prophet Muhammad[pbuh] in warfare, Muslim history and, in
fact, world history, would have transpired quite differently—indeed,
for the worse. Certainly, Islam wants to establish a social order where
people live in peace and security.

General characteristics of Islam in the Qur'an

Every religion has core teachings that characterise the religion and the
majority of its followers. It is important that we know what these are in
the case of Islam so that we can make a healthy analysis of the verses
of the Qur'an that talk about warfare and the behaviour of the Prophet
Muhammad[pbuh] in military engagement. In order to illustrate the point,
consider for instance, the following quotations from Jesus[pbuh]:

> But those enemies of mine who did not want me to
> be king over them; bring them here and kill them in
> front of me.[2]

> Do not suppose that I have come to bring peace to
> the earth. I did not come to bring peace, but a sword.
> For I have come to turn a man against his father,
> a daughter against her mother, a daughter-in-law
> against her mother-in-law. A man's enemies will be
> the members of his own household.[3]

Are we to conclude that Jesus[pbuh] has taught violence? We know that
the core message of Jesus[pbuh] was one of love and compassion. A
well-intended examination of these verses and the context leads to
the understanding that Jesus was really talking about the inevitable

consequence of a conflict that would arise between those who believed in him and those who did not accept his message. In a similar way, the Qur'an should be read with the same intent and the reader should understand the verses within the general spirit of Islam.

So what is this spirit? It is beyond the scope of this chapter to look at all the characteristics of Islam. It should, however, suffice to look at the general tone of the Qur'an with respect to human life, the nature of the mission of the Prophet Muhammad[pbuh], and how Islam seeks converts.

Derived from the root word 's/l/m', which has the meanings of 'peace' and 'submission', Islam as a religion claims to have been revealed to the whole of humanity with a peaceful message of good news and devotion to God. The Qur'an says, 'And We have not sent you (O Muhammad) except as a giver of glad tidings and a warner to all mankind . . . '.[4] The emphasis on mercy and compassion in the mission of the Prophet Muhammad[pbuh] is highlighted more in the verse, 'And We have sent you (O Muhammad) nothing but as a mercy and grace for the worlds'[5] of humans and creatures.

When the Prophet was wounded in the Battle of Uhud, some suggested that he curse the 'idolaters', and the Prophet Muhammad[pbuh] replied, 'I am not sent for damnation. O Lord! Guide my nation, they don't know.'[6] Aisha, the wife of the Prophet Muhammad[pbuh], reported that whenever the Prophet was confronted with an issue he always chose the path that was easy or better for people. In another instance of a Bedouin who urinates in a mosque, people in the mosque become infuriated by this behaviour and start to push and shove him. The Prophet emerges from his room to see what the commotion is about. Upon finding out what has happened, he scolds people, telling them that the Bedouin man does not understand what he has done. He needs to be educated. The Prophet then utters his timeless remark that underscores the right Muslim attitude in mission, 'Facilitate (ease) things to people (concerning religious matters), and do not make it hard for them and give them good tidings and do not make them run away (from Islam)'.[7] These examples give us an insight into the character of the Prophet Muhammad[pbuh] as a peaceful, humble person who empathised with the needs and feelings of people.

The teachings of the Qur'an hold human life in great respect. Without making any distinction of race, colour and status, the Qur'an teaches that human beings are 'created in the best of composition'[8] and have 'been honoured with goodness'[9]. Since only 'God gives life and causes death',[10] then 'it is forbidden to kill anyone except for a just cause'.[11] Therefore, if anyone kills a person—with the exceptions of proven murder by a court of law, or in lawful warfare—'it would be as if he killed all mankind'.[12] Furthermore, human nations and societies exist so that 'they may know one another not to despise one another'.[13]

For convert-seeking religions, there is a temptation to use violence and coercion to force people into the faith. This is particularly so, if they hold power over people. The justification is that people do not know what is true and false. Once they are in the faith, albeit forcefully, they will appreciate it and thank those people who forced them into it.

Although Islam seeks converts, it does not see any reference in the Qur'an and in the actions of the Prophet Muhammad[pbuh] that forced conversions were sought through conquest and domination. In many verses of the Qur'an, the Prophet is reminded that his duty is only to convey the message of God[14]. The Qur'an also warns the Prophet that he is not to force people into faith. 'So inform them (O Muhammad), you are only one who reminds. You are not a dictator over them.'[15]

Before Islam, one of the tribes in Medina had a peculiar practice. If their children died in infancy, they would give an oath to God that if their next child survived infancy, they would raise them as a Jew or a Christian, thinking that these were superior religions and therefore their prayer was more likely to be accepted. Consequently, when Islam came to Medina some of the Arab children were Jews or Christians. The following verse was revealed when their parents tried to force their children to convert to Islam: 'There is no compulsion in religion. Verily the right has become distinct from the wrong . . . '.[16]

It is clear, therefore, that Islam taught grace and mercy, gave great value to human life, and did not seek to advance its teachings through forced conversions. We, therefore, need to examine wars and other events that resulted in deaths during the lifetime of the Prophet Muhammad[pbuh] in this frame of reference.

The concept of *jihad* and the Qur'an

A closer examination of the Qur'an reveals that no word meaning 'holy war' is used. As a matter of fact, we don't see the use of this phrase in the authentic sayings of the Prophet Muhammad[pbuh] or in major Islamic works. The Arabic term for 'military war' is *harb* and for 'fighting' is *qital*, not necessarily *jihad*, as would be expected by most people today. *Jihad* has a broader meaning of 'struggle' against adverse circumstances within a person and externally in a society for good purposes. *Jihad* is covered in the Qur'an in many contexts:[17]

recognising the Creator and loving Him above any other;[18] resisting the pressure of relatives, peers and the society to do wrong;[19] staying steadfastly on the straight path of faith and equilibrium;[20] striving to do righteous deeds;[21] having the courage and steadfastness to convey the message of Islam;[22] defending Islam and the community as well as helping allied people who may not necessarily be Muslim;[23] removing treacherous people from power;[24] gaining freedom to practise Islam as well as to educate and convey the message of Islam in an open and free environment;[25] and freeing people from tyranny and oppression.[26]

Military engagement in the Qur'an

A military *jihad* or war becomes lawful as a last resort in self-defence against aggression. Both the defensive nature of war and its legitimate justification can be seen in the following verses that were revealed in the first year of migration to Medina:

> Permission to fight is given to those who were attacked for they have been wronged. Only God is able to give them victory. They are those who were driven from their homes unjustly and for no other reason than that they said 'Our Lord is God'.[27]

According to this text, there are basically two main justifications for military warfare: firstly, being driven from one's home or land unjustly by a foreign power; secondly, Muslims being forced to change their faith or losing their freedom to express their faith.

Even in these cases, there are important principles to follow. There is to be no aggression on the part of Muslims, since 'God loves not the aggressors.'[28] The Qur'an also provides detailed guidelines and regulations regarding the conduct of war; who is to fight and who is exempted;[29] when hostilities must cease;[30] and how prisoners should be treated.[31] Most importantly, verses such as 2:294 emphasise that warfare and response to violence and aggression must be proportional; 'Whoever transgresses against you, respond in kind'.[32] Peaceful solutions to disputes are preferred to military ones. In the event of unavoidable war, every opportunity to end the war must be pursued. The Qur'an directs, 'But if the enemy inclines towards peace, then you must also incline towards peace . . . '.[33]

Critics of the Qur'an often quote the first part of the Qur'anic verse 9:5, 'When the sacred months have passed, slay the idolaters wherever you find them and take them and confine them and lie in wait for them at every place of ambush . . . ' to argue that Islam is inherently violent. This is the same passage that religious extremists use to justify their violent actions in recent times. When one takes this passage out of the context of the complete verse and the other verses that come before and after it, the real intent could be easily missed. The verse continues to say, ' . . . but if they repent and perform prescribed prayers and give charitable alms then let them go their way, for God is Oft-Forgiving and Most Merciful.'[34]

We need to bear in mind the historical context of the set of verses in chapter 9 of the Qur'an. These verses were revealed in 631 CE, a year after the peaceful capture of Mecca by Muslims that ended the aggression led by Mecca towards Muslims, who thereafter legitimately held popular power in Arabia. Although organised aggression against Muslims ended, small bands of individuals and tribes were still attacking Muslims in a way that we classify today as terrorism. The greater Muslim population was subjected to acts of terrorism by a few remnant 'idolaters' and small tribes who refused to accept the conclusive Muslim victory and government of the Prophet. This chapter is an ultimatum to these individuals and tribes, telling them to end their aggression.

Verse 9:4 clearly asks Muslims to fulfill their obligations towards tribes with whom they have a treaty. Verse 9:6 also commands Muslims to treat well any 'idolater' refugee who seeks protection with Muslims and asks them to be escorted to a place where they can feel safe. From all of this additional information we understand that 'slaying those idolaters' mentioned in verse 9:5 only applies to those individuals who are carrying out acts of terrorism against a peaceful society and a popular and legitimate government. This is quite similar to the current (2004) American policy to kill Al-Qaida members wherever they find them because they feel these terrorists are in turn at war with them. Therefore, Muslims historically never understood verse 9:5 or other similar verses[35] as an open licence to kill non-Muslims. An overwhelming majority of Muslims, with the small exception of those who resort to terrorism, are still of the same understanding.

Circumstances that lead to wars engaged by the Prophet Muhammad

The Prophet Muhammad[pbuh] followed an active non-violence strategy for the thirteen-year mission in Mecca. Although he and his followers suffered opression, persecution and even murder, the Prophet never resorted to violence even though some of his followers urged him to take arms. He bluntly refused, saying that he was not commanded to do so.

In order to escape persecution, Muslims finally migrated to Medina in 622 CE and a fledging Muslim community was established. A City Charter was drafted, which was the first such document defining a puluralistic society. The Charter served as a constitution of the new city polity with remarkable emphasis on citizenship rights and responsibilities regardless of religious conviction. Jews, for example, were allowed to practise their faith freely and even to have their own laws. They were exempt from the application of Islamic law and military service. Interestingly, there was still a large pagan population in the city.

The migration of Muslims to Medina did not end the hostility of the Meccans towards Muslims. On the contrary, it appears that it had even increased it, despite the fact that Muslims were no longer in the city to influence their pagan tradition. This intractable hostility inevitably led to military conflicts. The Prophet Muhammad[pbuh], being the Prophet and the temporal leader of Muslims, had to lead them in these difficult times and to defend them in order to ensure the very survival of his followers and Islam.

In this struggle for survival, history notes that the Prophet never initiated aggression. Military wars that the Prophet Muhammad[pbuh] or Muslims had to engage in were either purely defensive or they were pre-emptive strikes against the other party who were preparing to attack Muslims. In the case of a pre-emptive strike, intelligence gathered was confirmed by independent sources and investigated prior to taking action.

It is beyond the scope of this chapter to look at the causes of the military skirmishes and battles fought in the lifetime of the Prophet Muhammad[pbuh]. I will only examine the significant ones in order to see some pattern. The three major wars were defensive in nature. Firstly, there was the Battle of Badr (623 CE). When Muslims migrated to Medina they had to leave all their assets and heavy possessions behind. Meccans set up a large trade caravan to Syria to sell the confiscated assets of Muslims.[36] Muslims in the Prophet Muhammad's command lead a lightly armed force, 313 men to intercept the caravan. When Mecca heard this move they raised an army of more than a thousand men to prevent the interception. While the caravan escaped, Muslims won a clear victory in the ensuing battle at Badr.

Then there was the Battle of Uhud (625 CE). Little more than a year later, Mecca raised an army of 3,000 men and moved to attack

Medina to avenge the loss at Badr. The Muslim army, numbering 700 men, led by the Prophet Muhammad[pbuh], faced the Meccan army near Mt Uhud. An initial Muslim victory was turned into a loss when the Muslim army broke ranks, thinking the war was over. Then the cavalry led by Khalid bin Walid led a surprise attack from the back. Satisfied that they had taken their revenge, the Meccans did not further attack Medina. The Prophet was injured in this battle.

Finally came the Battle of Trench (627 CE). With the facilitation and instigation of the Banu Nadir Jews now living in the fortress city of Khaybar, the Meccans raised an inter-tribal coalition army of over 10,000 warriors and laid a month long siege to Medina. Muslims defended the city by digging trenches near the exposed parts of the city. The siege was unsuccessful and the result was a decisive victory for Muslims.[37]

The following examples are the major pre-emptive strikes involving the Prophet. It is important to note that an offensive strike to an enemy force in a long-standing military conflict is an expected military tactic. One does not always wait for the enemy to strike.

The first pre-emptive strike was the Banu Mustaliq Expedition of 627 CE. The Banu Mustaliq tribe started to prepare for an attack against the Muslims. The Prophet Muhammad[pbuh] learnt of the plan and moved first with a pre-emptive strike catching the tribe by surprise.[38] The next strike was the City of Khaybar Expedition in 628 CE. The Jews living in the fortress city of Khaybar were protecting the Banu Nadir tribe, who were the main instigators of the siege of Medina. The Muslims believed that this conspiracy had to be dealt with; if it happened once, it was likely to occur again. The city was captured after an expedition and a siege.[39]

The third strike was the Muta Expedition of 630 CE. A large delegation sent by the Prophet to neighbouring countries was captured and killed by tribes in southern Syria. The Ghassan tribe, allied to the Byzantines, then killed another envoy of the Prophet. There was a need, therefore, to confront these tribes that had killed the Prophet's envoys. The Prophet Muhammad[pbuh] then sent an army of 3,000 men to the north, which was met by an opposing force of 100,000 comprising Byzantine and tribal troops. The ingenious military skill of Khalid bin Walid saved the Muslim army from annihilation and the Byzantine army was forced to retreat.[40]

Finally, there was the Tabuq Expedition of 631 CE. Another warning of a large Byzantine army in Syria reached the Prophet. The Roman emperor, Heraclius, was intent on invading Arabia and

Medina. An army of about 30,000 men was raised and led north by the Prophet. No fighting took place as the Byzantines retreated and the Prophet Muhammad[pbuh] renewed his existing treaties with border tribes and made new allies.[41]

Critics often cite the conflicts between Muslims and the three Jewish tribes in Medina as evidence that the Prophet Muhammad[pbuh] was not a peaceful person at heart and had a special animosity towards Jews. The truth of the matter is that all three tribes violated the City Charter that they had agreed to without any coercion.

While the Banu Qaynuga tribe laid an open military challenge to the Prophet after a fight in the marketplace between a Jew and a Muslim,[42] the Banu Nadir tribe secretly attempted to assassinate the Prophet.[43] Both tribes were asked to leave the city. The crime of the third Jewish tribe, the Banu Qurayza, was even more serious. During the heat of the siege of Medina in the Battle of the Trench, the Banu Qurayza, the citizens of the same polity in Medina, declared their agreement null and void and conspired with the enemy ignoring the serious warnings of Muslims. Their crime equated to treason. When the siege was lifted, the Prophet left the judgement of the fate of the Banu Qurayza to someone that they would select. They selected Sa'd ibn Muadth and the Prophet promised he would not alter the judgement. Sa'd asked the Jews what was the punishment for traitors according to Jewish law. The punishment for treason in the Torah was death. Sa'd passed judgment according to Jewish law and decreed that the men should be executed. The Prophet Muhammad[pbuh] could not intervene because he had already given up his right to alter the judgement.[44]

Jews continued to live in Medina. Just before the Prophet Muhammad[pbuh] died, he pawned his armour to a Jewish citizen. After witnessing the fairness and openness of the Muslim rule, the Jews of Khaybar were extremely happy and commented, 'this is Paradise created by Muslims on earth'.[45] Muslim–Jewish relations were exceptional for the next fourteen centuries, such that Jews call the era under Muslim rule the Golden Age of Judaism.

It is important to note that the total number of people who died in all military battles is only a few thousand by the most pessimistic estimations — a number remarkably low for the times.

Military engagement in the actions of the Prophet Muhammad

It is a fact of history that the Prophet Muhammad[pbuh] led a number of battles in his ten-year leadership in Medina. His involvement in wars provides Muslims with a solid example of principles of behaviour in warfare. I will continue my examination of this topic by looking at how the Prophet acted in wars and how he treated civilians and prisoners of war.

Significantly, in some of the examples I will give below, it will appear that some of the early Muslims were not living up to the standards of Islam. One should bear in mind that all of these events occurred in the formative years of Islam when the followers of the Prophet Muhammad[pbuh] were going through an educational process. We see that after the death of the Prophet Muhammad[pbuh], these early Muslims[46] staunchly upheld the standards of Islam. Most importantly, the behaviour of the Prophet outlined below might seem normal by today's standards. However, even today these standards set and practised fourteen centuries ago are not reached by the civilised world as we have discovered in graphic pictures of the 2004 Iraq war.

War as the last resort

There is ample evidence that the Prophet Muhammad[pbuh] tried to resolve conflicts through diplomacy and signed many treaties with neighbouring tribes. We have no record of the Prophet dishonouring these treaties. In order to ensure peace, he even signed disadvantageous treaties, such as the treaty of Hudaybiyah (628 CE), with the Meccans much to the dissension of his followers. One of the terms of this treaty, for example, was that if a Muslim from Mecca escaped and took refuge in Medina, he or she had to be returned to Mecca. According to the Qur'an, peace is the real victory as the Qur'an called this treaty an 'open victory'.[47] The treaty of Hudaybiyah had a ten-year term, but the Meccans broke the treaty after two years.

Perhaps, as an unparalleled feat in history, the Prophet Muhammad[pbuh] pulled off a diplomatic victory and captured the city without a battle. All measures were taken to prevent a battle. The Prophet asked the assembled Meccans, 'O people of Mecca, What do you think I am going to do with you?' He continued to address the silent crowd, 'There is no blame on you this day. Go to your homes, you are all free.' This was a general amnesty for the people of Mecca despite the fact that these were the same people who persecuted and attacked the Prophet and his followers for twenty years.[48]

Not to be merciless towards the enemy

The Prophet Muhammad[pbuh] did not aim to crush his enemies either physically or psychologically, even in times of warfare. When the news that Khalid Bin Walid had killed a few prisoners of war after a battle reached the Prophet, he lifted his hands to the sky and said, 'O Lord, I am far from what Khalid has done. I did not command him what he has done.'[49]

After the Khaybar siege, Bilal was taking away two female prisoners of war and inadvertently passed them through the dead bodies of their relatives. Seeing the scene, the women started to cry. The Prophet reprimanded Bilal saying, 'O Bilal! Is your sense of mercy removed from your heart that you are passing these ladies among the dead.' Surprised by the Prophet's response, Bilal apologised.[50]

Prohibition of torture

The Prophet Muhammad[pbuh] did not allow inhumane practices of torture. Suhayl bin Amr was a poet who was captured as a prisoner of war in the Battle of Badr. Knowing that poets can be more damaging than warriors in shaping public opinion, Omar ibn Khattab suggested to the Prophet that Suhayl's front teeth be removed rendering his destructive poetry ineffective. The Prophet replied, 'No I cannot torture him. If I torture him God would punish me. Besides one day perhaps he could say something you may like.'[51] A prophecy that came true later when Suhayl became Muslim.

Prohibition of the mutilation of dead enemy soldiers

The mutilation of the dead bodies of the enemy warriors was a common practice in Arabia. After the Battle of Uhud, the Meccans mutilated the dead bodies of the Muslims including the Prophet's beloved uncle Hamza. When the Prophet saw the mutilated body of Hamza, in sorrow he vowed to mutilate thirty dead bodies from the enemy side next time if he was victorious. As a result of this the Qur'anic verse 16:126, 'And if you punish (your enemy), then punish them with the like of that with which you were afflicted. But if you endure patiently, verily it is better for the patient ones' was revealed.[52] The verse clearly prohibited excessive response to aggression and even advised patience. The Prophet retracted from his vow and paid the compensation for breaking an oath.[53]

Not to attack civilians

After the conquest of Mecca, a number of tribes got together and attacked the Muslims. The Muslims were winning the ensuing battle at Hunayn. The Prophet saw a female body among the dead. When he asked what happened to her, he was informed that the forces of Khalid killed the woman. He sent a courier to Khalid prohibiting him from killing women, children and servants. When the courier exclaimed, 'O Prophet of God aren't they the children of idolaters?' the Prophet replied, 'Weren't the best of you once the children of idolaters. Every child is born in a natural disposition.'[54]

When the Prophet was sending an army to the north to meet another Byzantine expedition just before his death, he gave the following guidelines to a young commander named Osama:

> Only fight with the aggressors. Do not breech your word. Do not cut down fruit bearing trees. Do not damage livestock. Do not kill women, children and monks who are withdrawn from the world and worship in monasteries. Do not wish to meet the enemy. You never know, you may be inflicted with a calamity as a result.[55]

The most striking example in this area is the behaviour of Hubayb ibn Adiyy. In 626 CE, the Meccans captured Hubayb and his Muslim friend Zayd ibn Dasinnah. They were both to be killed in the middle of the city in a public spectacle. While waiting in chains for his certain death, Hubayb asked a servant, Mawiyah, for a razor to shave himself. Unwittingly, she sent a razor to Hubayb with her three-year-old stepson. When she realised the potential danger and ran towards Hubayb, she screamed seeing the child sitting on the lap of Hubayb with the razor in Hubayb's hand. Hubayb let the child go saying, 'Are you scared that I will kill the child? God forbid, I would never do such a thing. Taking life unjustly is not one of our attributes. You are not the ones trying to kill me are you?'[56]

Act under legitimate authority

It was important to the Prophet Muhammad[pbuh] that no one took the law into their own hands and acted on their own accord without the decision of a central authority. When a few incidents occurred beyond his control, he scolded those who were responsible and made sure that compensation was paid to the families of the victims. One particular case occurred when Abdullah ibn Jahsh led a small patrol battalion. Abdullah intercepted a Meccan caravan. In the struggle one man was killed and two captured with the caravan. When they returned to Medina, instead of the expected acclaim, the Prophet reprimanded them, saying, 'I did not instruct you to fight during the sacred months.'[57]

Investigate intelligence before striking

The risk in pre-emptive strike is that if the intelligence is wrong, the act of war would no longer be legitimate. In cases where the Prophet received intelligence information about preparation for war by a hostile tribe, he always confirmed the news by independent sources and made sure there was solid supporting evidence.

For example, after the conquest of Mecca, the Banu Mustaliq tribe became Muslim. The Prophet Muhammad[pbuh] sent Walid ibn Uqba to collect *zakat* (alms) from the tribe. When the people saw Walid approaching, they went out to greet him. However, Walid became afraid and ran back to Medina to report to the Prophet that the Banu Mustaliq tribe had tried to kill him and were now preparing to attack Medina. The Prophet sent Khalid ibn Walid to confirm the news. Once Khalid had learnt the truth of the matter, no further action was necessary.[58] After this incident, the following verse was revealed: 'O you who believe! If a seditious person comes to you with news, verify it, so that you don't harm people in ignorance, and afterwards you become regretful to what you have done.'[59]

Not to cause Muslim casualties as collateral damage

One of the current issues with certain terrorist acts or resistance movements against foreign occupation is that Muslim civilians are killed in some attacks as well as the target group. In the lifetime of the Prophet Muhammad[pbuh], the lives of Muslims were not knowingly put to risk. According to the Qur'an, one of the reasons why the Prophet signed the treaty of Hudaybiyah, rather than fighting the Meccans, was in order not to risk the lives of Muslims who could not migrate and were still living in Mecca, 'Had there not been believing men and women whom you did not know, that you may have killed them and on this account a sin would have been committed by you without knowledge . . .'.[60]

Humanitarian help to enemy

One of the best examples of the good intentions of the Prophet Muhammad[pbuh] is the way he gave food aid to the Meccans during the years of bitter conflict. This is even more remarkable, considering that it was the same people who subjected the Prophet and his tribe to economic sanctions for three years prior to the migration to Medina. During a drought in Mecca, the Prophet Muhammad[pbuh] sent financial aid to them in order to purchase food. While some Meccan leaders such as Umayyah bin Halaf did not want to accept the aid, Abu Sufyan accepted the aid in embarrassment.[61]

In a similar tone, when the tribe of Yamama stopped the shipment of food to Mecca because of maltreatment of one of its tribesman, Meccans asked the Prophet to intercede. The Prophet asked the tribe to continue the food shipments and the tribe of Yamama started selling food once again.[62]

Conclusion

It would be stating the obvious that conflict and war is a reality of human existence. In human history, there have always been aggressors who wanted to achieve their goals by force and sought to transgress the freedom, land and wealth of others. It seems almost certain that warfare will continue to be part of the human condition for as long as humans live on this planet.

While it is not realistic to rid the earth of warfare, it is possible to control what falls in one's circle of influence. Certainly, the decision to start wars, the conduct of soldiers in warfare, and the treatment of civilians and prisoners of war, are all within this circle of influence. The fundamental sources of Islam, the Qur'an and the actions of the Prophet Muhammad[pbuh], lay down principles to ameliorate warfare, principles that were far advanced for their time. It appears that even today, modern societies are having problems in following universal principles, despite international conventions, declarations and laws.

The fact that the Qur'an includes verses that discuss warfare and that the Prophet Muhammad[pbuh] led armies in battle, may seems counterintuitive to religion. Rather than being a liability, however, this fact has really been an advantage, as it sets high standards of behaviour during war-time and guidelines for Muslim rulers throughout history. Without these guidelines, both Muslim history and world history would have been quite different.

Since Islam as a religion sets high standards of behaviour in times of conflict, we can therefore confine the present day events involving Muslims to a particular time and space and conclude that the violence conducted by Muslims today is an aberration of history and will eventually cease when the prevailing circumstances no longer exist.

In some cases, people will do things in spite of the teachings of Islam. Once, when the Prophet Muhammad[pbuh] was speaking to a man, a child passed by. The Prophet Muhammad[pbuh] displayed such love and affection for the child that the surprised man said, 'We do not do this to our kids where I come from'. The Prophet looked at him amazed and replied, 'What can I do if God took away love and compassion from your heart?' So, what can Islam do today, if some people's hearts are so deprived of love and compassion that they do not hesitate to kill innocent people in cold blood.

Endnotes

1. The acronym 'pbuh' is short for 'peace be upon him'. It is a statement of reverence practised by Muslims for all prophets including Prophet Muhammad.
2. Luke 19:27.
3. Matthew 10:34-36.
4. Qur'an 34:28.
5. Qur'an 21:107.
6. Bukhari, *Anbiya,* 37.
7. Bukhari, *Ilm,* 12; Muslim, *Jihad,* 6.
8. Qur'an 95:4.
9. Qur'an 17:70.
10. Qur'an 3:156.
11. Qur'an 6:151.
12. Qur'an 5:32.
13. Qur'an 49:13.
14. See verses from the Qur'an such as 3:20, 5:92, 5:99, 13:40, 14:52, 16:35, 16:82.
15. Qur'an 88:21–22.
16. Ibrahim Canan, 'Islam as a Religion of Peace and Tolerance', *Yeni Umit* (Jan-Mar 2004), 21. The Qur'anic reference is 2:256.
17. Richard Bonney, *Jihad from Qur'an to Bin Laden* (United States: Palgrave Macmillan, 2004), 26–27.
18. Qur'an 9:23–24.
19. Qur'an 25:52.
20. Qur'an 22:78, 3:142.
21. Qur'an 29:69.
22. Qur'an 41:33.
23. Qur'an 22:39–40.
24. Qur'an 8:58.
25. Qur'an 2:217.
26. Qur'an 4:75.
27. Qur'an 22:39–40.
28. Qur'an 2:190.

29. Qur'an 48:17, 9:91.

30. Qur'an 2:192.

31. Qur'an 47:4.

32. John L Esposito, *What Everyone Needs to Know About Islam* (New York: Oxford University Press, 2002), 118.

33. Qur'an 8:61.

34. Qur'an 9:5.

35. Qur'an 2:190–3, 8:59–70, 9:12, 9:30, 9:38–9, 61:4.

36. Yahiya Emerick, *Muhammad* (Indianapolis: Alpha, 2002), 159.

37. *Ibid*, 216.

38. *Ibid*, 227.

39. *Ibid*, 241.

40. *Ibid*, 269.

41. *Ibid*, 276.

42. *Ibid*, 184.

43. *Ibid*, 208.

44. *Ibid*, 222–26.

45. Ali Akpinar, 'Religion of Peace, Prophet of Love', *Yeni Umit* (Jan–Mar 2004), 49.

46. The Muslims who converted to Islam in the lifetime of the Prophet Muhammad have the special title of *sahaba,* companions. This title was given to them by the Prophet who did not like calling them his followers or disciples. So he simply called them 'my friends'.

47. Qur'an 48:1.

48. Emerick, *Muhammad*, 248.

49. Akpinar, 'Religion of Peace', 50.

50. *Ibid*, 50.

51. *Ibid*, 51.

52. *Ibid*, 51.

53. In Islam, the compensation for breaking one's oath is to feed a poor person for ten days.

54. Abu Dawood, *Jihad*, 111.

55. Akpinar, 'Religion of Peace', 52.

56. Bukhari, *Magazi*, 28.

57. Emerick, *Muhammad*, 157.

58. Akpinar, 'Religion of Peace', 52.

59. Qur'an 49:6.

60. Qur'an 48:25.

61. Akpinar, 'Religion of Peace', 52.

62. *Ibid*, 52.

Gandhi, Scripture and Non-Violence

William W Emilsen

The extraordinary film called *Water* (2005) — the third in Deepa Mehta's trilogy, *Fire*, *Earth* and *Water* — is a flawless movie dealing with the plight of widows (sometimes girls as young as eight) in India in the late 1930s. Without a husband, these women are labelled worthless, they are ostracised, they live in a ramshackle 'widows' house', they struggle to survive by begging and, often, they are forced into prostitution. The widows are victims of a narrow and rigid interpretation of sacred texts like those found in the *Laws of Manu* which state that should a widow remarry, she 'violates her duty towards her (deceased) husband, brings on herself disgrace in this world, and loses her place with her husband (in heaven)'. Even '(after death) she will enter the womb of a jackal and is tormented by diseases (the punishment of) her sins.'[1] The film *Water* demonstrates superbly the theme of the essays contained in this volume — the shameful and crushing consequences of religion when it validates violence and violates faith.

Towards the end of the film there is a glimmer of hope in the figure of Narayan, a young law student and follower of Mohandas Karamchand ('Mahatma') Gandhi (1869–1948). Narayan rejects the abusive literalism that enmeshes the widows, challenges his father's distorted and privileged understanding of Hinduism, helps liberate Chuyia, a young girl from the widows' house, and leaves Varanasi in the closing scene on the same train as Gandhi and his followers.

In 1938, the year in which *Water* is set, Gandhi, a staunch opponent of enforced widowhood, was sixty-nine. A year later, the distinguished philosopher and, later, India's second president, Sarvapalli Radhakrishnan, presented Gandhi on his seventieth birthday with a collection of essays and reflections on his life and work from eminent people around the world.[2] Among those tributes, for example, Maude Royden, England's first woman preacher, admitted that it was a strange thing that many Christians felt that Gandhi, a Hindu, was the best Christian in the world.[3] EM Forster, the novelist, believed that Gandhi was likely to be regarded as the greatest person of our century.[4] The American Unitarian minister, John Haynes Holmes, had no doubts about Gandhi's greatness. Almost twenty years earlier (in 1921), he had declared in a sermon to his Community Church in New York that Gandhi was the greatest man in the world.[5] Now he extolled

Gandhi as the great among all the great of ages past. He compared him to nationalist leaders like Washington and Kosciusko, to emancipators like Wilberforce and Lincoln and ranked Gandhi alongside St Francis, Thoreau and Tolstoy, as a teacher of non-violence. Indeed, Holmes concluded, Gandhi holds his place with 'Lao-tse, Buddha, Zoroaster, Jesus, as one of the supreme religious prophets of all time'.[6]

As Europe was rapidly sliding into war, Gandhi was seen by many in the West as the great 'light-bearer' of the day. Central to almost all the tributes in Radhakrishnan's celebratory volume was Gandhi's 'working gospel' of non-violence and what it might mean for a world seemingly doomed to self-destruction. Since then there has been no evidence to suggest that interest in Gandhi's ideas on non-violence has abated; if anything, the dropping of the first atomic bomb on Japan in 1945, the race riots in the United States in the 1960s, the nuclear threat in the 1980s, and the so-called 'war on terror' today, have only intensified interest in the life and thought of Gandhi. Joan Bondurant's *Conquest of Violence* (1958), Arne Naess's *Gandhi and Group Conflict* (1974), Martin Green's *The Origins of Non-violence* (1986), and Richard L Johnson's *Gandhi's Experiments with Truth: Essential Writings by and about Mahatma Gandhi* (2006) are just a few of the many studies drawing upon Gandhi's life and thought in an effort to find a 'new way' of dealing with conflict.

In India, as well, Gandhi's reputation has generally remained high though his influence in the area of non-violence has not been the same as that outside India. Yet, even in the 1940s, the most difficult period in Gandhi's life, Sarojini Naidu, the Indian poetess, called 'the Nightingale of India', gave a memorable broadcast speech on Gandhi's birthday in 1947, the year before he died, where she summed up the feelings of many Indians. She said:

> Who is this Gandhi and why is it today that he represents the supreme moral force in the world? Throughout history, age after age, in every country, there have been very distinguished men and great men—kings, warriors, lawgivers, poets . . . Their names have survived and they are fresh today in their radiance, as they were in their own times—Buddha, Jesus Christ and Mohamed, and a few others whose gospel was an exaltation to the spirit of man. Today, there is Gandhi . . . he passes meekly through the years, he faces embattled forces, he overthrows

empires, he conquers death, but what is it that has given him this power, this magic, this authority, this prestige, this almost god-like quality of swaying the hearts and minds of men?

It is a quality he shares with that small band of great teachers of the world, who inaugurated great religions . . . With Christ he shares the great gospel that love is the fulfilling of the law. With the great Mohamed he shares the gospel of [the] brotherhood of man, [the] equality of man and [the] oneness of man. With Lord Buddha he shares the great evangel that the duty of life is not self-seeking but to seek the truth, no matter at what sacrifice . . . He [Gandhi] was born like other men, he will die like other men, but unlike them he will live through the beautiful gospel he has enunciated, that hatred cannot be conquered by hatred, the sword cannot be conquered by the sword, that power cannot be exploited over the weak and the fallen, that the gospel of non-violence which is the most dynamic and most creative gospel of power in the world, is the only true foundation of a new civilisation, yet to be built.[7]

In the past decade, among the many Indian books published on Gandhi's relevance for the twenty-first century, it is not uncommon to find him named as the greatest Indian after Buddha and one of the greatest figures of all times.[8] KBK Singh, for example, in a recent collection of articles on *Gandhi and 21st Century* described him as 'not only a great man' . . . but 'a genius, a thinker, a saint, a philosopher and a theorist par-excellence'.[9]

One could be forgiven for dismissing these laudatory and pious eulogies, but it should never be forgotten that for two decades this physically frail individual, this 'apostle of truth and non-violence' as Gandhi was called, conducted a national movement of non-violence involving millions which has hardly any other parallel in history. In the succeeding decades, estimates of Gandhi's significance have scarcely diminished. He is listed in the Sun Books *100 Great Lives* (1969) of all time. The Horizon Book of *Makers of Modern Thought* (1972) places him among thirty-seven undeniable giants like Newton, Darwin and Marx. And in 1999 *Time* magazine named Gandhi and Franklin Rosevelt second to Albert Einstein as its 'Person of the

Century'. Today, almost sixty years after his death, Gandhi appears more than ever to carry a message of hope for humanity.

Gandhi was not revered by everyone, and least of all, by many Hindus. It is not surprising that it was a Hindu, Narthuram Godse, editor of a Hindu Mahasabha extremist weekly, who assassinated Gandhi. At his trial Godse argued defiantly before India's High Court, 'My provocation was his constant and consistent pandering to the Muslims . . . I declare here before man and God that in putting an end to Gandhi's life I have removed one who was a curse to India, a force of evil, and who had, during thirty years of . . . harebrained policy, brought nothing but misery and unhappiness.' [10] Godse's militant ultra-Hindu fanaticism was (and is) unfortunately shared by thousands of conservative Hindus. Godse was hanged but there are still many Hindu nationalist especially among the former ruling party in India, the Bharatiya Janata party (BJP), and other organisations seeking to promote Hindutva ('Hinduness') and wishing to make India a Hindu nation, that would look upon Gandhi's assassination as an act of Hindu 'salvation'.

As early as 1924 Gandhi had upset many reactionary Brahmins with his opposition to untouchability. His deep conviction that untouchability was the 'great satanism of Hinduism' brought him into head-on conflict with many high-caste Hindus who believed it was supported by scriptural authority.[11] They were further enraged when Gandhi consistently placed his own moral judgements above the declarations of all that was traditionally considered the fundamental authority in Hinduism: the *Vedas* and the *Shastras* and their living interpreters, the *shastris* (theologians, scholars) or pandits. Gandhi made it quite clear what he thought of the authority of the *Shastras* and their traditional interpreters: 'If I discovered that those scriptures which are known as *Vedas*, Upanishads, *Bhagavad Gita*, *Smritis*, etc, clearly showed that they claimed divine authority for untouchability . . . then nothing on this earth would hold me to Hinduism. I should throw it overboard as I should throw overboard a rotten apple.'[12]

In order to appreciate fully Gandhi's attitude to scripture (of any religion), it is important to understand his insistence on accord between belief and action; it was the way a person lived, not the recital of a verse or a prayer or a hymn from scripture that made someone a good Hindu, or a good Muslim, or a good Christian. Gandhi was a *doer*, a man of action. With him *deed* was everything and *doing* was believing; belief without deed was nothing. In other words, the teaching of any scripture that could not be put into practice was, effectively, no scripture at all.[13]

Moreover, in Gandhi's estimation, the only legitimate interpreters of scripture were those who have put their injunctions into practice, not necessarily learned specialists.[14] Essentially, Gandhi considered persisting with texts that could not be put into practice, a waste of time.[15] The following quotation summarises Gandhi's pragmatic understanding of the meaning and purpose of sacred writing:

> Shastra [scripture] does not mean the pronouncements of men of spiritual experience in the past. It means the words of living men today who have had first-hand experience, that is, who have realised the Brahman. Shastra is something which is daily embodied in somebody's life. What exists only in books and is not followed in life may be philosophy, or it may be foolish chatter or mere hypocrisy. Shastra must be immediately capable of realisation in experience, it must spring from the living experience of the person who utters it. It is only in this sense that the Veda is eternal. All else is not Veda, but theorising about Veda.[16]

In Gandhi's view, if two or more meanings of a specific text were possible, it was only on the evidence of experience that the truth would eventually be determined. For instance, it is one thing to understand at an intellectual level the meaning of a text about non-attachment, but it is quite another thing to *be* non-attached to the consequences of one's actions, and learn through experience the significance of the text.

Gandhi also aroused opposition for his views on the historicity of sacred texts. 'The *Mahabharata* is not to me a historical record. It is hopeless as a history.'[17] For Gandhi, as well, not even the *Gita* was a historical book, but a religious allegory.[18] Its author, in Gandhi's opinion, had seized the occasion of the war between the Pandavas and the Kauravas for drawing attention to the war going on in our hearts between the forces of good and evil.[19] It was not important to Gandhi, for example, whether Krishna or Rama were historical figures. The same attitude applied to Jesus. He wrote: 'God did not bear the cross only 1900 years ago, but He bears it today, and He dies and is resurrected from day to day. It would be poor comfort to the world if it had to depend upon a historical God who died 2,000 years ago. Do not then preach the God of history, but show him as he lives today through you.'[20]

Despite accusations of heterodoxy by some caste Hindus, it was in Hinduism that Gandhi primarily lived, moved and had his being. He firmly believed in transmigration or rebirth which is one of the hallmarks of Indian religions. He often claimed to be a '*sanatani* Hindu', a Hindu with roots in ancient traditions, because he believed in the sacred texts and the traditional values and concepts of Hinduism. The book which became Gandhi's strongest bond with Hinduism, as well as the greatest influence on him, was the *Bhagavad Gita*. Though Gandhi drew inspiration from other religions, such as Jainism, Christianity and Islam, he was thoroughly Hindu in character. Most Indians saw him as a devout Hindu, a great Hindu, a Mahatma, the great-souled one.

Although Gandhi was a Hindu, he read the scriptures of all the world religions. He considered a sympathetic study of the world's scriptures to be a 'sacred duty', the mark of a cultured person, a first step towards understanding others and towards lasting peace on earth.[21] Furthermore, he had discovered from long experience that the study of the scriptures of other religions deepened and broadened his own understanding and experience of being a Hindu. From the age of nineteen, Gandhi had read the Bible and the *Gita*, and later, the Qur'an, the *Guru Granth Sahib*, the *Zend Avesta,* as well as the various Hindu 'scriptures', especially what Hindus call *shruti*, ('revealed writings' or *Veda*, which, interpreted in a broad sense, includes the *Upanishads* (*Vedanta*), the enormous volume of later writings known as *smrti* ('tradition'), which includes the *Puranas* (myths and legends), the *Ramayana* and the *Mahabharata* (the great Indian Epics), and various codes of law such as the *Manu-smriti*.[22] Though Gandhi had not studied these works in their original languages and did not consider himself a scholar of them, he did however, claim 'to know and feel the truths' of the essential teaching of the world's scriptures.[23] Thus, to Parsis he could say, 'I have read your scriptures in Gujarati and English, as many as I could get';[24] to Sikhs, 'The *Granth Saheb* and the Gurus are as much mine as theirs';[25] and to Muslims that he studied the Qur'an regularly and based his life on the significant truths found in that 'inspired book' and in the example of the Prophet.

Gandhi respected all scriptures. To accept the Bible as a source of revelation did not mean rejecting, say, the Qur'an, or vice versa.[26] He refused to elevate one above the other. He believed that they all had the potential of helping people live truly religious lives. He gave the Parsi scriptures the same reverence as the *Vedas* or the *Upanishads* or the *Gita*. He thought there was no significant difference between the

Qur'an and the *Upanishads* on important matters such as the necessity for total self-abandonment to God.[27] He was particularly struck by the Sermon on the Mount, which, for him, was equal in moral authority to the *Bhagavad Gita*.[28] He also believed that there was much in the Qur'an that Christians and Hindus could endorse, just as there was much in the *Gita* that Muslims and Christians could agree with. When, for example, Christian missionaries sought his advice on their work in India, Gandhi regularly challenged them to read the scriptures of the local people with as much reverence as he read the Bible. It was not sufficient, he insisted, for Christian missionaries merely to read the Qur'an and the *Gita*; they should read the Qur'an with Islamic spectacles and the *Gita* with Hindu spectacles, just as they would expect him to read the Bible with Christian spectacles.[29] Gandhi frequently grounded what amounted to a principle of respect upon the Biblical commandment to love one's neighbour: people were to respect the other's scriptures as they would have others respect their own. During times of inter-communal tensions, Gandhi chastened Hindus disposed to 'new-fangled' notions of reviling the Qur'an and the Prophet by reminding them that it was once the custom in India to speak of the Prophet with reverence and for Hindus to compose songs paying tribute to Islam.[30] For Gandhi's expression of these ideas, the one who was often accused of being an 'almost Christian' also earned the sobriquet 'Muhammad Gandhi'.

Yet, what about the competing claims of scriptures demanding equal respect? Gandhi, as is well-known from the subtitle of his autobiography, *The Story of My Experiments With Truth*, took a firm stand on truth, especially lived or embodied truth.[31] Immutable truth or revelation, in his estimation, was not the exclusive property of any single scripture, nation or religion.[32] Nothing should circumscribe the power of God. Echoing Raychand (or Rajchandra) Mehta, the Jain sage, he argued against Hindu orthodoxy that not even the Vedas were exclusively and divinely inspired.[33] The Bible, the Qur'an, and the *Avesta* were as much inspired as the Vedas. Eternal truths were to be found in all scriptures. Gandhi considered the belief that God was revealed only in one particular scripture akin to Hindu idol-worship, innocent enough, and, perhaps even devotionally beneficial, but, nonetheless, mistaken.[34] He rightly perceived that the real threat to religious harmony lay not in the competing claims of the different scriptures but between the representatives thereof, and then, between those who did not, and those who did, reject the authority of the scriptures altogether.[35]

Yet, Gandhi's reverence for the authority of the world's scriptures did not mean that these scriptures should be exempt from criticism. Though he was personally reluctant to criticise the scriptures of other faiths, or to point out their defects, error could claim no exemption even if it were supported by all the scriptures of the world.[36] In any conflict between reason and authority, whether personal or scriptural, however high, Gandhi would always follow reason. His detection of error was deeply influenced by the rationalism of the *Ramayana* from which he quotes: 'A saying sound in reason should be accepted, though it proceed from a child; and the contrary one rejected as a straw, though it purport to proceed from the God Brahma.'[37] Nothing, Gandhi believed, should be accepted as the word of God unless it could stand the test of reason. Reason was the best guide to what might be regarded as revealed and what might not.[38] Thus, interpretations repugnant to reason should be firmly rejected; scriptural practices and modes of conduct offensive to reason should be either changed or abandoned.[39] Gandhi had no hesitation in rejecting scriptural authority that supported principles that related to conditions at a particular place and time. In his endless debates on untouchability, for example, Gandhi repeatedly asserted that any scripture, including the *Laws of Manu* that claimed it was a sin to touch a *Bhangi* (outcaste), was no scripture at all. Untouchability, in Gandhi's estimation, was an evil, a 'delusion of Satan',[40] and it should not be defended on the grounds of its antiquity. When BS Moonje, the Hindu Mahasabha leader, tried to prove that untouchability was an integral part of Hinduism, Gandhi retorted, 'happily for me, my Hinduism does not bind me to every verse because it is written in Sanskrit . . . in spite of your literal knowledge of the shastras, yours is a distorted kind of Hinduism.'[41] The scriptures, in Gandhi's estimation, existed to purify reason and illuminate truth; they should not be used to endorse irrationality.[42] Every formula of every religion had to submit to the acid test of reason if it were to command universal assent, otherwise it should be rejected.[43]

Reason by itself, however, had its shortcomings and could be abused and distorted. Just as matter misplaced became dirt or plants in the wrong place became weeds, so reason misused became lunacy.[44] Various experiences had taught Gandhi the specific limitations of reason. He had found that mere appeals to reason were futile in the face of age-long prejudice. He was also acutely aware that any number of evils could be justified from the Bible, the *Vedas*, the Qur'an and other scriptures: particularly detestable was the fact that some Muslims justified stoning for illicit sexual relations on the authority of the

Qur'an and the *hadith*, and some Christians justified war and capital punishment on the authority of the Bible.[45] When the Muslim leader, Maulana Zafar Ali Khan, challenged Gandhi on his interpretation of the Qur'an, arguing that it 'is an unalterable law which transcends the ever changing policies and expediencies of puny humanity', Gandhi responded that even the teachings of the Qur'an could not be exempt from criticism, that every true scripture only gains by criticism. Gandhi argued that 'intolerance of criticism even of what one may prize as dear as life itself is not conducive to the growth of public corporate life and surely Islam has nothing to fear from criticism even if it were unreasonable'.[46]

Alongside the appeal to reason, therefore, Gandhi adopted a second principle of interpretation—the appeal to the heart, morality or conscience. Important as reason was for Gandhi, it must not usurp the heart.[47] Never accept anything as God's word, cautioned Gandhi, that causes violence and is repugnant to one's moral sense.[48] Shastric injunctions ought not to be employed to justify child-marriage nor to force young girls into prostitution as was the practice in some temples in Madras Presidency.[49] As an example of Gandhi's general approach to scripture, he cited a couplet from his beloved Tulsidas' *Ramayana*, 'The drum, the fool, the Sudra, the animal and the woman—all these need beating.' Not even Gandhi's love for Tulsidas could blunt his guiding principle of non-violence; either, Gandhi concluded, the couplet was an interpolation, or, if it was Tulsidas', it is limited by history and geography or it must have been written without much reflection.[50] Gandhi was adamant that not every Sanskrit saying was a scriptural precept and 'the general habit of regarding women as inferior beings' must be resisted at all cost.[51] Though Gandhi was generally reticent to criticise the scriptures of other religions, we learn from Mahadev Desai's dairy (4 March 1925) that Gandhi was deeply shocked when he was told that his Muslim colleague, Maulana Shaukat Ali (1873–1938), not only affirmed, along with most Muslims, that violence might be necessary in certain situations, but also subscribed to 'the law of an eye for an eye and a head for a head', and, as well, had argued that 'if there is a mention of stoning to death in the Qur'an, the act must be accepted as right and proper'.[52] Similarly, on another occasion when Gandhi was told that the Prophet Muhammad had prescribed the use of the sword in certain circumstances, Gandhi replied:

> I suppose most Muslims will agree. But I read religion
> in a different way. Khan Saheb Abdul Ghaffar Khan

derives his belief in non-violence from the Koran, and the Bishop of London derives his belief in violence from the Bible. I derive my belief in non-violence from the *Gita*, whereas there are others who read violence in it. But if the worst came to the worst and if I came to the conclusion that the Koran teaches violence, I would still reject violence, but I would not therefore say that the Bible is superior to the Koran or that Mohamed is inferior to Jesus. It is not my function to judge Mohamed and Jesus. It is enough that my non-violence is independent of the sanction of scriptures.[53]

Gandhi was unequivocal, no scriptural sanction was valid if it resulted in unjust, inhuman, sinful or violent practices.

Every scripture, then, Gandhi insisted, should be tested by the twin principles of reason and non-violence, 'the anvil of truth with the hammer of compassion'.[54] Any passage or text that was inconsistent with this 'infallible canon of interpretation' should be rejected. Likewise, that which was consistent with it should be appropriated. Even then, and in spite of his canon of truth and non-violence, difficulties of interpretation might arise. They, in Gandhi's view, had to be solved on the authority of the 'inner voice', or the 'voice of God', not God speaking through him, but rather some kind of inspiration which is open to anybody who makes the necessary spiritual effort.[55] The final authority in matters of religion was the voice within; no single text or pandit was entitled to override that voice.

Gandhi did not hesitate to re-interpret the Hindu scriptures in accordance with the promptings of his own inner voice. Whenever Gandhi felt puzzled he would retire into himself and, through a process of self-analysis and self-purification, try to clear his mind in order to listen to the 'still small voice within'. He stressed that there were certain conditions that needed to be fulfilled before one could claim to hear correctly that voice and come to know and understand the scriptures. These conditions entail keeping the following five vows which Gandhi called 'the life breath of truth': truthfulness (*satya*), sexual restraint (*brahmacharya*), non-violence (*ahimsa*), poverty (*aparigraha*), and non-coveting (*asteya*).[56]

The scripture that was Gandhi's favourite was the *Bhagavad Gita*. For him the *Gita* represented the very essence of religion. It was the key to the scriptures of the world, a means to unravelling the deepest mysteries in them.[57] Gandhi spoke of the *Gita* as his infallible guide, his reference dictionary, and his consolation in times of sorrow, trouble and conflict.[58] It was the one book, in his view, that could be to Hindus what the Bible was to Christians or the Qur'an to Muslims. The esteemed Indian National Congress leader, Chakravarti Rajagopalachari (1879–1972), once quipped, when asked to deliver a lecture on Gandhi's teaching and philosophy to students at the Univerity of Poona, that his lecture needed to contain nothing more nor less than what was contained in the *Gita*.[59] This rather small book which is an episode in the great epic, the *Mahabharata*, is not strictly *shruti*, revelation proper, but rather, it belongs to the sacred books called *smriti*, or tradition. Mahadev Desai, Gandhi's secretary, compared the *Upanisdads* to the New Testament and the *Gita* to the Gospels,[60] but a more accurate comparison might be, at least from a Christian perspective on scripture and tradition, to compare Gandhi's intense focus on the *Gita* with a Christian's sole concentration on Thomas à Kempis's great spiritual classic, the *Imitation of Christ*.[61] Nevertheless, Gandhi's acceptance of the *Gita* as the essence of the Hindu scriptures was not exceptional; many modern Indian interpreters of the *Gita* virtually elevate it to the status of *shruti*, considering it a spiritual distillation of the *Upanishads* and the essential 'gospel of Hinduism'.[62]

Gandhi chose the *Gita* for several reasons: like the *Vedas* it was accepted by all Hindu sects as authoritative; yet, unlike the *Vedas*, its language was simple and its teachings relatively accessible; and, most importantly, its central theme of selfless action or renunciation resonated with Gandhi's higher principle of *ahimsa* or non-violence. When Gandhi was asked whether *ahimsa* or selfless action was the central theme of the *Gita*, he admitted that selfless action was undoubtedly central, but added, that the practice of non-violence was necessary and preliminary to the practice of selfless action.[63] This is why Gandhi often repeated that the overall teaching of the *Gita* was non-violence rather than violence. In the end, the validity of the *Gita* or of any other scripture, according to Gandhi, has to be decided in relation to non-violence. The test of any particular teaching from any scripture, including the *Gita*, has to be based upon a refusal to do harm to anyone or anything. Non-violence, Gandhi held, is 'the law of our being'; it is not merely 'a garment to be put on and off at will'.[64]

Endnotes

1. *The Laws of Manu*, translated by Georg Buhler (New York: Dover Publications, Inc, 1969), V: 161, 164.
2. S Radhakrishanan, *Mahatma Gandhi: Essays and Reflections on his Life and Work* (London: George Allen & Unwin, 1939).
3. Radhakrishanan, *Mahatma Gandhi*, 258.
4. Radhakrishanan, *Mahatma Gandhi*, 289.
5. John Haynes Holmes, 'Who is the Greatest Man in the World?', in *The Enduring Greatness of Gandhi: An American Estimate*, edited by Haridas T Muzumdar (Ahmedabad: Navajivan Publishing House, 1982), 3–24; John Haynes Holmes, 'The Meaning of Gandhi' and 'Who Is the Greatest Man in the World?', in *The Americanization of Gandhi: Images of the Mahatma*, edited with an introductory essay by Charles Chatfield (New York and London: Garland Publishing, Inc, 1976), 574–75, 599–621.
6. Radhakrishanan, *Mahatma Gandhi*, 114.
7. DG Tendulkar, *Mahatma: Life of Mohandas Karamchand Gandhi*, 8 volumes, (New Delhi: Publications Division, Ministry of Information and Broadcasting, Government of India, 1963), 8: 144.
8. Vishwanath Prasad Varma, 'Mahatma Gandhi and His Message and Their Relevance to Modern Times', in *Gandhi and [the] 21st Century*, edited by Janardan Pandey (New Delhi: Concept Publishing Company, 1998), 17.
9. KBK Singh, 'Pragmatism of Gandhian Values in [the] Contemporary World', in *Gandhi and [the] 21st Century*, 129.
10. 'Official Account of the Trial of Godse, Apte, and Others for Murder and Conspiracy, with Verbatim reports of Speeches by Godse and Savarkar' in *Rex versus Godse* (Glasgow: The Strickland Press, nd, but after 1950), 49–50.
11. *The Collected Works of Mahatma Gandhi*, 100 volumes (New Delhi: The Publications Division, Ministry of Information and Broadcasting, Government of India, 1967) 19: 149, hereafter cited as *CW* followed by volume and page(s).
12. *CW*, 57: 7; 21: 246.
13. *CW*, 41: 98.
14. *CW*, 28: 316–17; 15: 312–13; 33: 384; 34: 89; 35: 367; 41: 92; 43: 85; 56: 341; 63: 153.
15. *CW*, 32: 228.
16. *CW*, 53: 348–49.
17. *CW*, 25: 86.
18. *CW,* 28: 318–21.
19. *CW*,15: 288.

20. *Selections from Gandhi*, edited by Nirmal Kumar Bose (Ahmedabad: Navajivan Publishing House, 1948), 12.
21. MK Gandhi, 'Foreword', in *The Sayings of Muhammad*, edited by Abdullah Suhrawardy (London: John Murray, 1941), 7.
22. *CW*, 18: 451; 51: 344–45.
23. *CW*, 21: 246.
24. *CW*, 20: 26.
25. *CW*, 88: 21.
26. *CW*, 52. 345; 62: 334.
27. See Qur'an 33: 72.
28. *CW*, 48: 483.
29. *CW*, 63: 92. In all probability, Gandhi read the 'Old Testament' with Christian spectacles as well.
30. *CW*, 25: 178.
31. 'Truth is embodied not in words but in persons and in their living.' For a discussion of the Hindu personalist-humanist view of truth, see Wilfred Cantwell Smith, *What is Scripture? A Comparative Approach* (Minneapolis: Fortress Press, 1993), 138, 305 n 36.
32. *CW*, 25:180; 25: 178.
33. On the Jain influences upon Gandhi, see Stephen N Hay, 'Jain Influences on Gandhi's Early Thought', in *Gandhi India and the World*, edited by Sibnarayan Ray, (Melbourne: Hawthorn Press 1970), 29–38.
34. *CW*, 52: 96.
35. *CW*, 62: 423.
36. *CW*, 26: 202, 226.
37. *CW*, 36: 87.
38. *CW*, 26: 226; 63: 153.
39. *CW*, 21: 246.
40. MK Gandhi, *My Religion*, edited by Bharatan Kumarappa (Ahmedabad: Navajivan, 1955), 22, 151.
41. Raghavan Iyer, *Moral and Political Thought of Gandhi* (New York: Oxford University Press, 1973), 380.
42. *CW*, 20: 7.
43. *CW*, 29: 398.
44. *CW*, 31: 497.
45. *CW*, 32: 314. *Hudud* penalties : a punishment fixed in the Qur'an and *hadith* for crimes considered to be against the rights of God. The six crimes for which punishment are fixed are theft (amputation of the hand), illicit sexual relations (death by stoning or one hundred lashes), making unproven accusations of illicit sex (eighty lashes), drinking intoxicants (eighty lashes), apostasy (death or banishment), and highway robbery (death).

46. *The Moral and Political Writings of Mahatama Gandhi*, 3 volumes, edited by Raghavan Iyer (Oxford: Clarendon, 1986), 1: 478–79.

47. *Harijan*, 12 December 1948, 346.

48. *CW*, 31: 392; 64: 398.

49. *CW*, 20: 7–8.

50. JTF Jorden, *Gandhi's Religion: A Homespun Shawl* (Basingstoke: Macmillan Press Ltd, 1998), 131.

51. *CW*, 14: 32.

52. Mahadev H Desai, *Day-to-Day with Gandhi: Secretary's Diary*, 8 volumes (Varanasi: Sarva Seva Sangh Prakashan, 1970), 6: 48.

53. *CW*, 64: 399.

54. *CW*, 24: 320.

55. *CW*, 33: 355; 21: 419; 49: 85.

56. *CW*, 21; 246; 49: 311; see also Iyer, *The Moral and Political Writings of Mahatma Gandhi*, 2:167.

57. *CW*, 62: 334.

58. *CW*, 21: 249; 33: 384.

59. C Rajagopalachari, *Gandhiji's Teachings and Philosophy* (Bombay: Bharatiya Vidya Bhavan, 1974) 4–5.

60. Mahadev Desai, 'My Submission', in MK Gandhi, *The Gospel of Selfless Action, or The Gita According to Gandhi*, translated by Mahadev Desai (Ahmedabad: Navajivan Press, 1970), 19.

61. See JTF Jorden, *Gandhi's Religion: A Homespun Shawl* (Basingstoke: Macmillan Press Ltd, 1998), 129.

62. PM Thomas, *20th Century Indian Interpretations of Bhagavadgita: Tilak, Gandhi and Aurobindo* (Delhi: ISPCK, 1987), 10–11.

63. Thomas, *20th Century Interpretations of Bhagavadgita*, 97.

64. See *Gandhi on Non-Violence: A Selection from the Writings of Mahatma Gandhi*, edited and with an introduction by Thomas Merton (New York: New Directions Publishing Corporation, 1965), 24–25.

Part 3
Violence in History and Theology

Unpicking Retribution's Knots:
Churches as Cultures for Peace

Heather Thomson

In this chapter I examine the work of James Gilligan, a contemporary American psychiatrist who has worked for forty years with men convicted of violent crimes, mostly murder, in American prisons. From his experience, Gilligan has produced several books which outline his agenda for 'preventing violence'. His interest is as much in culture as it is in the psyches of the individual violent men. Gilligan argues that the cultures of the prisons do nothing to heal the violence in the criminals and in fact make the violence worse. However, it is possible to change the prison culture considerably to dispel, heal and even prevent violence, even for convicted murderers.

My interest is in what we may learn from Gilligan's work about the types of psyches and cultures that maintain and produce violence, and those that cultivate peace. What may we learn from this for the culture of Christian communities, signs and sacraments of the new creation? Theology often turns to the social sciences for wisdom, guidance and understanding (and occasionally, if it is brave enough, to face critique). In this case I am looking for wisdom on what it is that marks a culture as being part of the old creation (still living under the law with its demands for retribution and punishment, still caught in hierarchies of inequality and exclusion, still cultivating hurt and violence) and the marks of a culture that leads to peace.

Further, I feel the need for wisdom from the social sciences, from some source outside the Christian tradition and its scriptures, on the question of violence. Within and throughout the Christian tradition there is ambiguity regarding violence and its relation to God. Vengeance and retribution, forgiveness and peace, all claim to speak in the name of God. So I turn to James Gilligan, not as a source of theology *per se*, but to help us discern what, in our desires and in our cultures, may guide us into new ways of thinking and being so that we may 'choose life and good', not 'death and evil' (Deut 30:15). From this I will draw out from scripture certain metaphors for church as the community of the new creation, one that cultivates peace.

By the time he wrote his book, *Preventing Violence*, in 2001, Gilligan had had nearly forty years of experience in American prisons,

attempting to understand the acts of violence of the convicted criminals
he met in those institutions. His first twenty-five years were with the
Massachusetts prison system as a psychotherapist, then as Medical
Director of the prison mental hospital for the criminally insane, and
later as Director of Mental Health Services for the prison system as
a whole.[1] He could see no better laboratory in which to view, from
the inside (so to speak), the working of violence in the form of crime
and punishment. The prisons in Massachusetts at that time were a
'virtual war zone', particularly the Maximum Security prison, which
they used to call the 'maximum insecurity prison'.[2] He describes
the violence throughout the prisons as 'an epidemic of homicides,
suicides, riots, arson, gang rapes, hostage-taking, and self-mutilation
(prisoners gouging their eyes out, cutting off their genitals, pulling
out their toenails, swallowing razor-blades), in which prisoners, prison
staff and visitors were being killed or grievously injured'.[3]

After legal action was taken on behalf of inmates who had been
injured or killed, Gilligan and the staff of the prison mental hospital
were asked to expand their services to the whole prison system in
Massachusetts. For the next ten years they implemented violence
prevention programs, working with both prisoners and correctional
staff, in an experiment that yielded positive results. In the first five
years, the violence within the prison system was drastically reduced,
and in the next five years there were 'no riots, no hostage-taking, and
a total of one homicide and two suicides throughout the state prison
system; that is, there were some full years with no violent deaths in
any of the prisons'.[4]

Gilligan went on to produce similar dramatic reductions in violence
in the prison system in San Francisco. He does not go into details on
how this was achieved, but refers readers instead to numerous books
and websites now available that detail such programs, including the
Centre for the Study and Prevention of Violence at the University of
Colorado, Boulder.[5] Rather, Gilligan wishes to draw on his experience
in such programs to convey some basic principles underlying the
causes and prevention of violence as he sees it. And the first principle
is this: 'it is possible to prevent violence virtually anywhere, in even
the most violent of environments, if you want to badly enough and are
willing to devote sufficient time and effort to the task'.[6]

The second principle is that such programs will not succeed unless
we abolish the traditional moral and legal approach, whereby violence
is understood as a behaviour to be punished rather than a sickness to be
healed. Moral condemnation and punishment of violent acts has been

tried as a way to prevent violence, to 'teach people a lesson', or to deter further violence. However, as Gilligan points out, four thousand years is more than long enough to test any hypothesis. The experiment has failed, and the condemnation and punishment approach only makes things worse.[7] The number of people in prison in America, per capita, has continued to rise, not fall, and is higher than it ever was in Russia, or in South Africa under Apartheid.[8]

Dennis Pierce concurs with this view from his experience in prison chaplaincy and prison reform in America. Arguing that the 'correctional systems for the most part have traded the rehabilitation model for the punitive model', he speaks of the 'human breakdown' created by the prison system itself.[9] *Restraint* of violent people is one thing, and is needed for the protection of others, but *punishment*—the deliberate inflicting of pain (whether bodily or psychologically)—does not stop violence. It only exacerbates the problem—violence for violence, an eye for an eye.

Rather than requiring punishment, Gilligan sees violence as requiring treatment and therapy, for individuals and communities. It is an issue for public health and preventative medicine. Violence is a disease, an illness, a pathology. 'We treat illnesses', he says, 'we do not punish them'.[10] Punishment is 'an ill-conceived, mis-directed social crime for which we pay dearly'.[11] Pierce regards punishment as a 'substantial evil', which 'is what our society does to its juveniles and to its young adults, the poor, the oppressed, and the uneducated who fill the cells of our prisons to the bursting point. Society's answer is to build more places of incarceration'.[12] His ministry is from a place of compassion that seeks 'healing and wholeness'.[13]

Gilligan speaks of violence in terms of preventative medicine: risk factors, secondary and tertiary prevention strategies. But he is not about to simplify a complex and difficult topic. 'Human violence', he admits, 'is much more complicated, ambiguous and, most of all, tragic, than is commonly realised or acknowledged'.[14] And the tragedy includes the perpetrators as well as the victims of violence. Seeing violence as an illness to be healed, leads one onto the path of compassion, for the perpetrators as well as the victims of violence.[15]

While Gilligan's work deserves a close reading, I will draw out some further summary points that he makes in attempting to understand violence, which may help us in thinking through churches as cultures of peace.

In referring to violence as a disease, Gilligan names it as a *contagious* disease, rather than an *hereditary* one. In other words, psychological and social factors are more important in the causes of violence than biological.[16] A sense of self and personal identity comes from the process of interaction with others, from relationships and culture. The psyche is as dependent on culture for its nurturing as a body is dependent on food.[17] Good cultures provide people with self-esteem and establish mutual, universal respect for each other's human dignity.[18] But the men that Gilligan worked with—the criminally violent and insane—were products of environments, usually childhood abuse and violent communities, that had severely damaged their sense of honour and self-worth.

Gilligan argues that our greatest pain is to be insignificant, to be without a voice, or without control over one's life and decisions; as an adult to be treated like a child or an animal. And a number of the prisoners he knew recognised that in prison they were worse off than the animals in zoos, for at least there had been some zoo reform by then.[19] This is why punishment does not help the situation, but only exacerbates it. Those who are already damaged in their psyches and suffering from such humiliation and shame that they will dominate and humiliate others to feel at least *some* sense of power, are not going to be cured by being shamed and humiliated further. Rather, a change in culture can heal such wounds.

> We have to recognize that the only basis on which we can live with each other without violence is one of mutual respect, a respect that is so deep and unconditional that it is not dependent on achievement or behaviour, but is respect for human dignity, for the inviolability of the human soul and personality, and a determination not to subject anyone to shame . . . [20]

Still working with his metaphor of violence as a disease, Gilligan argues:

> If cleaning up the sewer systems could prevent more deaths than all the physicians in the world, then perhaps reforming the social, economic and legal systems that systematically humiliate people can do more to prevent violence than all the preaching and punishing in the world.[21]

Inequalities of any kind, when built into a social system, lead some people to feel inferior in relation to others, and lend themselves to the feelings of shame and lack of self-worth. This is one of the risk factors that lead some people, at least, to lash out violently, or suffer violence as victims.

For all that has been said so far, what has not been explained is why men are by far greater perpetrators and victims of violence than women, when you take into account all wars, homicides, suicides, gang-wars, fights, rapes and domestic violence. For Gilligan, this is again a matter of socialisation. Men more than women, particularly under patriarchal cultures, are socialised to think that to want love and care from others is to be passive, dependent, a 'wimp', unmanly.[22] This is certainly the case with the men that Gilligan worked with in the prisons, and a factor in their violent behaviour. He says that:

> Violent men's deepest fear is that they will go out,
> not with a bang but a whimper; which is why they try
> so hard to create the biggest and loudest bang they
> can, in an effort to drown out their shame-inducing
> whimper . . . the whimper of the wish to be loved and
> cared for.[23]

At this point I want to make some transitionary remarks that will move us from Gilligan's work to thinking about churches as cultures of peace. I found it hard to discern what was motivating me, what were the connections that I had intuited between the two, and on reflection it is this. I recognise myself as a recovering moralist. The waters I swam in during my childhood, the cultures that formed me, were punitive cultures that shamed and humiliated those who did not conform—at school, at home, and at church—though they also had strengths, love and support. Plenty of double-messages there to muck me up for a few years. Coming from such cultures, it is not hard to incorporate the retributive justice and punitive thinking that is built into certain theories of atonement and eschatology, judgement, heaven and hell. Perhaps this is why God-ordained retribution and punishment have such a strong hold on the Christian psyche—so many of us come from such cultures.

As a recovering moralist I have come a long way, but it is James Gilligan who has shown me how ill-conceived and misguided a punitive mentality is. Not only is it not loving, but the very desire to want others to 'get what they deserve', to want payment and punishment, is the same mentality belonging to those who commit the violence we call 'criminal acts'. Both parties work from their own sense of 'justice', and both are motivated by retributive, not restorative, justice.

Gilligan has two chapters on the violence of punishment, and they form the most disturbing part of his book.[24] It was upsetting enough to read through previous chapters where, in order to explain how he came to understand the motivations and 'causes' of violence, Gilligan had to describe some of the murders and mutilations that these prisoners had committed. But he goes on to talk about the legally and state-sanctioned violence, part of the accepted culture of the prison designed to humiliate, degrade, isolate and dehumanise, on the assumption that these men are worse than animals and deserve what they get. Then I could see that 'punishment' was difficult to discern from any other act of violence, even those that the punishers condemned.

The most disturbing part of this section on punishment was the discussion of rape in jails—the extent of it, the culture of it, and how it is allowed by prison authorities and politicians as part of the punishment that criminals deserve when they go to jail. Within this we hear the story of a young man, about nineteen year old, who was admitted to jail for a non-violent crime.[25] He was gang-raped on three separate occasions, once so brutally he had to be sewn up afterwards. It turned him mad, which is why James Gilligan came to see him. There were two things in particular that upset me about this story. One was that it, and all the other rapes in jails, are happening in a Christian country where there is a strong Christian voice for punishment, law and order: it is common knowledge that rapes happen in jail, so if someone doesn't want to be treated like that they should have thought about that before committing their crime! If such punitive thinking leads to so much violence and suffering, then this story has helped to unpick any remaining knots I had that tied me to retributive justice.[26]

The second reason I found this story particularly disturbing is that I have a nineteen year-old son, and I have to admit that some transference came into play. The lioness was stirred to protect and care, but she felt the anguish of knowing that for this young man it was all too late. His life had been literally buggered up. It was my empathy for him, and all my male relatives and friends, that helped unpick retribution's knots even for those who have committed violent crimes. No-one deserves to be treated violently.

There is one more piece to this transition from Gilligan's work to thinking about churches as cultures of peace. It was Patricia Brennan who put me onto James Gilligan. She was the founding president of the Movement for the Ordination of Women (MOW) in the Anglican Church of Australia, and was a spokeswoman during the 1980s and 1990s for feminist concerns, church and theology with various media in Australia. Brennan is also a medical doctor, and has worked for the last ten years or so in the area of child sexual abuse. She sees little children—three months old, five years old—who have been sexually abused one way or another, and prepares the medical side of the evidence for the court cases.

What would you expect from a committed feminist working in child sexual abuse when almost all the abusers are men? That she would be anti-men? That she would become a man-hater? No, not in her case. While working for justice and healing for the victims of abuse, I have heard Patricia Brennan speak with compassion about the perpetrators of these acts—for their lonely, sick, sorry, despised lives, and heaven help them if they go to prison. She is on the same wavelength as James Gilligan.

So where does this take us in terms of the church and its ability to cultivate peace? For one, we will not get very far so long as Christian people keep moralising and calling for punishment. James Alison in his book, *On Being Liked*, has a chapter entitled, 'Unpicking atonement's knots'.[27] What I am trying to do here is unpick retribution's knots—the knots that tie punitive desires to our hearts and souls, and to our theology, especially in theories of atonement and eschatology.

When it comes to considering the cultures of our churches and how they may contribute to cultivating peace, we can be inspired by James Gilligan to move as much as possible to cultures that are egalitarian, accepting, loving and dignifying for all, and as non-patriarchal as we are able. There are certainly biblical warrants for this, and the work of Elisabeth Schüssler Fiorenza is one contribution among many that captures the vision of the early Christian community as a radical 'discipleship of equals'.[28]

This is not to derive our theology from Gilligan, but to allow him to help us discern among the different cultures of church that exist within the scriptures and tradition, those which will promote peace rather than contribute to violence either directly or indirectly. However, I am heading towards a specific biblical model of church that in my view theologically unpicks retribution's knots, so that retributive justice is untied from any lasting association with the will of God. This is found in the metaphor for church in 1 Peter 2: 4–12, and contributes to our understanding of church as the community of the new creation. The new creation in this instance is a new building, a different architecture of relationships between its members. And since the Christian community itself is meant to be the sign and sacrament of what God wants for all human communities, the models and metaphors we work with are important.

The writer of 1 Peter mixes several metaphors from the Old Testament and applies them to the Christian church. After referring to his readers as 'living stones' he urges, 'let yourselves be built into a spiritual house, to be a holy priesthood, to offer spiritual sacrifices acceptable to God through Jesus Christ' (2:5). What would this 'spiritual house' look like? It is built upon a foundation stone, one rejected by mortals, yet chosen and precious in God's sight (2:4). Here we have the first Old Testament reference from Isaiah 28:16:

> See, I am laying in Zion a stone,
> a cornerstone chosen and precious;
> and whoever believes in him will not be put to
> shame.

This is a building in which none will be put to shame (cf Rom 10:11). The Isaiah text goes on to add, 'I will make justice the line, and righteousness the plummet'. The relationships in this community are given their measure from the cornerstone. They are aligned by justice and righteousness, and they are built up from below.[29] The writer of 1 Peter then adds another metaphor of a stone, this time from Psalm 118:22:

> The stone that the builders rejected
> has become the head of the corner.

These images together have profound implications for a community, built up from the stone that was rejected. The 'rejected one' in New Testament texts refers to Jesus, the one who was pushed out, punished for breaking the law, humiliated and killed in the name of 'justice' and of God. Psalm 118:22 is quoted in the parable of the vineyard to refer to the son who is rejected, and implies the rejection of Jesus later in the gospels (Mark 12:10–11; Matt 21:42; Luke 20:17–18).[30] The point is brought home even more strongly in Peter's speech in Acts 4:8–12. Peter tells the Sanhedrin in Jerusalem that his power to heal comes from 'Jesus Christ of Nazareth whom you crucified', referring then to Psalm 118:22: 'This is the stone that was rejected by you builders, but which has become the head of the corner' (Acts 4:10–11).[31]

If the Christian response to Jesus' death is to blame those who killed him and seek retribution, then we have learned nothing, and have nothing revealed to us by Jesus, the revelation of God. But Jesus himself, in the stories of his resurrection appearances, did not return with a sword, or with hatred and vengeance. He came speaking peace. Jesus' own way is a scandal and stumbling block to those who see justice as requiring punishment and payback. If we have eyes to see, punishment is not what God requires, and nor should we. In the name of punishment, humanity 'killed the Author of life' (Acts 3:14–15).

Jesus' life and death enable us to see things differently, and to live according to new relationships with God and with each other. The foundation stone of our new community is not one who was punished on our behalf because we deserved it, but one who was 'rejected my mortals' (1 Pet 2:4). He was expelled in the name of retributive justice, and suffered violence under the law. How can any community built up from this foundation continue to exercise retributive justice, or even have a heart for it?

The Christian community gathered and built up in Christ's name, is not standing on the body of a victim as if we are victors and conquerors. Rather, we are built up from being *aligned to* this victim, identifying with him, against the kinds of powers that call for violence in the name of justice and of God.

Justice must still be done for the victims of violence, and in our societies, that may entail imprisonment, but *punishment*, as in the deliberate infliction of pain, humiliation and degradation, remains 'an ill-conceived, mis-directed social crime for which we pay dearly'.[32] When we, like Paul, shift our allegiance from those who call for punishment, to those who suffer from it, then we see something of what the 'new creation' is about.

I am talking hermeneutics here—horizons and points of view. An horizon is as far as you can see from where you are standing. But where you are standing matters. James Gilligan spent his life's work among the lowest of the low, the insignificant and disregarded, the hated and humiliated. He tried to understand them from their perspective and to read his culture through their eyes. In doing so he revealed the heart of darkness within the type of justice that works from retribution and punishment. Jesus, as the one who was punished, rejected and killed, reveals the heart of darkness when retribution is tied to God and religion.

When the crucified one is our hermeneutic, then the new creation is more than individual Christians being made anew through their relationship with God. It involves a whole new way of being community, having a new culture, one that is aligned in such a way that each 'living stone' is honoured and respected, where no-one will be put to shame, and where justice and righteousness are restorative, reconciling and healing, not condemning and punishing. In such a culture we are called from a heart of darkness, 'into God's marvellous light' (1 Pets 2:9).

James Gilligan's work, together with the vision of Christian community found in 1 Peter 2:4–9, make fruitful contributions towards my campaign to unpick retribution's knots.

Endnotes

1. James Gilligan, *Preventing Violence* (London: Thames & Hudson, 2001), 15.
2. *Ibid*, 15.
3. *Ibid*.
4. *Ibid*, 17.
5. *Ibid*, 9; The Centre for the Study and Prevention of Violence has a website: http://www.colorado.edu/cspv
6. *Ibid*, 17.
7. *Ibid*, 7.
8. James Gilligan, *Violence: Reflections on a National Epidemic* (New York: Random House, 1997), 23.
9. Dennis W Pierce, *Prison Ministry: Hope Behind the Wall* (New York: Haworth Pastoral Press, 2006), 60, 65–7, 79ff.
10. Gilligan, *Preventing Violence*, 19. See also, Gilligan, *Violence*, 17.
11. Gilligan, *Violence*, 140.
12. Pierce, *Prison Ministry*, 134.
13. *Ibid*, 115.
14. Gilligan, *Violence*, 5.
15. For a discussion of compassion, see Pierce, *Prison Ministry*, 115–17.
16. Gilligan, *Violence*, 105.
17. *Ibid*, 96.
18. *Ibid*, 213–14.
19. *Ibid*, 181.
20. Gilligan, *Preventing Violence*, 75.
21. Gilligan, *Violence*, 239.
22. *Ibid*, 237.

23. *Ibid*, 214. See also 225–36 for a chapter on this topic, 'Culture, Gender and Violence: "We are not women"'. Gilligan also devotes a chapter to this topic in, *Preventing Violence*, 56–65, 'Violence as Proof of Masculinity'.

24. *Ibid*, chapter 6: 'The Symbolism of Punishment', 139–61, and chapter 7: 'How to Increase the Rate of Violence—and Why', 163–90.

25. *Ibid,* 166f.

26. Pierce also discusses rape in prisons, see *Prison Ministry*, 73–5.

27. James Alison, 'Unpicking Atonement's Knots', in *On Being Liked* (London: Darton, Longman and Todd, 2003), 17–31.

28. ES Fiorenza, *Discipleship of Equals: A Critical Feminist Ekklesia-logy of Liberation* (London: SCM Press, 1993).

29. Achtmeier convincingly argues for 'cornerstone' as the correct term here, against those who would translate the 'stone' as the keystone of an arch, the highest stone of a building. Its position as the foundation, and as a stone that can cause one to stumble, makes it more likely to refer to a cornerstone from which a community is built up. See Paul J Achtmeier, *1 Peter* (Minneapolis: Fortress Press, 1996), 159–60. Compare Eph 2:19–22.

30. John H Elliott, *1 Peter: Anchor Bible* volume 37B (New York: Doubleday, 2000), 410.

31. Elliott, *1 Peter*, 410.

32. Gilligan, *Preventing Violence*, 19.

The Location of God, Theories of the Atonement and 'Redemptive' Violence

Chris Budden

Suicide bombers, terrorist attacks, the invasion of Afghanistan and Iraq, the military activity of the State of Israel or Hezbollah, or talk about *jihad* pose questions about the connection between religion and violence, the connections between religious bodies, war and terrorism. One particular part of that conversation, one that has caused significant theological debate, concerns the way theories of the atonement within the Christian tradition, and the understanding of God that they imply, encourage and help to justify violence in our society.

As the word suggests, 'atonement' is concerned for bringing parties together, making them one. It is about the reconciliation of two parties to each other. In Christian theological discourse, reconciliation refers to the person and work of Jesus Christ and the new relationship he brings between God and humanity. There are various metaphors and models used to describe this atoning work. Gustaf Aulén[1], for example, places these models under the headings of *Christus Victor* (Christ as victorious over the powers, however understood), moral-influence (Abelard), and satisfaction (Anselm).[2]

A significant area of discussion in theological circles has been whether there is a relationship between the place of the church in society, the major theories of the atonement used in the church, and the support such theories give for violence in society. For example, J Denny Weaver argues that the early church was a counter-cultural community living in opposition to state authority and violence, which held to a theory of *Christus Victor*, and was opposed to violence. However, as the church aligned itself with power during the time of the Emperor Constantine, and found itself needing to justify violence, it sought to find a model of the atonement that did not emphasise confrontation with the world (the 'powers' in their many forms). The primary theory of the atonement that developed during this time spoke of the need for Jesus to die to appease the anger of God (sacrificial theory) and of the role of violence in redemption.[3] Redemptive violence was then used as a justification for state violence and war.

There has been significant disagreement with Weaver's position, including the work of Hans Boersma who claims that Weaver's position is historically inaccurate. Boersma contends that Constantine continued to use the cross as a symbol of victory, and was able to do this because he could draw on, even as he changed, *Christus Victor* themes.[4] On a broader front, Boersma is suggesting that there is no simple correlation between the church's position in society and the dominant theories of the atonement that exist at any time.

While my concern is with the relationship between theories of the atonement and violence, I want to suggest that on its own the effort to link theories of the atonement with particular political and social movements is not productive. A community's or a person's theological position is significantly shaped by the constellation or cluster of themes which they connect to the issue under discussion, the relative importance of the different themes to the overall pattern of their thought, and their point of entry into the discussion.[5]

In this chapter I want to suggest that a central factor in the way theories or models of the atonement are understood, and the mimetic (i.e., imitative) impact they have in regard to violence, is the way people understand the location of God, as revealed in Jesus Christ.[6] My central claim is that the metaphors we use to express the theological location of God are crucial to our interpretation of models of the atonement and their impact on social behaviour, particularly violence. The metaphors we use to depict how God works in the world, where God is to be found and how God is present among us, will significantly influence how we see God's relationship to those in power, and the exercise of force and violence in a sinful world. The way we understand that theological location of God is important to the way we understand the social meaning of the atonement.

My purpose is to encourage a long-term conversation around atonement, violence and the location of God. I am seeking to name some of the issues and point to areas that need further exploration, to offer one framework and set of questions that might encourage that conversation to occur

Two foundational claims

There are two claims that need further explanation as we explore the connection between theories of the atonement, the theological location of God, and violence: (i) the mimetic role of religion; and (ii) the importance of metaphor for understanding models of the atonement.

The mimetic role of religion
One of the most significant functions of religion is to rehearse the

founding and shaping stories of life, to celebrate in ritual re-enactment, retelling, and rehearsal the events through which God has brought life and salvation. This provides the images which suggest what reality is about, what are the highest values, and how the world should be structured and made to be as God intended. Human behaviour imitates the behaviour of God as the source of ultimate values.

In terms of theories of the atonement, the claim is that the way we see the action of God in the cross, the way we understand the nature of God and reality in that event, will shape the way Christians and the church understand social reality, and what is appropriate behaviour for them as God's people. The difficulty with theories of the atonement which are inherently violent and based in punishment, is that their enactment in the church's life leads to a similar sort of view of how the world should be. Violence, punishment, and retribution become guiding principles for church and social life. As David Woods says:

> It is no accident that believers in brutal theories of the atonement tend themselves to be violent in their attitudes and behaviour. After all, we quite naturally reflect the god in whom we believe, fashioning ourselves in the image and likeness of idol or truth.[7]

Metaphor and models of atonement

In his chapter on metaphor, Boersma suggests that the primary, historical models of the atonement work with different metaphors, such as sacrifice, financial exchange, slave trade, healing, reconciliation, and military battle.[8] Those metaphors that become root metaphors (that is, the most suggestive ones) can become models.

> A model incorporates a number of other metaphors and thus forms a complex structure that can function as a paradigm or lens through which we can look at a particular doctrine. One fundamental way in which we look at the doctrine of sin, for instance, is through the metaphor of pride, while a very significant model for our understanding of God is the metaphor of father.[9]

It is not my purpose to explore the role of metaphor in theology (that has been already well done by people like Sallie McFague[10]), but to suggest two things. Firstly, metaphors not only help us interpret our world, they also give meaning. As Boersma says: 'Metaphors don't just present certain propositional truths; they first of all relate normatively how we want to view the world around us and how we believe the world should change'.[11]

Secondly, models of the atonement are not simply built on metaphor, they are interpreted in the light of other metaphors. The implication of this is that it is not simply a shift of models for the way people behave that is important at different periods in history, but the choice of metaphors that are used to interpret and understand the model and its implications.

Atonement, violence and the location of God

Where is God to be found? Among whom does God reveal Godself? How and where is God present in the world? The issue of God's location has to do with the nature of relationship, the exercise of power, the issue of hospitality, and the way we treat the 'other'. If, as Christian faith confesses, Jesus is the presence of God in our lives and history, then Jesus most clearly reveals how God works in the world, where God is to be found, and how God is present among us.

The way the church has interpreted the theological location of God has changed, I wish to suggest, from the time of the early church and the scriptural witness, to the understanding held as the church became part of the Roman Empire, to what is still the case today.

Jesus and our understanding of atonement

For almost 300 years, Christians were largely on the margins of society, essentially powerless and counter-cultural, and often persecuted. The decision to join the church involved a significant commitment and change of social space, and led to a lengthy period of preparation and formation. Those who enquired about Christ, or joined the Christian community, did not simply hear about the meaning of the cross, but learned about Jesus' life, message and death, and what this meant for their life of discipleship. New Christians were not simply called to believe something different about God and about Jesus, but to discover the new way of life implied in those beliefs. It was to enter a world in which their primary identity was as disciples of Christ, not citizens of their nation. One of the challenges, and words of hope, for the early disciples was the way in which the message and promise of atonement gave expression to the location of God in the world.

There are three locations of God that seem to me to be crucial. Firstly, there is the location of God in the incarnation and ordinary human life of Christ, the real first-century, Jewish, laughing, crying, suffering, bodily life of Jesus. In the incarnation, God shares with humanity and is immersed in human struggles and life, rather than exercising power from a distance, or delivering rules for life from afar.

In the life of Jesus, God is revealed as the one whose dancing life flows into the world to name it and to call people as sons and daughters, inviting people into God's dance of life, and offering hospitality and championing the struggle of, the most marginalised, excluded, oppressed. One of the great summaries of the life and location of Jesus, and thus of God's place, is 'he mixes with sinners and eats with them' (Lk 15:2). The early church saw Jesus located on the margins of society, giving expression to the covenant love and hospitality of God, and deeply opposed to ideas of retaliation and retribution.

Secondly, there is the location of God that we discover in Jesus' servanthood, and his sitting with the powerless, and protesting against power (for example Mk 10:17–22), his location in the world with the poor and marginalised and in the parables that shaped and constructed surprising ways of seeing (for example the rich will find it hard to enter the kingdom of God; see Lk 18:24–25). When Jesus begins his ministry in Luke 4, and speaks of Jubilee, he is speaking of remission of debt, the refusal to keep a balance, the offering and receiving of that which is not deserved.

Jesus says that we are not to resort to an eye for an eye and a tooth for a tooth (Matt 5:38, a law intended to limit vengeance), and when he says that we are to turn the other cheek to those who would harm us (Matt 5:39), speaks about anger (Matt 5:22), and demands that we not repay evil for evil (Matt 5:38–48). In these commands, he speaks of a world that is not always morally balanced, where there is not always a clear relationship between goodness and reward, evil and punishment, and he undercuts the idea that there must be vengeance and payment for sin. When the father in the parable we know as the Prodigal Son (Lk 15:11–32) is wronged, he forgives and restores a broken relationship. Despite what the older brother might desire, there is no retribution. Jesus undermines all efforts to build a theory of the atonement that uses violence, insists on retribution, or returns 'evil for evil'. God could not, in Jesus, have told us not to be angry, yet have burned with anger towards us and demanded the death of Jesus to appease his anger. The way Jesus lived had to be reflected in his death and its meaning.

Thirdly, there is the location of God in Christ in the suffering of the cross, rather than in acts of retaliation and rescue.[12] This is Christ who refuses to collude with injustice and violence, to reinforce that world by doing as others do. As Simon Barrow says: 'The cross, borne by God in Christ, turns out to be God's shocking, real, political satire of the death-dealing ways we are immersed in as both secular and religious people'.[13]

When Jesus says, reflecting Hosea 6:6, that he desires mercy and not sacrifice, he undermines the whole system of atonement and social relationships based on sacrifice, violence and payback. When he refuses to oppose those who would kill him, refuses the way of equal force and violence but takes the way of non-retaliation, he challenges all those theologies that are punitive and claim God as the vengeful, violent one.

Metaphors that speak of the location of God in the life of Christ point towards peacemaking and non-violence as central ways for understanding the atonement. To speak of God being found in Christ suggests images of solidarity, hospitality, forgiveness, non-violent treatment of others, care of enemies, of deep immersion in people's lives rather than the pronouncement of laws from a distance. The early church understood that it was only in a peaceful, non-retaliatory, graceful, turn-the-other-cheek, radically equal and servant community that there would be no poor, losers, excluded or second class citizens, and no injustice or institutional violence. What Jesus brought in his proclamation of the reign of God and his offer of hospitality was not just a promise that God was on the side of those who were excluded, but that God's reign had no room for those things that led to exclusion. This is hope and liberation for victims, the abused, the excluded, and the sinned-against.

I realise that, in taking this position, I find myself in one of the significant dilemmas faced by the church: how do we sustain this sort of peaceful, non-retaliatory community in the face of violence, evil and war? Can any genuine atonement or salvation be achieved without violence? There is, in this time between the promise of Christ and its fulfillment, dreadful abuse and suffering, violence and marginalization, that leaves people desperate and without voice. If there are no boundaries, no power that can protect, then the church may fail the victim. Indeed, this is the point of Hans Boersma's critique of the Anabaptist tradition represented by Weaver. These are the issues which Miroslav Volf wrestles with, in the concrete context of the horrors of the Balkans, in *Exclusion & Embrace*.[14] This is why the Church has wrestled with the two-kingdom tradition, pacifism, just war, the role of perfection and spiritual elites, and the belief that only in the future kingdom will we be able to live as Christ called us to live.

There is not the space in this chapter to explore all these issues, or to provide a full justification for the decision to locate the argument towards the non-violent, even pacifist end of the theological spectrum. However, there are three things that need to be taken seriously in further exploration of this issue.

Firstly, there are significant questions to address. Why, when God is hidden and powerless in the face of suffering, does the church insist on claiming another role? Why do we wish to fill the pain and space with violence that will give the result we desire? Is it our task or God's task to deal with violence, and how can we be other than faithful disciples who seek to make God known in the world? However it is that we find a way forward in relation to the continuing existence of violence, we must take seriously the *theologia crucis*, with its bold claim of death within God and of God who claims space in the world through suffering and weakness. There is a need to take seriously the claim that, in the crucified Christ, God identifies with the godless and those abandoned by God.

Secondly, the task of the church is to act in *responsible correspondence* to the life of Christ in the world. That is, we will take responsible decisions and act in ways which will reflect the identity of Christ in our world, in order to show God as the ultimate reality. The identity of Christ was one of suffering servanthood.

Thirdly, if the church does move to the point of justifying violence and force to restrain evil, it is not redemptive force. It is not violence used to restore the balance of the world, nor violence used rightly. It is violence to hold the world in check, and it is entered as a way of sharing in Christ's bearing of the world's sin. It is violence that is still wrong, that still betrays the nature of the church, yet it is a betrayal we take upon ourselves in solidarity with Christ. It is not violence to protect ourselves, or violence to destroy enemies and achieve our ends. Turning the other cheek is our first discipleship demand, and violence cannot be redemptive or community-building.

The primary model of the atonement in the early church, and one that continues to have a place in many people's life and theology, is that of Christ who is victor over dark forces and oppressive powers, who conquers evil and death, and liberates people from oppression. Yet, in the light of the understanding of God's place in Christ that has been suggested here, this cannot not be understood as a sign of God's violence or our own right to be violent.

To follow Jesus is a difficult journey of discipleship in which people seek to live out the social, economic and political implications of his life and teaching, rather than seeing discipleship simply as an act of belief. This is well reflected in the book of James, who insists that the true measure of faith is the actions which flow from it (2:14–26).

To construct a theology of the atonement around the cross was, for the early church, a strange thing. It was to place at its centre a symbol that would bring forth revulsion, and was a sign of subversives, criminals and rebellious slaves. As the authors of *Storm Front* remind us, crucifixion was not a general form of capital punishment, but was reserved for those who committed particularly violent and repugnant crimes, for sedition, and for slaves who rebelled. Crucifixion was intended to be as horrifying and gruesome as possible, a way of terrorising those seen as dangerous to the security imposed by Rome, providing the greatest deterrent to those who would act against the established order.[15] To speak of crucifixion was to suggest a community which would align itself with what was subversive, and to be a community that in a fundamental way called into question the way the world is.

> The message of the cross invites us to look to a God who works from the bottom up and from the margins inward, rather than from the top down. Christianity has not often functioned with spiritual vitality in the mainstream of a culture. There's something about that location which often seems to blunt the energizing and disruptive power of the cross.[16]

What happens, though, when God is claimed by the powerful, when God is forced to shift places? What happens to the church's view of forgiveness, punishment, atonement and violence, and what practices in church and society flow from that shift?

The Church and Christendom

When Constantine decided to adopt the Christian faith, and to make it the official faith of the Roman Empire, the Christian community found itself shifting from the edges of society, from being a counter-cultural community standing over against government persecution and oppression, to being at the centre of power.

In the middle of a section entitled 'Disestablishment as Opportunity', in which he asks whether the church really was designed to be an established faith as it was in Christendom, Douglas John Hall says that in Christendom there were significant things that had to be downplayed or simply neglected:

> the primacy of love; the demand for justice, especially toward the underprivileged; the insistence upon forgiveness (not just once, but seventy times seven!); the equality of all human beings, without reference to race, culture, creed, gender, and all else; above all, I think, the insistence upon a continuous and prophetic orientation toward truth and a concomitant vigilance against hypocrisy, subterfuge, and oversimplification. None of these things . . . are natural allies of power . . . [17]

> And some of us have begun to realize how the biblical concern for the poor and outcast, for the dispossessed, for the victims of oppression and abuse and injustice, for children and women—how all this had to lose its central bite, its inherent critique of power, to be reduced at best to a matter of charity toward the underclasses.[18]

As Stuart Murray points out, the relationship of church to state in Christendom, the growing wealth of the church, and its association with those who had wealth and power meant significant changes in the way the church thought and acted. The church required a model of atonement which did not question the church's relationship to the powerful, even if it did not provide good news for the poor and dispossessed. The God who supported the politics of Christendom, the God of art and liturgy, was remote and vengeful, and ever ready to punish those who threatened this order destined by God, and the theory of atonement which developed tended to reflect this image. The Christendom church abandoned the early church's message of peace in favour of just war and redemptive violence. The notion of justice became 'retributive and punitive rather than restorative, forensic rather than relational', and in this form supported the doctrine of penal substitution, and the myth of redemptive violence.[19]

The old theology of the work and preaching of Christ was an embarrassment in Christendom. To become an ally of those in power and, eventually, to justify violence and war, God had to be shifted from the edges to the centre. Whatever theory of the atonement was used, whatever metaphors were now seen to be significant to explain the meaning of the life and death of Christ, they were understood in the light of a new place for God.

This shift is nowhere more clearly illustrated than the way in which the affirmation 'Jesus is Lord' changed its meaning. 'Jesus is Lord' (1 Cor 12:3) is the central Christological affirmation shared by the church through the centuries and often used as the basis for Christian co-operation. Yet, as Susan Brooks Thistlewaite[20] shows, there is a deep political meaning in this affirmation that is not shared by all Christians. When the early church, as a persecuted minority in a large and powerful Roman Empire, said that Jesus is Lord, they were also saying that Caesar is *not* Lord. The early Christians affirmed the Lordship of Christ as a challenge to the militaristic and expansionist Roman understanding of power and community. It was a way to construct Christian identity, a site of resistance that allowed a new and inclusive community to arise.

When the situation of the church changed, so that it functioned as the official religion within the Holy Roman Empire, the phrase 'Jesus is Lord' became invested with a different meaning. Rather than 'Lord' being the language of protest and struggle against the power of Rome and other authorities, it became the language which supported the place of the church in society. Political rulers were now lords who acted on behalf of the 'Lord', and the world was seen to be organised in an hierarchical fashion with the lords on top. To call Jesus 'Lord' was to suggest one who blessed a society stratified through gender, race and class, with himself as the first, and then the church, and the political ruler. Jesus was no longer the one who was owed sole allegiance, and who stood with people against those who abused power. Instead, allegiance to Jesus was shown through paying homage both to church authority and to political lord; in this context, Jesus was always seen to be standing with those in power.[21]

Douglas John Hall makes the point that the church has always struggled to combine a belief in divine otherness with an affirmation of God's participation in the world. He asks:

> How is it possible to insist upon God's infinity, eternality, omnipotence, omnipresence, and so on, and at the same time affirm that our God is compassionate, long-suffering, merciful, just, faithful, patient and kind?[22]

Hall's answer to this question is:

> It would seem that historical Christianity resolved
> this knotty problem for the most part by accentuating
> the attributes that depict the divine power and
> transcendence, and causing its Christology to fit that
> theological mold.[23]

God is removed from creaturely suffering, and becomes the one
who lives in unapproachable majesty. God is not only relocated to
the political centre of society, but becomes unapproachable and
dispassionate. God emerges as the one from whom all tenderness is
removed, the God of power and might, who requires the Church to
mediate God's life.

God changed places, and the practices of discipleship that
transform Christians into a kingdom people are spiritualised, and that
kingdom or reign is moved into the future. This change in the location
of God, and the alignment of the church with political power, impacted
on the way atonement was understood.

Firstly, theories of the atonement reflect one of two archetypal
ways in which we can understand the theology of the Easter event:
'one is structured around the notion of retribution; the other around
the notion of forgiveness'.[24] On one side is a position that insists on a
morally balanced universe, and the need for sin to be paid for, punished,
and balanced in some way. The scales of justice must always be righted
by retribution, by the payment of a price, and Jesus pays for human sin
by his own suffering and the shedding of his blood. The other position
understands that life rests in forgiveness and undeserved grace, that
retribution and balance are not always necessary or possible.

With the move to the political centre, the framework that shaped
the church's understanding of atonement became that of balance and
retribution—the same framework as the Roman legal system—rather
than forgiveness, redemption and restoration (and covenant love)
among those in a community with Christ. It was the framework of
citizenship rather than discipleship.

Secondly, to the extent that the earlier *Christus Victor* theory
was maintained, it was seen to be less about the defeat of the powers
that threatened the people of God, less about victory over all the evil
powers that denied God and robbed people of life, than it was about
the cross as a sign of blessing upon the power and victory of rulers.

The victory of Christ was over those who opposed the lord who represented Jesus.

At the same time, there began the slow movement from the centrality of the *Christus Victor* theory of the atonement, to a theory concerned for Jesus' substitutionary death as that which appeased God and set the world right. In the early church people faced the anxiety of death and powerlessness, and Christ was liberator. In Christendom needs are spiritualised. People face the anxiety of guilt and condemnation, and Christ bears our guilt.[25] Christ moves from the one that scripture says died 'for' us, to one who 'died in our place', an act of violence from a God whom Jesus revealed to be non-violent.

The church moves from a theology of the cross—God located in suffering solidarity with the outcasts outside the gate—to a theology of glory—the reign of Christ at God's right hand, located in heaven, and a glorious church.[26] The church becomes a religious institution that sees itself as a priest to the kingdoms of the world, the one between God in glory and a still sinful world that must cope with sin through violence and control by the princes (who now serve God).

When the church became an imperial religion, its theological writings began to develop an account of the righteous empire and, eventually, justifiable war. The outcome of this move is such theological work as Augustine's in which the political realm and the kingdom of God are so closely aligned that Christians can be called to take up arms to defend the *polis* against all enemies without and within. It culminated in Anselm's *Cur Deus Homo?*,[27] a defence of the honour of God through a solitary death, that found its metaphors in feudal society, hierarchy, and honour owed to the lord.

From its role as priest the church imposes a universal and detached ethic. It knows what is good and evil, who is friend and enemy (without anguish, doubt or involvement), and why the world should remain as hierarchical as it is (for this reflects its life, which is a reflection of God). Faith becomes correct belief (determined by the church), not obedient discipleship to Jesus (and certainly not in terms of the social, political and economic implications of how Jesus himself lived). Christ's death and resurrection are separated from his life. Indeed, there is no place for Jesus' real humanity, for God being incarnated in one particular person. The particular, first-century, Jewish humanity of Jesus becomes a generalised, theoretical humanity that does not touch his saving work. The theological debate was about whether he was really human (as well as God)—in a general way—and not about his humanity, location and saving life.

God has moved place, from being the companion of the poor to the protector of those in power. Violence is justified as necessary to protect the God-appointed ruler, the ordained order of society, and the kingdom of God found in the new world. It is possible to do this because God is no longer the one who defies the powerful to establish a peaceful kingdom, but the one who sacrifices his son in an act of violence in order to balance the universe and protect God's holy honour (rather than loving heart). Violence is now seen as redemptive, and war and violence can be justified.

Today

While the substitutionary theory may have developed further since those early centuries, and particularly since the Reformation, so that the most widespread theory is now one of *penal* substitution,[28] the essential groundwork had been laid: redemptive violence, God on the side of those in power, the church in a priestly role.

The myth of redemptive violence has become the major myth underlying the foreign policy of the United States of America and, by association, of Australia. The link between a retributive doctrine of the cross and a politics of violence and pre-emptive strike, that is able to justify torture to defeat terrorism, and leads to the belief that the blood spilled on September 11 must be paid for with blood, is the sense that God is on our side, and our enemies are God's enemies.

In this situation, a doctrine of 'Just War' is too restrictive. Theories of a 'Just War' sought to restrict war, to indicate the criteria which must be met to enable a government to wage war. They understood that the goal is peace-making, and that there is a great human propensity for evil. They understood that God was Lord of heaven and earth, and was not simply on our side. But in the modern situation God takes sides. God fights with us, and our acts of violence are what God would desire so that the enemy can be destroyed. What is necessary to balance the world is the capacity for first strike or pre-emptive strike, to use whatever violence is necessary so that blood can be shed to balance terror. Warfare is now retribution and revenge, not the limiting model of the just war theory. Retributive violence is the same myth that shapes movies, culture and foreign policy. And it is articulated and defended by the religious right whose theology is one of penal substitution.

In a penal substitutionary theory, backed by a metaphor of God as imperial support, there is no good news for victims, the poor and marginalised (black people, women, etc). Christ, sacrificed by the

Father and submitting meekly to this abuse, is an unhealthy model for women abused by husbands or children sexually violated by important males in their lives. 'A model of passive, innocent suffering poses an obstacle for people who encounter conditions of systemic injustice, or an unjust status quo produced by the power structure'.[29] This is particularly so when the church then urges victims to submit to such abuse, using Jesus as a model, hierarchy as the justification, and the place of God with those in power as happened with apartheid, slavery, the abuse of women, the invasion of Indigenous lands, or the military occupation of Palestinian autonomous areas. The idea that the world must be in some sort of moral balance leads Christians to support the death penalty, insist on lengthy jail terms, and oppose genuine prison reform.

Conclusion

The myth of redemptive violence, interpreted through metaphors about the location of God as the one who is with those in power, does not, in fact, lead to redemption—particularly for those on the edge of society or those who have been named as the enemies—but to more violence. It does not lead to the hospitality of God, to people being drawn into the divine dance, to forgiveness, the love of the enemy, the turning of the other cheek, or the going the extra mile, but to exclusion, punishment, and the spilling of more blood.

The idea of redemptive violence is actually self-contradictory, for violence does not lead to redemption but to further violence. Theories of the atonement which depend on violence underpin violence in society. The cross tells us that God is known in suffering. It challenges the view that God cannot suffer or share with outcasts, and affirms that God is indeed in those seemingly deserted places offering life. It challenges our sense of where God is, and with whom God shares life.

If we are to find a metaphor that will enable us to explore the atonement in ways that tackle modern meaninglessness and violence, we need something that is incarnational, that places God within our journey, is able to be transformed by new experiences and discover salvation with us. We need a metaphor, an image, of God on the margins and edges or, maybe, in the centre where the non-retributive cross stands.

Endnotes

1. Gustaf Aulén, *Christus Victor: An Historical Study of the Three Main Types of the Idea of the Atonement*, translated by AG Herbert (London: SPCK, 1970). There has been increasing criticism of the way Aulén has 'forced' the various ways of speaking of the atonement into these three models. For example, in *Saving Power: Theories of Atonement and Forms of the Church* (Grand Rapids: Eerdmans, 2005), Peter Schmiechen suggests that there are ten theories of the atonement which can be gathered under four headings (Christ died for us; liberation from sin, death and demonic powers; the purposes of God; and reconciliation).

2. Much of the discussion of those theories which are placed under a broadly Anselmian umbrella are concerned for ways in which the atonement does something for God: 'his honour or justice is upheld (satisfaction, punishment), or his anger and wrath are assuaged (propitiation). In other words, reconciliation involves some kind of economy of exchange'. See Hans Boersma, *Violence, Hospitality, and the Cross: Reappropriating the Atonement Tradition* (Grand Rapids: Baker Academic, 2004), 158–59. Included in this is the post-Reformation concern for penal substitution.

3. J Denny Weaver, *The Nonviolent Atonement* (Grand Rapids: Eerdmans Publishing Company, 2001).

4. Boersma, *Violence* 154ff. He lists a number of significant critiques of Weaver's work in, for example, footnotes 6 and 7 on page 156.

5. For example, Boersma enters the debate about atonement and violence through the ideas of hospitality and its limits, election, the reality of violence and sin in the world, and the need for boundaries and punishment in this world. In *Consuming Passion: Why the killing of Jesus really matters*, edited by Simon Barrow and Jonathon Bartley (London: Darton, Longman & Todd, 2005), the various authors reflect a Mennonite–Anabaptist concern for discipleship (rather than intellectual belief), the way that Jesus' life, death and resurrection together contribute to our salvation, the life and teachings of Jesus, and the centrality of non-violence and peace-making. Douglas John Hall, on the other hand, has a concern for the suffering and loving heart of God, and the way God is found in the cross. See *The Cross in our Context: Jesus and the Suffering World* (Minneapolis: Fortress Press, 2003).

6. My concern for the location of God had its genesis over thirty years ago as I read Dietrich Bonhoeffer's *Christology*, translated by John Bowden (London: Collins/ Fontana, 1971). Bonhoeffer suggested that the Christological question was not how is it possible for Jesus to be the Christ (or to be God-man), or is revelation a fact, but *who* is Jesus Christ? His concern was to describe the form of Christ's presence in

the world, and to show how Christ's existence could be described as his personal being-there-for-humankind. In order to show Christ as one whose presence is also his existence, Bonhoeffer turned to the language of sociology and logic, space and structure rather than event and history. In my opinion it is the form of Christ, Christ's concrete existence in the world, that changes throughout Bonhoeffer's writings. (See Chris Budden, 'A Response to Aveling's "Dietrich Bonhoeffer's Christology"', *Colloquium*, volume 16 (May 1984): 39–42.) Together with liberation and contextual theologies, this Christological concern has nurtured my sense of the importance of the theological location of God.

7. David Wood, 'Finding Light in the Shadow of the Cross', in *Consuming Passion*, *op cit*, 115.
8. Boersma, *Violence, Hospitality, and the Cross*, 99.
9. *Ibid*, 108–9.
10. Sallie McFague, *Metaphorical Theology: Models of God in Religious Language* (Philadelphia: Fortress Press, 1982).
11. Boersma, *Violence, Hospitality, and the Cross*, 103–4.
12. In Matt 26:52–53, Jesus responds to the action of one of his disciples who defends him with a sword with the words, 'Put your sword back into its place; for all who take the sword will perish by the sword. Do you think that I cannot appeal to my Father, and he will at once send me more than twelve legions of angels?'
13. Simon Barrow, 'The Cross, Salvation and Politics of Satire', in *Consuming Passion*, *op cit*, 109.
14. Miroslav Volf, *Exclusion & Embrace: A Theological Exploration of Identity, Otherness, and Reconciliation* (Nashville: Abingdon Press, 1996).
15. James V Brownson, Inagrace T Dietterich, Barry A Harvey and Charles C West, *Storm Front: The Good News of God* (Grand Rapids: Eerdmans, 2003), 60–61.
16. *Ibid*, 62.
17. Hall, *The Cross in our Context*, 167–68.
18. *Ibid*, 172.
19. Stuart Murray, 'Rethinking Atonement after Christendom', in *Consuming Passion, op cit*, 32.
20. Susan Brook Thistlewaite, 'Christology and Postmodernism: Not Everyone Who Says to Me, "Lord, Lord"', *Interpretation*, volume XLIX, number 3, (July 1995): 267–80.
21. *Ibid*, 274.
22. Douglas John Hall, *Professing the Faith: Christian Theology in a North American Context* (Minneapolis: Fortress Press, 1993), 53.
23. *Ibid*, 53.

24. Giles Fraser, 'The Easter of hawks, doves, victims and victimizers', in *Consuming Passion, op cit*, 16.

25. Hall, *The Cross*, 131–33.

26. This is not to suggest that there is no concern in the early church for Christ raised in glory. Yet this concern is always secondary to, and held in tension with, a theology of the cross and the suffering of God in Christ. This tension largely disappears in Christendom as a theology of glory takes centre stage.

27. Anselm of Canterbury, 'Why God became a Man (*Cur Deus Homo*)', in *Anselm of Canterbury, Volume Three*, edited and translated by Jasper Hopkins and Herbert Richardson (Toronto and New York: Edwin Mellen Press, 1976).

28. The theory of penal substitution draws on metaphors of law and the courts. Sin is a violation of covenant law, and human beings, having been judged guilty of breach of the law, are under penalty of death. The issue is satisfaction of God's justice. Jesus dies in our place, as a substitute, and satisfies the law's demand for punishment, thus freeing us from the penalty of the law.

29. J Denny Weaver, 'Jesus' Death and the Non-violent Victory of God', in *Consuming Passion, op cit*, 49–50.

Jews and Violence

Rachael Kohn[1]

There is a convention among critics of the Bible that the God of the Jews is a vengeful and violent God, who is moved to punish, indeed even smite, those who do not live up to his expectations. By contrast the figure of Jesus in the New Testament is exceptionally forgiving, and instead of punishing his enemies, he instructs his followers to love them. This comparison, regularly rehearsed by Christians and post-Christians, such as Richard Dawkins, has ingrained the contempt that Christians have for Judaism, because it goes far beyond the initial irritation with Jews as 'unbelievers'. It appears to provide a rock solid argument that Jews are morally inferior to Christians because they worship a violent God. It stands to reason that people who worship a violent God are repugnant: either they are cowards, depending on God for protection, or they are inclined to be violent themselves. This is such a tenacious view that even those who have long departed from their Christian heritage continue to cite it, particularly inhabitants of the New Age. A recent example blames the violence of the Western World for the last 3000 years on the Book of Genesis and the God of the Hebrews.[2]

There is a deep irony, of course, that any informed reader would immediately recognise, which is that for almost 2,000 years Jews have had a pacific history, with no standing armies and no wars to fight. Even more remarkable, this has been the case despite Jews being deemed 'the antichrist' by the Church throughout that entire era and bearing the burden of regular pogroms, mass expulsions (from France, England and Spain), synagogue burnings (infamously at the direction of Martin Luther and later the Nazis), confinement to ghettos and deprivation of basic freedoms. Jews learned to live with those disabilities for so many centuries, such that when the final curtain fell in Nazified Europe, there was minimal violent reaction when thousands of businesses and synagogues of Germany and Austria were ransacked or razed to the ground on 9–10 November, 1938 and almost 26,000 Jewish civilians were arrested. The subsequent rounding up of Jews into ghettoes from which they could not escape, and their shipment off to concentration camps where they were slated for extermination (unknown to most of them of course) was met with only sporadic revolts, such as the Warsaw Ghetto Uprising, and the remarkable blowing up of Crematorium IV at Auschwitz in the summer of 1944, led by the twenty-three year old Rosa Robota. Jews who managed to escape the round ups and who were allowed to be members of the fiercely nationalistic partisan movements, did partake in organised resistance, but almost six million Jews lost their lives in the collective pursuit of Hitler's dream to annihilate the Jews of Europe. In contrast, Christendom, both Roman and Byzantine, as well as the Islamic caliphates have a long history of religious wars, both amongst themselves and with each other. Christian Sovereigns and Knights as well as conquering Caliphs vied for territory across the Middle East and Europe. After the Reformation, the contest was escalated when the two main wings of the Church, the Protestants and the Catholics, struggled for supremacy in wars that would consume much of Europe, and in the brutalities of the Inquisition.

Why did the Jews refrain from open warfare? One very obvious fact is that they were a subject people wherever they lived (except for India and China, where they prospered in small communities, such as Cochin and Kai Feng respectively). But subjugation does not account for their pacific history, since it is usually the very stimulus for armed revolt. Unlike Christians and Muslims, however, for the last 2,000 years the Jewish people were not driven by a theological imperative to convert others to the fold. Nor did they embark on a conquest of peoples and territories for the greater glory of God. Their God had promised them but one land and made one covenant with them. Both had been tested over the millennia, and their land, tiny compared to the empires that surrounded it, had been dominated and at times wrested temporarily from them by a litany of conquerors, the last being the Romans. Nonetheless, for the Jewish people, trust in both the promise and the covenant was and is essential to their faith and tradition.

The final destruction of the Jerusalem Temple in 70 CE, the consequent dissolution of the priestly cult, and the failure of the last revolutionary battle by the Jewish messianic leader, Simon Bar Kochba (Kosiba) against Roman rule in the second century, left the people Israel in an existentially new situation. Nevertheless, their belief in God's promise, the original core of their tradition, remained unchanged. Expelled from their land, Jews were obliged to extend their hope of its fulfilment well into the future, where a return to Zion might take place in real time or in messianic time. In the meantime, however, their homes would be amongst strangers, and the law of the land wherein they dwelt was given authoritative endorsement by rabbis as the law while the safety of the ruling powers was prayed for at the weekly Shabbat synagogue service, a custom that is practised to this day. It was not just a strategy of survival, it reflected a profound ethic that cherished life, not death, and exhibited an abiding belief in the eventual realisation that they would be delivered once again into the Promised Land, as they proclaimed every year at Yom Kippur and Passover.

The Torah and war

This is not to say that the history of the Israelites before the Roman occupation was untypical of the ancient world, where warfare between kingdoms and tribes was commonplace. Like every other nation that claimed the land wherein others dwelt, the Biblical narrative of the Israelite possession of Canaan was given Divine sanction. Battles ensued, and the Israelites would struggle to govern themselves, at first, without a king, and then with great misgivings about the idea of kingship itself, under the royal line of David. Even the twelve tribes of Israel had their lethal battles with one another, most significantly with the tribe of Benjamin (Jdg 20:27–25), while their division of the land into the Northern and Southern kingdoms was the most obvious sign of hostilities within the fold. Yet the ancient Israelites did have a formal set of rules from the Book of Deuteronomy governing 'normal' war, as Norman Solomon has outlined.[3] Briefly put, they include recruiting only those who are courageous men of faith and do not have domestic commitments; offering peace to any city which is besieged; and if refused, only men are put to the sword, while food trees are not cut down, and some amelioration is offered to female captives. Whether these strict rules were actually followed in the Biblical period, or were a later addition to 'bolster the covenantal consciousness of Israel', as some scholars have speculated, is a moot point as some of its principles remain efficacious today.

Nonetheless, the accounts of wars and skirmishes recounted in the Bible do not in themselves reflect Jewish attitudes to violence. For one thing, the majority of modern Jews are Progressive or Reform and they read the ancient text as a light onto their past history, with moral implications to be sure, but not literally as a series of admonitions on how to behave. Indeed, even for Orthodox Jews, the Torah alone is insufficient as an ethical or legal blueprint, even though it is redolent with moral dilemmas and cautionary tales. In late antiquity, when the Bible was codified, it already required rabbinical interpretation to

extend, mitigate, generalise or individualise its meanings in accordance
with rabbinical precedent and the circumstances of the day. Different
schools of interpretation were established under the tutelage of The
Pairs, most famously represented by rabbis Hillel and Shammai. By
the second century, an even more inventive somewhat esoteric form
of interpretation (tending toward the mystical) was provided by the
convert Rabbi Akiba, who was gruesomely put to death by the Romans
because he supported the Bar Kokhba revolt against them. Simply put,
the Written Law of the Torah was inadequate without the Oral Law, as
compiled in the Talmud (codified in the fifth and sixth centuries) and
its later commentaries. What this means, in a nutshell, is that Christians
and others who read the Bible as a blueprint of Jewish thought and
practice, especially on violence, are grossly mistaken, since outside
the eighth-century sect of the Kairates and the isolated Ethiopians,
Jews everywhere did not rely on the Bible alone.

The Oral Law of the rabbis, which they developed in the houses
of study, was collated in the Talmud. Ironically, even that had its
limitations because its earliest core text, the Mishna, was codified long
after some of its content had ceased to have any immediate relevance
for the Jewish people, who no longer constituted a sovereign nation.
For example, rabbinic discussions of war, such as obligatory, optional
and preventive wars, were largely academic exercises because Jews
had been expelled from their land by the Romans and had embarked
on an exile that would last almost two millennia. However, in so far
as these same discussions revolve around the issue of self defence,
which continued to be an issue for Jews, they were instructive on the
rare occasions, for example, when small numbers of Jews organised
themselves in armed defence against the Crusaders. However, the
pursuit of expansionist wars, such as took place under King David,
were virtually ruled out in Talmudic discussion. Even if they were
physically possible, expansionist wars required authorization from
the Great Court of seventy-one justices (the Sanhedrin), as well as
approval of the oracle of the High Priest, none of which existed after
70CE.[4]

The eminent Torah scholar, Adin Steinsaltz, examined the
criminal law in the Talmud, and concluded that self defence is a basic
assumption. That is, if someone comes to kill you, it is permissible
to kill him first (Exod 21:12). Although that very principle prevails
in our contemporary secular law, Steinsaltz cautions, 'At the same
time, it is stated emphatically that violence should not be employed in
self-defence beyond the necessary and feasible minimum dictated by

circumstances. A man who kills his pursuer when he could have saved himself in some other way, may himself be charged with murder.' [5]

Other situations where it could be said that violence is used include the punishment of sinners, such as the stoning of the adulterer and the rapist. However, before the Roman destruction of Jerusalem, the system of offering sacrifices to the Temple as a means of compensating for one's guilt employed the concept of substitution and resulted in the mitigation of the sentence. Here the sacrifice is said to have substituted for self sacrifice or death of the sinner. 'The sinner deserves to die for his sins, but the Torah grants him the opportunity of offering up a sacrifice, on condition that he realizes that this symbolises sacrifice of his own self.'[6] Steinsaltz goes on to emphasise that the sacrifice alone does not atone for the sin, but must come after repentance and or restitution. Ritual sacrificial offerings, however, were no longer possible after the destruction of the Temple, and so other forms of compensation were devised, along with prayer and repentance.

Other examples of causing a violent death arise in discussions concerning the threat to an entire community. When, for example, a community was faced with extermination if it did not surrender one of its number, the rabbis counselled that the whole group should give itself up. However, if a known fugitive and criminal hid within the community, which would be threatened by mass extermination if it did not hand over the man, then it is permitted to hand him over. Even here, the sages are not always comfortable with the decision, and a story is told that when a man who killed a Roman princess and hid within the community was given up by the rabbi in charge, the rabbi was abandoned by Elijah the prophet, who chided him for acting just like one of the crowd and not as a great (pious) man.[7]

These piecemeal examples of Jewish attitudes to violence derive from the holy books, which are instructive as far as they go, but even a thorough account of them cannot provide the whole picture. Rabbinical thought, like any other form of theological writing, tends toward the ideal, whereas observations from the field of history have a more urgent realism that is evident, for example, during the period of religious strife in medieval Europe. Nachmanides, the great thirteenth–century rabbinic scholar from Catalonia, who was obliged to flee his home after he 'won' an official disputation with a Catholic opponent in Barcelona in 1263, commented on the vicissitudes of war. In particular, he was critical of the moral degradation that warfare entailed. He based his comment on Deuteronomy 23:9, 'You shall guard yourself from every evil thing'.

Scripture [warns us to be especially careful] at times when
sin is common. It is well known that when groups go to war
they eat every abominable thing, steal, do violence, are not
ashamed even to commit adultery and other detestable things,
so that even the most naturally upright of men is enveloped
in violence and anger when setting off to battle against an
enemy. Therefore scripture warns, 'You shall guard yourself
from every evil thing' for 'the Lord your God is in the midst
of your camp'.[8]

One can only assume that Nachmanides was commenting on
situations, such as the protracted war between Christians and Muslims
in Spain, where Jews would be enlisted to aid one side or another,
perhaps as suppliers since they were not generally permitted to carry
arms.[9] While some might have welcomed the opportunity to profit
from other people's war, other Jews would have looked askance at
their brethren's involvement in the violent campaigns of the Gentiles,
particularly on account of the immorality of wanton killing of innocents
and the suspension of religious observance. Generally speaking, war
was seen as a highly dubious undertaking unless commanded by God,
which in the case of the Jewish people had already taken place in the
annals of their divinely ordained history. As for the possibility that
God might instruct them to go to war, through divine revelation, the
likelihood was slim indeed, as Jews did not believe in such occurrences,
after a famous dialogue recorded in the Talmud that ruled out the 'Bat
Kol'—God's voice—in a legal dispute. For most Jews, the prayer for
deliverance back to their home in Zion from the four corners of their far
flung exile, *galut,* was a future hope that might some day come about
at the hands of the Messiah. But even here caution was uppermost, as
the messiah's identity was occasionally a cause of embarrassment and
punishment by the authorities, especially when dubious men claimed
the title.[10]

Nonetheless, the Jewish hope of return give ample opportunity to
Christians to remind Jews that their exile from Zion and homeless
wandering was divine punishment for not believing in Jesus as
their messiah. Hence, the deep discomfort of many Christians at the
Jews challenging this divinely ordained destiny by returning to their
homeland and proclaiming it a Jewish state.

Zionism and war

Before addressing the modern return of Jews to Israel, which plunges us into the currents of history and, at a conservative count, four wars and two intifadas, the religious nature of this hope must be considered. Given its centrality to Jewish sacred history and liturgical practice, it would be easy to imagine that the religious idea of a return to Zion gave rise to the violent history that has beset the modern state of Israel. That would be a trap for the uninformed. In fact, the most fervently religious Jews in Israel are the least supportive of the State and refuse military service. Indeed, when the numbers of ultra-Orthodox Jews were a mere 400, in the early days of the State, the first Prime Minister of Israel, David Ben Gurion, exempted them from compulsory military service under the Status Quo Agreement

The ultra Orthodox Jews, *Haredim*, who today make up over half a million Jews in Israel, live mostly in Jerusalem and follow an extremely avid form of Jewish observance. Their lives are meticulously circumscribed by the 613 commandments of the Torah, and the majority of their men, about seventy per cent, study Talmud and Torah as their daily 'work'. Their women, who on average have eight children, are the sole 'bread winners' which, given their maternal obligations, is extremely onerous. Therefore, almost fifty per cent of the ultra-Orthodox Jews live on government hand outs and communal charity which, even with their frugal lifestyle that usually does not include the usual amenities such as TV, is on or well below the poverty line. It is the price they willingly pay for being the most observant 'Torah True' Jews in the world.

This is a perplexing development and one that could be explained by reference to the eminent Jewish philosopher, Joseph Soloveitchik (1903–1993).[11] In his work *Halakhic Man*, Soloveitchik depicts the ultra-Orthodox Jew just described in the category of *homo religiosus*. This figure is the impractical Talmudist, deeply engaged in the holy task of studying the Talmud, serving only the Author of the Torah, and indifferent to the world around him. Such men fill the academies, the *yeshivot*, and study Torah for its own sake. They do so in order to one day ascend to heaven. Another type of man, whom Soloveitchik called 'Halakhic man', studies the Torah in order to bring heaven down to earth.

> They travel in opposite directions . . . *Homo religiosus*, dissatisfied, disappointed, and unhappy, craves to rise up from the vale of tears, from concrete reality, and aspires to climb

to the mountain of the Lord. He attempts to extricate himself
from the narrow straits of empirical existence and emerge
into the wide spaces of a pure and pristine transcendental
existence. Halakhic man, on the contrary, longs to bring down
transcendence into this valley of the shadow of death—ie,
into our world—and transform it into a land of the living.[12]

In drawing this comparison, Soloveitchik was making a case for a
Jewish life which is both religiously observant and socially realistic,
and therefore inseparable from the currents of history. Indeed, his call
to transform the world into a land of the living, while inspired by the
Biblical prophetic tradition, is given urgency by the fact that the world
of his youth had vanished into the land of the dead. Born in Poland
and educated in Germany, where he received a PhD in 1932, he was
safely in America by 1937, when most of the Jewish people in the
heart of modern Europe, including a large number of his extended
family, were expelled from their homes, rounded up and exterminated.
In drawing up his comparison of the two kinds of Jew (which can
be easily generalised to all religious traditions which have generated
world-denying and world-affirming streams), Soloveitchik echoed the
post-Shoah consciousness which is determined to live, and in whom
resounds the reminder to 'never again' allow the wholesale slaughter
of his people. Indeed, for many Jews that realisation came a generation
earlier, having endured the brutal anti-Semitic policies of Tzarist
Russia, which culminated in 1903, with the Kishinev Riots against
Jews that left forty-seven dead and ninety-seven severely wounded,
followed by more riots in 1905.

Tzarist oppression was among the first major catalysts for a
physical return to Zion, the modern Zionist movement that would be
led by the diplomatic efforts of the urbane journalist Theodore Herzl.
This multi-lingual Hungarian had already made a name for himself
in Paris covering the Dreyfus Affair (1894–1899), which revealed
the deep seated anti-Semitism in French society. Having witnessed
crowds yelling 'Death to the Jews' when Captain Alfred Dreyfus, the
French Jew, was falsely accused of sedition, Herzl wrote in his diary
of 'the emptiness and futility of trying to "combat" anti-Semitism' and
he went on to make a case for an independent Jewish state in a book by
that name.[13] Herzl tried many avenues of diplomacy but his overtures to
the British government and his convening of the first Zionist Congress
in 1897, out of which the World Zionist Organisation would raise funds
for the proposed state, were the key factors in the establishment of a

Jewish National Home in the British Mandate of Palestine. The story of the Zionist movement, with its several subgroups, representing its cultural, political, territorialist, and religious interests, is not to be entered into here, but it is crucial to realise in this discussion of Jewish attitudes to violence that the return to Zion was never envisaged or planned as a military takeover. It was above all a diplomatic, civilized and idealistic undertaking, which in the full bloom of nascent Western democracy was seen as its cherished product.

The Zionists' primary method of securing land was through its purchase from largely absentee Turkish landlords, a policy that was wholly legitimate but had unfortunate consequences for some of the local Arab farmers who had lived and toiled these tracts for generations. The Zionist aim was always to live with the Arab population, not to expel them (and the 160,000 who did not flee after Israel was declared a state, were given Israeli citizenship). However, when the Turkish government became hostile to the settlement of Jews (the Yishuv) in Palestine and switched its allegiance during World War I from a friend of the British to an ally of Germany, the once idealistic notion of living alongside the Arab population began to unravel. This was particularly painful for Turkish Sephardi Jews who had lived in cities like Hebron for generations, where in 1929, anti-Jewish riots broke out and Arabs killed more than sixty Jewish neighbours and children. A deal was struck between Britain and several Arab nations, which gave them independence—in exchange for which, Palestine was cordoned off and left under British control.

It was the Russian-born Jewish chemist, Chaim Weizmann, who most influenced public figures in England in favour of the idea of a Jewish homeland in Palestine. Educated in Switzerland and Germany, Weizmann obtained a readership at the University of Manchester, and went on to help the British war effort through his invention of synthesised acetone. Always an ardent Zionist, he soon convinced others, including his dear friends, Charles P Scott, editor of the *Manchester Guardian* and Henry Wickham Steed, editor of the *London Times*. He also gained the support of Winston Churchill, David Lloyd George and Arthur James Balfour. The central plank in this concord of sympathies was that Weizmann linked the future of Zionism with the triumph of the Western democracies.[14] It precisely mirrored the ethos in which Theodore Herzl, a thoroughly modern idealist, had pursued the Zionist dream. It would be a long and difficult process of diplomacy, however, because of the intervening Second World War and the Holocaust, before the Jewish National Home became a reality in Palestine.

It would be even longer before the United Nations General Assembly Resolution 181 called for the partition of the British-ruled Palestine Mandate into a Jewish state and an Arab state, on 29 November, 1947. Accepted by the Jews and rejected by the Arab League at a public meeting on 17 December (in which they declared they would use all means to nullify it, including armed intervention), anti-Jewish violence broke out almost immediately. Six months later on 14 May, 1948, Israel was founded as a democratic state with a socialist ethos. The next day, on 15 May, the armies of five neighbouring Arab states, Egypt, Lebanon, Syria, Iraq and Transjordan, invaded the State of Israel. Israel did not lose the war and the Palestinian problem was born.

Israel's history since then has been a long and protracted effort to deal with a local problem that has had international stake holders, most particularly the twenty-two Arab states surrounding Israel, which have insisted on keeping the Palestinians in refugee camps and in economically depressed conditions as a bargaining tool to force the dismantling of the Jewish State. Throughout Yasser Arafat's regime as head of the Palestine Liberation Organisation, he displayed the map of Palestine including *all* of Israel, which is why he rejected the two state solution brokered by President Clinton in 2000, with Ehud Barak offering him an independent state in all of Gaza and 90 per cent of the West Bank. Four years of a suicide bombing campaign followed, and after Israel's withdrawal from Gaza in 2005, Hamas launched a brutal takeover campaign, while the Iranian-backed Hezbollah launched an attack on Israel from Lebanon. Today Hamas, Hezbollah and Islamic Jihad (assisted by Iran, the former Iraq, and Syria) maintain a position of total rejection of the state of Israel as a concept and a reality, leaving President Abbas of the Palestinian Authority courting the financial and ideological support of the West. The Europeans have been only too happy to give it, while America currently leads all other Western nations in providing billions of dollars in aid and 'roadmaps to peace'.

Four conventional wars were initiated against Israel (1948, 1956, 1967, 1973) and two guerrilla wars or intifadas (1987–1993, 2000 onwards), plus a litany of battles, all of which have maintained the pressure on a state one seventh the size of Tasmania. A situation of constant siege has increasingly pushed the once profoundly Leftist nation of Israel into a more defensive, inevitably Right wing, position.

But these labels trivialise a central fact, which is that Israel, a nation with mandatory national service, where all babies born are issued a gas mask by the state, has been forced to use its defence forces throughout its entire history, not for expansionist wars (it has returned most of the land it won in the 1967 War) but for the right to protect its citizens and ensure its survival. It is an aim that looks increasingly tenuous today, not only because the Arab nations that surround it as well as those further afield want it to disappear, but also more significantly, because the Christian and post-Christian West insists that Jewish claims to the land, including Jerusalem, are negotiable 'for the sake of peace'. That no peace has resulted from decades of negotiations (as one leaflet puts it, 'Oslow = 1,300 Israelis murdered, 10 000 injured'), makes this once noble demand hollow indeed. And yet, with all this embattled history, Israelis still hope that negotiations will deliver a workable two state solution, which is safe for its citizens. Perhaps it is the legendary Talmudic tradition that trained 100 generations of Jews to find rational solutions to the thorniest of legal and ethical problems, which has given them an almost impossibly optimistic outlook when faced with the manifold problems of dealing with Palestinian factionalism and pan-Arab rejectionism. Rather than descend into total chaos or total war, Israel pursues negotiations, targeted missile attacks, and a 'normal society' all as part of its everyday life. Even its most hawkish former leader, the ailing (comatose) Ariel Sharon, relinquished Gaza in 2005 and dismantled its settlements in the hope that it would bring peace.

The situation of ceaseless war is enormously draining for both Israeli society and Jews around the world who look to their tiny land as a living expression of their faith; but after the Holocaust, they have little alternative but to remain strong. Jews cannot lie down and die again, despite the unceasing torrent of Jew hatred that is generated in the Arab world and broadcast throughout its media and on the internet. Nonetheless, a chorus of Christian and post-Christian nations and organisations, who are both spiritually and physically far away from the situation, and largely ignorant of Jewish history, continue to characterise Jews as intransigent, aggressive, and violent. No more apt example of this occurred in December 2007, when the National Council of Churches of Australia visited Israel/Palestine to report on the plight of Christians there. Despite an obvious desire to present a 'balanced' report on their impressions, the NCCA issued a statement that identified a key cause of Palestinian hardship as Israel's security measures, such as checkpoints and segregated roads, but did not acknowledge that these have been necessary due to the campaign of Palestinian suicide bombings in Israel which escalated in late September 2000 and claimed more than 900 people up to 2003. The NCCA media release did not mention a single instance of the violent demonstrations recently carried out by Hamas and Islamic Jihad, nor did it cite the recent Islamist killings of Christians in the West Bank and Gaza and the expropriation of their land. The official statement of the NCCA represents a certain Christian attitude to Israel, which on the one hand refuses to accord it a normal status by referring to it only as 'The Holy Land'; and on the other hand, is bent on making Israel the belligerent party whose actions 'stand in the way of a just peace'. One cannot help concluding that Christians actually resent Jews who have returned to their land and are happy to provide apologias for Palestinians who are at war with them. It is a short step from the traditional accusation that Jews are Christ killers to the more political observation that Jews are Palestinian killers. Given the unrelenting pressure on Israel

Endnotes

1. A number of the ideas in this chapter are canvassed in Rachael Kohn's Oration for The Council of Christians and Jews in Victoria, delivered on 16 October, 2007 and published as *Learning from History: Pre-War Germany and Now* (Kew, Vic: CCJ, 2007).
2. Julie Hunter, *The Myths That Make Us* (Christchurch, NZ: Hazard, 2006). Appropriately enough, the book is written by an advertising copy writer, who writes myths for a living.
3. Norman Solomon, 'Judaism and the Ethics of War', *International Review of the Red Cross* 87 (2005): 296.
4. Solomon, 'Ethics of War' 298, citing Mishna Sanhedrin 1:5.
5. Adin Steinsaltz, *The Essential Talmud* (New York: Basic Books, 1976) 173.
6. Steinsaltz, *Essential Talmud* 176.
7. Steinsaltz, *Essential Talmud* 203.
8. Cited in Solomon, 'Ethics of War' 302.
9. The exception being Shmuel Ha Nagid (993–1055), the vizier under the Granadian caliphs Habbus and Badis, who was military commander of the Muslim armies. He was also a poet who likened war to 'a beautiful maid at first, and in the end a despised hag who brings tears and sadness to whomever she meets'.
10. Several false messiahs arose, such as Messiah ben Joseph, in the second century BCE, and later figures like Simon Bar Kokhba in the second century CE, Solomon Molko in Italy and Sabbatai Zevi in Salonica; and it goes without saying that for most Jews in Roman Palestine, the messianic claim of Jesus was also a false hope.
11. Joseph B Soloveitchik, *Halakhic Man*, translated by L Kaplan (Philadelphia: Jewish Publication Society of America, 1983), 40.
12. Soloveitchik, *Halakhic Man* 40.
13. Theodore Herzl, *The Jewish State: An Attempt at a Modern Solution to the Jewish Question* (New York: Dover, 1989; German original 1896). The work was a manifesto that made a case for the 'question to be discussed and settled by the civilized nations of the world in council'. See also the *Yale Companion to Jewish Writing and Thought in German Culture 1096–1996*, edited by Sander Gilman and Jack Zipes (New Haven: Yale University Press) 225.
14. Howard Morley Sachar, *The Course of Modern Jewish History* (New York: Delta, 1958) 373.
15. Abd Al Bari Atwan, Editor in Chief of *Al Quds Al Arabi*, the international Arabic newspaper based in London, author of *The Secret History of Al Qaeda* (London: Abacus, 2007), and recent visitor to Australia as a keynote speaker at the Brisbane Writers Festival, was interviewed on Lebanese TV (ANB TV) on 27 June 2007, about the consequences of Iran becoming a nuclear capable nation. I interviewed him for ABC

Radio National's 'The Spirit of Things', but had not seen this interview in which Bari Atwan's prediction culminated in his hope, that 'if the Iranians strike Israel, by Allah, I will go to Trafalgar Square and dance in delight if the Iranian missiles strike Israel'. This interview was published at www.memritv.org.80/clip/en/1506.htm.

Religion and Violence:
A Macrohistorical Perspective

Garry W Trompf

Macrohistory, I should first explain, is looking at the past with a 'single imaginative experience', as Arnold Toynbee put it, or as it was earlier expressed, surveying the 'spectacle' of history 'in the mind's eye' (à la Bishop Bossuet and the philosopher David Hume).[1] Doing macrohistory is a very venturesome, indeed risky business, and here I do not undertake it lightly. The trouble is, the subject of the relationship between religion and violence inevitably raises extremely ancient and therefore prehistoric issues. In terms of current debates between Creationism and Evolutionism, it will be easy to tread on conservative toes, because I will be asking at the onset whether humans inherit their propensity for violence from an animal past.

To explain any nexus between 'religion and violence', I wonder whether we should be reading the works of ethologists, such as Konrad Lorenz's study of comparable *Aggression* in beasts and humans (1966), or Robert Ardrey's *The Territorial Imperative* (1967) on our shared 'defensiveness of property and boundaries' with animals.[2] Of course the trouble with that might be, for conservatives from those three great monotheistic traditions that inherit the six-day Creation story (Gen 1; Qur'an 57, cf Matt 19:5), the received distinction between us and the brutes gets blurred. And besides, a fear may well up about 'the great abyss of time' that constitutes so-called prehistory, going back to 'hominids' and 'missing links' hundreds of thousands of years before the conventional chronological placement of Adam and Eve.[3] I can only remind my readers that our sense of kinship with the animals goes back to the Bible itself—we are all connected creatures (Gen 2:18; 7 – 9; Num 22:31; Jas 1:18)—and that, long before modern evolutionary theory, spiritual thinkers contemplated 'the great chain of being' linking us to the earth itself. Why, mediaevals even conceived of a 'Scythian lamb', the body of an animal connected to a treelike stem growing from the soil, marking a bridge between vegetal and animal life; and consider the mystical insight of the Greek Orthodox Gregory Palamas (*ca* 1296 – 1359) that:

> the human is the concentration into one whole of
> all that is, the recapitulation of all things created by
> God, therefore being produced last of all.[4]

Besides, 'evolution' was a term first coined by a very spiritually sensitive Genevan biologist by the name of Charles Bonnet, who visualised all nature, in 'a continual progress' towards God, passing through various catastrophes towards a complexity and perfecting called *'évolution'*.[5]

However much such reflection may soften the blow, mind you, the most liberal of monotheists will still have to ask whether a stress on our animal past, acknowledging seriously its intrinsic violence (or 'the tooth and claw' aspects of biological evolution) takes our responsibility for violence 'off the hook'. In consequence, violence will then tend to be put down to instinctual behaviour, or to chemical drives (whether seen as 'natural' or as tragic expressions of 'neuronal disorder') that come into play when threat, frustration and hostility present themselves to us, leaving the implication open that we are not fully to blame for violence, and that it is an inevitable part of biospheric events. This is precisely why certain psychologists have reacted against theories of bio-ethological bases for aggression, contending instead that it is primarily *learned* in society.[6] Why, how interesting it is to go back further and find Alfred Wallace, as much the founder of modern evolutionary theory as Darwin, hastening to insist that, although we inherit animal bodies through processes of natural selection, this inheritance cannot apply to our intellectual or aesthetic faculties, let alone moral conscience (which are God-given).[7] Somehow the responsibility for our actions had to be salvaged, the very thing German thinkers at the time believed made us *free* rather than left stuck in nature.[8] And, because of this whole predicament, it is typical of biologically-oriented thinkers to avoid looking like moral nihilists; so that we as the 'dominant mammal' *à la* Macfarlane Burnet still have to face up to guilt, and Richard Dawkin's so-called 'selfish gene' conveniently finds itself in an 'altruistic body'.[9] No wonder a sensitive soul, imbedded in traditional religion, will shudder at a lack of clarity in evolutionary theory as to when we are dealing with us as animals and when (indeed whether!) we are to be considered as humans. That is integrally related to trying to pinpoint the time we sinned ('sinning', after all, making us more distinguishable from the animals than 'thinking' or 'reasoning'), and became estranged from the One from whom we need salvation.[10] How much easier for conservatives to accept the story of Adam and Eve at face value!

I cannot pretend to resolve all these problems being raised here, whether in this chapter or at any other time. Let me just assert that, as a trained prehistorian and archaeologist, the stratigraphic and artistic record puts human violence (to animals more commonly, but to humans as well) very far into the past. If Cain's killing of Abel comes early in the Bible (Gen 4:8), killing in prehistory is positively palaeolithic. That is to say, evidence of deliberately damaging skulls probably goes back as far as 200,000 BP (Choukoutien, China), more definitely to 55,000+ BP (Monte Circeo, Italy). Weapons, whether of attack or defence, have been excavated across all phases of the 'Stone Age', with depictions of fighting and warrior aggression located in Upper (or more recent) Palaeolithic contexts (from 20,000 BP onwards). Large scale acts of violence towards animals—as in the earliest signs of mass sacrifice (of reindeer with stone weights around their neck (near Hamburg, Germany)—come from this same era.[11] Debates about all these finds will go on, of course, and other ones with them. A clash lingers between the views of a Louis and Richard Leakey that the human being remained a 'peaceable hunter gatherer until the invention of agriculture some 10,000 years ago', and a Robert Ardrey who finds evidence for our carnivore habits and plant avoidance dating back as far as 40,000 BP.[12] Biologists will want to know if the presence of testosterone makes men more aggressive than women; while some feminists may be hoping for signs of prehistoric Amazonian matches to male prowess.[13] Conservatives might want to ask if we can tell whether situations differed before and after the Flood (Gen 5:1, 10:9 cf 1 En 8:1; 9:1; Qur'an 51:46; 71), and, interestingly, some of the finest prehistoric rock paintings of warrior life come from near Mount Ararat.[14] For our present purposes, though, the key issue is whether violence within our species (as well as against other life forms) is an extension of our animal past (albeit an unfortunate urge that crops up from time to time and which we have to manage) or else an internal propensity for which we have to take full responsibility. It is extraordinary how much energy is now being currently exerted, in social and highly theoretical analyses of violence, to uncover and excoriate the perpetrators of violence in all its dimensions, as if it now almost goes without saying that we are completely culpable for violent deeds whenever and wherever they occur.[15] Indeed, young, mainly secular intellectuals seem to have a voracious appetite to blame all violators—Foucauldians against remnants of 'over-discipline and punishment' in our institutions; world systems theorists and new Marxists against the hegemony of both metropoles and the rich over marginal groups and subalterns; feminists against males mistreating the female body; animal rights activists against speciesists.[16] And needless to say, such eyes are watching for 'religious perpetrations'.

Part of the agenda of my own research, especially in a late section of *In Search of Origins* (but also in the introduction to the work called *Payback*), is to pose awkward questions about the long distant beginnings of revenge action or blood feuding, along with motivations for it. After all, tribal tit-for-tat war and raiding is virtually endemic in small-scale traditional societies, and one naturally asks, as human groups first expanded across the face of the globe and yet still came into contact with each other, about the dynamics of the earliest tensions and clashes.[17] Why, this was a matter that pressed upon the brain of a 'titular founder' of post-modernism, Friedrich Nietzsche, who decided that thought itself, let alone religion, derived from the calculations earliest peoples had to make when engaged in both 'market exchanges' and recurrent fighting—winning or losing (and losing warriors) in any given conflict.[18] The primal mentality of 'payback', by implication, was the basis of rationalising action, of being able to say *why* one required one way or the other, even *justifying* one's course. It was also Nietzsche's thesis that the ancient principle of punitive revenge (*Rache*) came to be co-opted by the state, providing a reason why it had to be resisted (at the least psychologically)[19]—but that is a contemporary issue we will have to return to later. Here it suffices to say that *reasons* given for paying enemies back negatively and conceding to kin and current allies are found everywhere in the world of tribes and small-scale societies, both contemporary and historical, with the prior shedding of blood between groups constituting the almost ubiquitous cause for violence.[20] Providing *rationale*, normally consensual and not strictly personal, figures as a datum of *religion* because the capacity to explain one's actions belongs within a whole life-way, and 'reason-giving' is integral to collective survival. So the big question is whether this is the proper starting point for analysing the relation between religion and violence.

Nietzsche's approach is thoroughly Germanic in stressing the human quest for *Freiheit*; only in his case the rules and repressions of 'civilised' society lend themselves to his defence of warriorhood as an impulsion towards freedom, as a virtue or 'intrinsic moral strength' (and thus making possible the justification of a military society).[21] But his was in fact a reinvocation of an archaic extolling of the warrior's role, of a man imbued with 'spirit' (of a courage that breathed the air of the gods and ancestors themselves), not mere 'spiritedness'. This is a preconceived social understanding too common for us to neglect. It is enough to see *prima facie* that men need to be 'stirred' to kill, but it will then not come as much of a surprise that they will need and call upon higher spirit powers to carry out their deeds. Actually the principle of fighting simply to stay alive has been rare as a known justification for fighting, so much more pronounced has been the *honour* of dying in battle before the divine (and how hard it is to find, in modern times, legitimation for a skirmish through that 'desert of abstraction', the 'survival of the fittest'!).[22] In general, passing off violence as inherited biological mechanism will never be enough when signs of a distinctively human expressiveness — a shared acceptance of the group need for *élan vital* — show up very early indeed in art and excavation.[23]

The prehistory of religion and the archaeology of war and violence, then, probably amount to the same pursuit, even if we must admit that we will be forever testing a 'persuasive-looking hypothesis', fully aware that all the pieces of the jigsaw puzzle will never be recovered from silent objects, and that it is hazardous to extrapolate from contemporary anthropological materials back to the dark recesses of palaeolithic times.[24] We will have to admit in the end, too, that we will never really know how or when human consciousness (at least as relevant to our discussion) actually began, and whether it was a 'big bang' or an incredibly slow unfolding.[25] We only have footprints into the great distance. And this is where fostering a macrohistorical perspective becomes a highly useful, if not an imperative exercise. As a guide to history as a whole, serious note has to be taken of the way larger unities — early regional clusters of settlements, 'city-states', and at last empires — took over, absorbed and grew up on the back of countless small-scale cultures. Today we have around 7,000 such cultures somehow intact, all of them left vulnerable to varying degrees by expansionism, colonialism and imperialising energies. One's historical imagination requires but a nudge to appreciate that something like these small fry lay behind, or are prey to, all the emergent and documented 'great configurations' of the past, from Danubian neolithic 'coalitions'(?) of the ninth-century BCE, through Mesopotamia's Uruk and all that followed it in and on both sides of the Middle East, including even various efflorescences of empire in the Americas on the far side of the globe. Every one of the great social coagulations we call empire — from Akkad to the United States of America—spelt upheaval for discrete traditional societies, whose distinct languages and religions were typically forced to buckle under the weight of new overlordship. The farther we probe the past, perhaps, the more difficult it is to detect all the 'people without history', were it not for occasional authors—the great Herodotus and his '[ethnological] enquiries' (= *historiai*), for one—providing clues about the processes of spread, conflict, conquest and absorption.[26]

Now, far be it from me liking to squash the human past into an excessively broad sketch, one cannot be hanged for concluding that takeover by takeover in history required violence, usually actual, and only occasionally the mere threat of it. As a rule of thumb, moreover, it is not inappropriate to infer that notions of payback and the backing of expansive warrior exploits by socially persuasive reasons were drawn from the consensual tribalist principles I began sketching earlier. That inference, intriguingly, has given rise to one of the most influential political dicta of modern times, by the British political theorist Lord's Bryce, that, although with the coming of full-scale political society:

> every individual man is now under law and not in
> a State of Nature [as acephalous, tribal societies
> supposedly were], every political community,
> whatever its form, be it republican or monarchical, is in
> a State of Nature towards every other community.[27]

Empires not only absorb smaller social entities, they compete with, and even conquer larger groupings of enemies, even other empires. Let us face it, the history of the changing political face of the world, is precisely to do with the changing fortunes of military conflict— from Sargon's to George Bush Jr's Iraq, or from the first to the latest imperialisms, if you wish to put it in a nutshell. And a favoured legitimation of expansion is to mete out punishment to outside or border groups who are 'troublesome' or live under 'an unworthy way of life'—an adapted version of (apparently age-old) 'indigenous xenophobia'.[28]

Wait. Am I then arguing that there is something essentially in common with both tribal and imperial religions, as if one is a self-glorified extension of the others? Precisely. In fact, in one brash moment of theory I posed the possibility of disclosing the 'basic', the 'fundamental', the 'perennial' religion, and suggested for it two congenital characteristics—the twin celebration of fecundity and victory.[29] Why, nowhere is the configuration more imposing than in the house of *religio* itself, ancient Rome and the Roman empire, where the extolling of ('national') *prosperitas* and *victoria*, still so important for our own times, was vociferated.[30] So, it helps and is actually clarifying to my case, that the original users of our word 'religion' were energised by the same fundamental concerns dominant in documented traditional belief-systems — 'small-scale religions' — the world over. On the one hand they shared the desire for plentiful fruits from the ground (or harvests), healthy animals, virile males and pregnant women; on the other, they sought physical security, and better, hunter and warrior prowess. They looked to the spirit worlds to ensure these things above all else; and their sacrifices fit the logic of their orientation — they either needed special succour or the instruments to ward off inimical spiritual influences, or both. One wants to reciprocate with the gods and not to turn them into enemies by neglect or bad action, just as one exchanges and concedes to friends, knowing that relations are fragile and the enemy's frontier is always over the horizon.

Now, please do not take me as indulging in some kind of old-fashioned universalization, as if the 'savages', 'barbarians' and bearers of 'civilisation' all share essentially the same divinely inspired religious vision,[31] or in the New Age vogue that all religions are many paths to the same end. Actually, what I find as a specialist in comparative religion is an extraordinary array and complexity of *différence*, and when it comes to contemplating the tapestry of thousands of so-called 'primal religiosities', what variegation! Trying to find two ritual procedures precisely the same between two cultures is like trying to find two faces alike in a football crowd! And by 'recognising' in imperial religions an extension of the smaller traditional ones, I am far from saying religion is intrinsically imperialist. How empires arise remains a still partly mysterious matter of socially accepted power and organization (typically sacralised in the ancient world), but almost all in the whole host of indigenous peoples rarely ever managed such a thing. Some, if they escaped the bindings of territory, became wide-spreading marauders, but even the Scythians, whose border fighters might well fit into this category, protested how unjust it was that Alexander tried to imprison them within his imperial grasp.[32] That is only to underscore variations in size, territorial reach, relative opportunity and vulnerability in traditional societies.

The point of my argument is, rather, that the *structures* of a basic religion are discernible in spite of formal variances; its general underlying purposes can be intuited while the particular objects of worship are manifold.[33] This is why in the course of last century's developing theory of comparative religion or *Religionswissenschaft*, scholars came to write of 'natural religion', not in the old (rather Scholastic) meaning of a God-given sense of the divine shared by all humanity (thus Vatican 1, *De fide cath*, ii:2), but of a phenomenologically grounded insight: that peoples have been moved by inherited erradicable propensities to 'find their places in the sun' through 'working and securing' their territories. Their life-way, their customary way of binding effective economics and bravery, their culture, their 'organic' tradition, is the same thing as their 'religion'. This essentially remained true, even if one has to spot possible qualifications, for archaic empires—Middle Eastern (Akkadian, old Babylonian, Egyptian, Hittite, Assyrian, etc), Indian, Chinese, Graeco-Roman (Athenian, Macedonian, etc), Meso- and South American, and the Tongan one in the Pacific—that arose out of such bases. They were about 'success', in terms of wealth and military grandeur. In their expansions, force was an unquestioned embodiment of their heroic energy. There were principles of honour to uphold, perhaps, as, in the course countless engagements through time, each culture developed its rules of war, but who could imagine, or have the prick of conscience (at least among male warriors!) that 'great things' were not being decided on the field of battle? War was as natural as Enkidu's hunt, as Gilgamesh holding a lion by the throat. And why not honour Ishtar, goddess of the city and of love with the imperial capital's main gateway, as Nebuchadnezzar thought fit for Babylon? All very problematic, we can already see, but the fundamental inheritance of human history nonetheless.[34]

Thus it was that, during the last two centuries, such scholars as Hegel, Max Müller, Tiele, Siebeck, Kuenen, Bousset, Söderblom, and latercomers George Foot Moore and Robert Bellah, came to draw the distinction between these 'natural religions' (sometimes including 'national' and imperial ones) and those 'great universalising religious traditions' that dominate in textbooks of Religious Studies.[35] We find the somewhat obscure Hermann Siebeck, in fact, cleverly distinguishing '*salvation* religions' from the other ones,[36] because in emergent *Erlösungsreligionen* the 'assumptive worlds' of long-inured hard-edged practice—the traditions of 'warriorhood religion', as I am tempted to call them—start to be undermined.

Salvation religions raise issues that are not (or barely) faced by the hundreds of religions that pre-existed them, the ones earlier analysts called natural, but which I prefer dubbing basic, fundamental and perennial. Of course there are highly significant things raised by salvation religions that are not central to our purposes here, such as questions about the state of one's mortal or immortal soul. It is a typical feature of small-scale traditional religions that at death everybody goes to the same (usually happy) 'hunting ground'. In all my researches into Melanesian belief patterns, for example, into one quarter of the known discrete religions on earth, I could count the number of peoples who believed in some kind of 'heaven/hell' division in the afterlife on my hands.[37] But this projected dichotomy between the after-state of the blessed and the lost is a characteristic aspect of 'salvific' teachings, running from Zarathushtra (or Zoroaster) through Upanishadic and Orphic currents on to Buddhism, Jainism, various ancient Chinese systems, later Judaism, Christianity and Islam.[38] What is posited as 'salvation' in these emergent movements of belief, admittedly, is not uniform, and the matter of distinguishing their claims is an important business of Comparative Religion—whether the means of expurgating taints is stressed most, for example, or a new 'knowledge' extolled as a way out of the world's mire. In another context, I maintained that the teaching of salvation from sin by faith in a mediator is singular to Christianity, though the latecomer to the big traditions, Sikhism (or *Gurmat*), approximates to it.[39]

Whatever the fine distinctions, the orienting of worship and ethical life with post-mortem conditions in mind was to raise new issues that were not raised in 'natural religions'. You might say new notions on such matters were quite 'unnatural' to traditions that normally just assumed there was continued life for everyone after death. In most cases the after-world was more or less just the same as before for everybody (except for people who were unlucky enough to be killed suddenly and became ghosts, or did not follow the right spirit track to exit this life, or were given a bad send-off at their funeral, etc); in a minority of cases it was happier or sadly worse—with a Sheol or Hades. More to the point, however, founder figures of these so-called salvation religions critiqued the prior preoccupations with material wellbeing and victory over enemies as secondary, even unworthy of the spiritual life.

To varying degrees these prime-movers reject grand-scale animal sacrifices and each has his own way of controlling or opposing violence. Zarathushtra (c 2,000 BCE)[40] turned his back on patterns of bloody conflict between (large) tribes in the northeast Persian region, and sought to substitute Old Iranian animal sacrifices by a spiritual one of deeds and worship (for example *Gathas* 34:1; 48:7). Following a lead from Indian ascetic beliefs (for example *Brihad Aran Upan,* I, ii, 5–7; Vi, ii, 15; *Chandog Upan* VIII, xv, 1), the Buddha and the

Mahavir (sixth century BCE) are renowned for the messages of non-violence, and opposed the grand animal sacrifices prescribed in the Vedas (for example *Vin pacitt*, rules 61–62; Amitagati, *Sravak*, 6:34, 39). Further to the east (in the same century) 'Lao-tse' knows 'the Way does not rule when war horses breed in the park', and shows disdain of compassionless ritual and etiquette (*Dao de Jing* 38, 46, cf *Sun Tzu*), and Confucian teaching put 'family first' to curb the disintegration in China brought by 'warring states' (for example *Liyun Liki*, 9). And important long-term threads of Hebrew Biblical thought lamented excessive war and bloodshed, and animal offerings given at the expense of a contrite heart (for example, Is 2:4; 1 Chron 22:8; Ps 5:6; Eccles 3:8; Amos 5:22–24; Hos 6:6). When we come to Jesus and his followers, of course, war is totally subverted, no more indelibly than in the crucifixion (cf also Matt 26:52); and Christ's death, taken as rendering animal sacrifices unnecessary (Heb 9:12–13), was commemorated in a bloodless ritual replacement for them (1 Cor 11:24). Muhammad also confronted a complex mix of Arab tribal feuding and the great arraying of animal carcasses—as in the great feast (*'Atâïr*) before the idol Ocaisir. Around 625 he created instead a 'super-tribe' (the *Ummah*) that proscribed brother Muslims from killing each other (for example Qur'an 4.93), and apparently mixed sacrifices on the last stages of pilgrimage with the prohibition (at least for women) against harming any living thing (while at Zaribah).[41]

In the midst of all these calls for readjustment came some of the most powerful ideas on earth—of Zarathushtra's 'joyful acceptance' (*vohu*), the Hebrews' care (*hesed*), the Buddha's compassion (*metta*), the 'unconquerable goodwill' of the Christian *agapê*, of Allah the Merciful (*al-rahmin*). As I have put it elsewhere,[42] once the idea of love is presented as an overarching principle—pointing to peace, justice, mercy, truth—the world has changed forever. Love becomes the 'last judgement'; love thought through to its furthest implications becomes the means by which all actions can be assessed at depth, and all that is *un*loving, or compromised, or self-serving, can be exposed. (I admit right away, it is the criterion to which I would have to appeal in this very analysis of religion!)

The influence of such re-visioning has, of course, been immense, changing many, many cultures. When you examine some religious maps of today's world, you might wonder where all the 'old traditional' religions have gone—all those 'countryside religions' on the outskirts of empires and beyond we could still call *pagani*. The monotheisms alone (and here I include Zoroastrianism and Sikhism) seem to have seriously affected the belief patterns of over two-thirds of humanity. As we carry our story along, we may well ask (again) whether unnecessary problems have been brought to bear by new salvific messages on myriad archaic forms that were indeed more 'natural' for being closer to their particular environments, that seemed to grow up like plants— osmotically, organically, chthonically, however we put it—and were uncluttered by the really difficult questions of human existence. Were they indeed natural in the same way we were considering earlier, that is, evolutions for survival that inevitably entailed outbursts of violent activity, sometimes even orgiastic, intoxicant-induced activity, even 'sacred prostitution', in the name of collective generativeness,[43] for which no one could be blamed and no individual take sensitive responsibility? and about which, one might add, no one should feel a sense of shame? Is this the basic, the pristine set of religions that, in developing naturally, should never have been tampered with by the ever-growing, missionising 'faiths'? A host of belief-systems that did not have to contend with guilt, let us say, until representatives of some larger concern came to foist a sense of 'fallenness' on them? Traditions that could do without the conscience of a 'wider love' if they wanted to retain their old, blatant strength—their 'warrior virtue' (as Nietzsche perceived it)?

How many more difficult questions are we expected to ask! But I suspect, appealing to a likely consensus, most of us want to assert that there is enough conscious life and deliberation about all documented religions for us to assert that their custodians and supporters have 'taken responsibility' for them, otherwise we are left with myriad dreamers who would not know what it meant to defend and uphold a way of life.[44] Such artifacts of belief are not just footprints of some high-level analogue to naturo-sexual selection. As the forthright Weston la Barre would add, in talking of 'the human animal's' troubling propensity for religion, we do not talk about it as mere weeds or gangrene of thought, but as a type of 'psychosis' we will somehow have to learn to outlive as a species, because, unlike primates, we possess an uncontrollable 'power to symbolize'.[45] We can take La Barre as having exaggerated to make our point. There is a serious psychological investment in religion such that it expresses an identity for which humans have offered their workaday bodies, and if necessary their actual lives in violent death.[46] History is writ large with peoples' earnestness to keep up their relationship with the divine or the spirits; it was a fearful thing to do otherwise—flouting retribution—and every known change of religions has involved tensions over the issue of abandonment.

Perhaps it might look as if we discuss a body of human beings' 'natural beliefs', in David Hume's sense, because each of us is brought up in a whole life-way—in the grammar of a language and by parental socialization—that will slant our mentality one way or another without our questioning it.[47] But religion is ubiquitously entered into by initiation (often ordeals), monitored by custodians, and, however touched by the unconscious of its rituals[48] and myths may be, its rules have to be taught to youth. Religion and culture are traditionally indistinguishable, and, expressing the 'lifeworld-systemic nature of society', the claims they place on people are supervised and they can be used to wield individual power.[49] Humanity, I will now aver, ought to bear responsibility for religion, even if it is mysterious in origin and anomalous in outcome—the product, we might say in Biblical language, of 'naturo-psychological Man' (*psuchikos anthropos*), 'feeling after' but not yet arriving at spiritual depths (1 Cor 2:14; Acts 17:27).

For 'basic religion', I am maintaining, looms as intrinsically problematic. That is, to summarise my central theme, religion in its basic, fundamental, perennial guises is deeply implicated in violence. Arrant pacifist as I am, I should admit openly that religion deeply troubles me, if I remain nonetheless fascinated by its pull. Imbedded in it are elements very close to the heart of being human, more particularly the calculations of retributive thought, or the mind-sets of payback with their seemingly unfathomable beginnings. Its basic morality is one of *Helping Friends and Harming Enemies*, as the title of Mary Blundell's book on classical Greek religion aptly puts it.[50] Reciprocity and exchange activity for securing socio-economic well-being in it is usually matched by dealings with the gods. *Do ut des* ('I give in order that I be given to') and so sacrifice—actions of concession that expect favours in return—remains endemic in it. That is a datum underscored by the great French essayist René Girard, and he is also only too willing to see violence and the sacred enmeshed, because he considers all animal sacrifices derive from an original human one.[51] Be his special (and contestable[52]) view as it may, sacrificial rites in one form or another appear from one side of the globe to the other—from Achan bull-slaying to Fuyughe dog-killing—enticing James George Frazer into his famous definition of religion as the 'propitiation and conciliation of powers'—or the positive (if sometimes wary) operations of payback.[53]

Then, of course, there is the expectation of warriorhood. You might say it reached a veritable apex in the Roman *cursus honorum*, when every citizen above the poorest proletarian was expected to serve time in the most successful 'military machine' of all Antiquity. No fighting, no magisterial office. Why, not even the finest professional lawyer could escape the requirement; for do we not find Pompey writing to Cicero as a 'General' (*Epist* 20 Feb. [49 BCE])? Lying before and after such a phenomenon in the history of religions are countless initiatory ordeals youths had to face if they wanted to achieve manhood, including the taking of victims. The skull dangling against a young tattooed Marquesan brave's thighs was a veritable passport to high social acceptance.[54] The ethos of heroism goes *pari passu* with the archaic demand to win one's 'right of recognition'. One of my intellectual inspirers, Giambattista Vico, titular founder of Social Science (in the early eighteenth century), waxed eloquent about the Age of Heroes, through which every society must pass and which can forever hang around the 'mental dictionary' of human consciousness at large. This is a framing of existence wherein virility rules, dying is for honour, leadership (accompanied by legal commands) is strong, if brash and peremptory, and mighty daring deeds bring forth epic poetry.[55] Women may be saved, yet men may die in the doing; peace achieved but at the cost of lives; men may die in battle by the hundreds, but under the illusion they will be remembered forever.

An art to be cultivated in the study of religions is to work out how each of the larger (or 'great') religious traditions has related to such a background. I will have to warn that the story is far from easy to tell, and that my broad brush-strokes can only stand as a *grand tour d'horizon*. (Here I also have to relinquish the temptation of killing off my overall case with a thousand qualifications!) Earlier I wrote of critiques by founder figures and in currents of thought, but one will still be left asking whether such critiques were complete or to varying degrees relative subversions of the old religiosity, whether indeed they might have been radical re-fabrications or re-styling of the same essential 'structure'. Contexts and degrees of effects differed. Processes in Israelite–Jewish experience were obviously incremental; compared to their neighbours, Israel's legal punishments were much less violent, and she arrived at exemplary principles of internal justice; but, locked in between Egypt and Mesopotamia, and then divided between north and south, she could never be weak-kneed militarily (see Jer 46–51!), while a centralising of the sacrificial cult made for the increased religious and national unity through the vicissitudes of time.[56] China presents the case of reformist elements being grafted on to imperial ceremonial and official practice, with one or another of the great influences—Confucian, Taoist, Buddhist—gaining advantage, yet with 'mandarin elitism' dominating in economic affairs and security, having only a superficial effect in the countryside.[57] What we may call the meta-technological assumption of religion, in any case, generally prevails: do what is prescribed—and blessings will follow, even if for high practitioners, such as ascetics, physical victory and riches were abhorred, and even though the advice might be to 'work out your own salvation', as the Buddha put it (*Mahâparin.* [*Digha-Nik, sutta*] 16).[58] To tell you the truth, the only drastic undermining of religion one can find in the ancient world, or the only text that 'sees right through religion as such', is St Paul's *Epistle to the Romans*. In this letter (especially chapters 5–9) one finds the *locus classicus* of 'faith' against *religio*, where religion means persuading God (or the divinities) to be on your own side and to secure you the benefits and the building up of merits you desire. Religion entails controlling or manipulating the cosmos in our interests rather than trusting, aware of the ultimate uselessness of human achievements to secure ultimate salvation, and falling into the hands of the living God (cf Heb 10:31; 11:1).[59] But who, then, can hold back such an irresistible force—the enticement that we ourselves can do something to move the divine Power apparently offered as our chance of a final grip on this life? 'Can God himself blame a Man' when religion is so persuasive? And what tradition, when you find you are being 'anxious about tomorrow' (Matt 6:34)—in your own terms and circumstances—is going to leave you discouraged and offer you no sense of tangible blessing? Certainly a whole social group will need the vision of a brighter and better terrestrial future (unless it be a suicide cult!).

The trouble is, the basic, fundamental religion is also the perennial one. It will not be put down; but keeps on bobbing up to the surface, and it irrepressibly infiltrates the lives even of all those who have questioned it. I am not here discussing the 'perennial tradition', by the way, as others have presented it—the 'ancient theology' or body of truth lying independent of the Bible, as in Steuco; the deep heart of the great tradition according to Schuon or Nasr; or the mystic thread *à la* Aldous Huxley.[60] I am taking into account, rather, the resilience of multiform pressures for physical power and generativeness that well up from humanity's wide and deep 'Background Factor'. The preterite of the past with a premonition for the future. Because, for all their subversions of archaic *habitudes de l'esprit*, the trouble is that the salvation religions remain forever vulnerable for being taken back over by 'the natural one' (generically speaking). The former stressed spiritual victors, the latter actual victory. If the *Gîtâ* spiritualised the tribal contest of the *Mahâbhârata* into a call for duty (*dharma*), the text could just as easily be read as a call to a validated war.[61] If the *Qur'an* means the greater *jihad* to be a spiritual struggle in the heart of the believer (9:112–3), there were protagonists ready to agitate for a lesser one of conquest (2:187, etc). The grail story was to set the minds of mediaeval knights on higher things (the ultimate in life being the vision of the *sang real*, the transubstantive mystery of the Mass),[62] yet certain knights had physical crusading at the forefront of their minds. Over many centuries, if the many local histories of it could be retold, football was the device of missionaries to divert battleground energies into the collective kicking of a 'pig's bladder', but of course this attempted sublimation of tribal fighting has not always succeeded—there have been small wars over score results.[63] The vulnerability applied equally to the economic sphere: if sages taught restraint, just reciprocity, and spiritual blessing, voices evoking grandeur, material plenty, and group prosperity were always there to be heard. The need to celebrate military triumph and fecundity, an all too human need, never faded.

At the heart of the problem, we can say, was 'politics', that is, politics wrapped up with the old religious impetuses. The world is the better for loving and peaceable behaviour, but changes to its great territorial configurations are not created by them. Macrohistory is the history of empires, and they went rising like billows long after Ancient Times receded into the mists: the Byzantine, the Abbasid, the Holy Roman, the Khmer, the Mongol, Tamerlaine, the Moghul, the Ottoman, the Portuguese, the Spanish, the Dutch, the British, the Russian, the Austro-Hungarian, the Franco-Napoleonic, the Manchu, the German, the Japanese, the American. They were often settled in place by peace treaties, and by compromises of the well intentioned. These empires were all filled with religious people; as complex institutions they all needed religion to cohere within themselves and to legitimate their causes. Wonderful people lived out beautiful spiritual lives within them, 'making their own [inspirational] history', to adapt Marx, yet not normally 'under circumstances of their choosing'[64]—but under polities, nations and empires, whether premature or successful, following hard-nosed agendas that would often drive any peace-loving idealist to despair. And sometimes 'grey eminences'—high-achieving religious leaders, and professionals assumed to follow decent ethical standards—shocked their peers into veritable disbelief by their prosecutions or vindications of terror.[65]

Perhaps I am beginning to sound like that early post-modernist Alexandre Kojève, who was tempted to deduce from Hegel that 'bloody strife—and not "reason"—is responsible for the progress of events'.[66] Certainly I have my problems with most history as with most religion; I have a passion to learn about both of them, to 'place' all the plights of my fellow beings, to understand, empathise with all the struggles that went on. But I invest no ultimate hope in either. For me, both history and religion are cumbersome vehicles of temporality pointing beyond themselves. And as time has goose-stepped into the present, the extraordinary attempts to transform both 'the general course of history' and 'the general configuration of religion' into a peaceable order have faltered, never more noticeably than in 'our time'. Yes, at the end of this macrohistory, we have experienced two World Wars (allegedly but falsely 'to end all wars'), the burgeoning Communist movement as a neo-'spiritual' surrogate of all those belief-systems that sought to 'free' people from 'evils and vices' (brought by capitalism), and then, with Communism almost disintegrating, we have witnessed the globalization of a victorious, paradoxically self-righteous capitalism, that other 'pyramid of sacrifice', with a continuation of the structural and actual violence it already entailed.[67] Since the League of Nations was inaugurated (1920), nationalism and national borders are a given; and it is a myth always awaiting invocation, that every sovereign state should be 'powerful' and have 'dominion over all the country'.[68] Religious pacifism lost ground when, after Hitler, people could insist more strongly that tyranny had to be actively stopped with arms.[69] In rampant processes of secularization and scientific achievement, moreover, the discourse of salvation has been weakened by a massive return to this-worldly concerns—to winning and not losing in a competitive world, manoeuvring for kick-backs, sacrificing for tax concessions. It is a world in which the 'natural', lower common denominator morality has returned, even been philosophically recommended, that of helping friends and getting even with those who give you a bad time.[70]

How it all happened the way it has is a matter of scholarly vigilance. Part of the story of the persistence of the basic religion is to be expected. Its multitude of forms were usually grafted on to the large, expansive traditions, and when any takeover occurred, a degree of blending was probably a better thing to have happened than not—for the sake of cultural health. Autochthonous culturo-religious habitude is hard to break, mind you, and it is important to assess what the chief protagonists of the big salvation religions required of pre-existing 'shows'. Great traditions that already allowed for polytheism and ancestor worship were more accommodating towards tribalist modes—the so-called Hindu tradition, the Chinese 'system' of things, and to a lesser extent Buddhism. Monotheisms were more demanding—especially in their call to eliminate 'idolatry'. But there are interesting degrees of accommodation nonetheless. Catholicism and Orthodoxy allow images, for example, and the former are more concessive than Protestants to the idea of turning to the dead (as saints) for assistance.

These comments already suggest another explanation for the tough qualities of 'organic' *religio* in its aged dresses and proclivities. It is generally more colourful—more festive and celebratory in expression—than salvific verities. Although every comparison may be arbitrary, this one can be neatly expressed as the difference between a Shankara meditating with his fellow monks to attain the high state of *samâdhi* and crowds in awe as an elephant is processed through a temple.[71] By implication, we can go on to say, 'the fundamental religion' can appeal to the basic instincts more consistently; it is less physically restraining, even if it has its own discipline, certainly more accommodating as to what is considered 'right action', for placing high value on military valour. Indeed, in its very syncretic pull, it carries possibilities not only of subverting salvation religions, but of transforming them into something they never intended to be by their earliest purveyors. The temptation in the wilderness has voiced itself again and again, seducing every follower of an '*ahimsa*-practising Messiah with fame, dominion, ambition'.[72]

The history of the religious validations of violence would almost inevitably follow, not only because religious complexes produce in each other some peculiar chemistry, so that populaces shift one way or another in terms of relative peacefulness or belligerence. That may come into it, and may call on our best methods of detecting collective temperamental variations across the globe. But the real problem arises with the uses of religion politically. Every political economy depends upon a mythic sustenance, on a latent *religio* either waiting to be made visible or is indeed manifestly drawn upon in one country or another. This is the primal impetus to achieve prosperity and security—if necessary victory—against the foe. And no matter how hard the voices of justice and peace vociferate against it, its perennial power persists.

I do not want to leave you with the impression that nothing has been achieved for the better in this macrohistory that has taken violence and religion together. Even in small-scale traditional cultures, we find common stories that wild behaviour has had to be left behind—those days when frightening men ate raw meat and ogre-like characters indulged in blood lust. Primal payback thinking also set in train sanctions and incipient legal principles for governing conduct within a human group as well as for making peace between antagonists.[73] In our common psychological depths, archaic worldviews have done us benefit: its heroes, for all their bloodletting, are capable of inspiring us into forms of greatness that can save rather than take lives.[74] At the end of Antiquity, what is more, someone dared to 'deconstruct' historiography as the noble act of writing about military affairs, and ventured to believe that the Incarnation made worldly affairs softer. This was the Christian deacon Orosius, whose history work is the only one with a large compass surviving intact from Graeco-Roman times, and who saw in the empire-making and extravagant slaughters of the past humanity's utter *miseriae*, and hoped, under the Theodosian order, that Christianity was going to make a real difference.[75] Perhaps, along with influences of other great salvation religions, it has. At least the days of purely warrior societies are virtually over; now we have professional (mainly standing, if sometimes mercenary) armies, and the great mass of people are not expected to lift a weapon.[76] However tainted the history of punishments, humanising influences have come to hold something of an edge over 'barbarities'.[77] Addressing the abuse of women and children is now a high profile issue internationally. The transference of physical heroism from war to sport is another sign of progress.

Has not humanity, also, achieved 'civilisations'? and are not its works, from the sphinx to the Sydney Harbour Bridge, truly wondrous? History experiences its massive power changes, but there is some point in acknowledging 'Hume's law', as I have dubbed it, that in between the conquests of one empire or another, the majority of people in any affected region will soon get back to the same old business of making a living.[78] A sensible point enough; yet while we are glad that humanity has had some stretches of time attaining its 'civilisation', who but the odd cranky prophet, likes to remind us how easily the walls of any Jericho can come tumbling down? and who wants to see themselves descendants of cannibal raiders and vicious conquerors (whether we are phylogenetically connected to their activity or not)? In any case, might there not be a logical slide in concluding that we have 'evolved' to civilisation when we have really only 'learned' and been 'socialised' into conditions we call by that name, and with defiant minds (so formidable a figure as Nietzsche among them) now paradoxically calling us to resist its repressions?[79] Certainly religions have contributed to so-called civilisation. National and imperial ones have nursed them, and in the 'stratigraphy of time' they are more their children than any other socio-religious forms. Representatives of salvation traditions have been more the restrainers, and those complainants who want the most freedom are likely to blame them for civilisation as repression; but of course matters have been nowhere near as simple as that. The real repressiveness has arisen more out of the distinctly political preserve, with its right to coerce, or out of a totalistic mix of political force and religion or some ideological surrogate. To bring off this kind of social mode the 'configurational stubbornness' of an attitude that loves to 'hold its own', 'command' and 'win' without a shadow of 'sissiness', with no special 'pie in the sky', and to show off its riches—its material cargo—is the most useful.[80] That is the steady weight of *religio*—what *religion* basically amounts to—upon the whole human story.

We are living in highly confusing days. In the West, once godless Communism collapsed, a new enemy apparently had to be created, Islam, with the growing implication that Christians and Jewry now have a 'fearful religion' to contend with close to hand.[81] The technology of violence leaps exponentially 'high'; bombs and large planes can reduce skyscrapers to rubble. 'Terror talk' abounds. As strange as it seems, even those who want to save animals from experiments, or save foetuses from abortion, have been branded 'terrorist' for their extreme actions based on high ideals.[82] And among general populaces, xenophobia, ill feeling, and an almost crusading mentality have risen above sentiments of respect, while the gospel of success and prosperity deeply threatens principles of fairness and moderation.[83] The mixing of religious ideas with self-defence practices has never been more popular; gangs and resistance elements stressing initiatory tests and shared secrets have burgeoned; the sky-rocketing (tele)visualization of violence may be more an unknown grim-reaper through imitation and its effects on the imagination than we can ever tell. All these shifts play more and more into the hands of the nation states, whose leaders will mix managing and enlisting religion for their own ends, appropriating long-inured rhetoric of glory, stealing heroism for its cause (with Hollywood-style war and cowboy movies being grist to the mill), and compromising all people of goodwill 'to hell'. In that vast arena of the world affected by Christianity, this is especially poignant. Jesus died pacifistically, and was crucified; yet from Constantine to George Bush Jr, we have had acts that do not square with his challenge to enter into the peaceable 'Order of God' and his primal martyrdom. We need a massive reactivation of pristine *faith*; and let 'the premise of all criticism be the criticism of *religion*'.[84]

Endnotes

1. A Toynbee, *A Study of History*, volume 1 (Oxford: Oxford University Press, 1935 edition), 5; JB Bossuet, *Discours sur l'histoire universelle* (1681), I, *av-pr* [col 685]; III, I [col 922] (this work being part XII of *Théologie historique*, found in *Œuvres complètes*, edited by F Lachat, Paris: Migne, 1866, volume 10, cols 683ff); D Hume, 'On the Study of History', in *Essays: Moral Political and Literary*, edited by EF Miller (Indianapolis: Liberty Press, 1985), 565–66. For a comparable seminal statement, see ARJ Turgot, *On Progress, Sociology and Economics*, translated and edited by RL Meek (Cambridge: Cambridge University Press, 1973), 41.

2. K Lorenz, *On Aggression*, translated by MK Wilson (New York: Bantam, 1969); R Ardrey, *The Territorial Imperative: A Personal Inquiry into the Animal Origins of Property and Nations* (London: Fontana, 1969); see also Ardrey, *The Hunting Hypothesis: A Personal Conclusion concerning the Evolutionary Nature of Man* (London: Fontana, 1977).

3. On the West coming to terms with a very distant past, P Rossi, *The Dark Abyss of Time: The History of the Earth and the History of Nations from Hooke to Vico*, translated by LG Cochrane (Chicago: University of Chicago Press, 1984).

4. J Harpur and J Westwood, *The Atlas of Legendary Places* (New York: Weidenfeld & Nicolson, 1989), 12; Palamas, 'The Ascetic and Theological Teaching of Gregory Palamas', translated by B Krivosheine, *The Eastern Churches Quarterly* 4 (1938): 3. See also AO Lovejoy, *The Great Chain of Being* (Cambridge, Mass: Harvard University Press, 1964); and for important long-term implication, see the potential ambiguity in Augustine's reference to Adam as *corpus animale* (*De civit Dei*, III, xxii, 2, etc).

5. C Bonnet, *Palingénésie philosophique*, in *Oeuvres d'histoire naturelle et de philosophie* (Neuchâtel: Samuel Fauche, 1770), volume 7, 149ff. *Evolutio*, note, is perfectly respectable classical Latin for 'unrolling'.

6. Start with *The Making of Human Aggression*, edited by H Seig (London: Quartet, 1971). Other critics of Lorenz are introduced by RI Evans in his *Konrad Lorenz: The Man and his Ideas* (New York: Harcourt Brace Jonavich, 1975), chapter 5. (For interest, the earlier quotation derives from Tennyson's *In Memoriam*, lvi; and notice how violent events in nature more generally, not only in the animal kingdom, might be used

to legitimate human violence, as dramatically illustrated by Dennis Lehane's novel *Shutter Island* (New York: HarperCollins, 2003), 279.

7. A Wallace, *Darwinism* (London: Macmillan, 1889), chapter 15, implicitly questioning Charles Darwin's *The Expression of the Emotions in Man and Animals* (London: Murray, 1873), though handling only mental not emotional issues.

8. Following Immanuel Kant, see especially his *Lectures on Ethics*, translated by L Infield (New York: Harper, 1963), 11ff. For the popularity of Neo-Kantianism in the second half of the nineteenth century, see KC Köhnke, *The Rise of neo-Kantianism: German Academic Philosophy between Idealism and Positivism*, translated by RJ Hollingsdale, (Cambridge: Cambridge University Press, 1991), especially 143–8; and on Freud's reaction against the overstress on conscience, replacing it by the *Überich* (translated as super-ego) and barely mentioning conscience, see N Symington, 'An Exegesis of Conscience in the Works of Freud' in his *The Blind Man Sees: Freud's Awakening and Other Essays* (London: Karnak, 2004), chapter 3.

9. F Macfarlane Burnet, *Dominant Mammal: The Biology of Human Destiny* (Melbourne: Heinemann, 1970), chapter 8; *Richard Dawkins: How a Scientist Changed the Way we Think*, edited by A Grafen and M Ridley (Oxford: Oxford University Press, 2006). For late nineteenth and early twentieth-century background on race degeneration theory and criminology (with the continuing imputation of blame), see A Hermann, *The Idea of Decline in Western History* (New York: Free Press, 1997), chapters 1–2.

10. As brilliantly argued long ago by Søren Kierkegaard; see *The Concept of Anxiety*, translated by R Thomte (Kierkegaard's Writings 8), (Princeton: Princeton University Press, 1980), book 1. See *Animal Problem Solving*, edited by AJ Ropelle (Penguin Modern Psychology, UPS 7), (Harmondsworth: Penguin, 1967) and subsequent literature. Another early modern way of distinguishing human beings, that they 'invented' (thus Bossuet, *De la connaissance de Dieu et de soi-même* [Lyon: Antoine Perisse, 1845], 251) seems to have been thrown into the balance by recent observations of gorillas and chimpanzees 'making' elementary tools for foraging. See B Fontaine, PY Moisson and EJ Wickings, 'Observations of Spontaneous Tool Making and Tool Use in a Captive Group of Western Lowland Gorillas', *Folia Primatologica* 65, 4 (1995): 219–223; [Reuters], 'Chimpanzees' Tool Time Sheds Light on Early Humans', *Sydney Morning Herald* (25–26 May 2002): 18. A more recent observation is that they both invented and communicated; see KP Oakley, *Man the Toolmaker* (London: British Museum [Natural History], 1953), 1. This has to face new theories of 'animal language': start with *Language and Communication: Comparative Perspectives*, edited by HL Roitblat, LM Herman and PE Nachtigall (Comparative Cognition and Neuroscience), (Hillsdale, NJ: Lawrence Erblaum,

1993. The definition of humans as uniquely reflective, moreover, has to deal with evidence of minimal reflection in dolphins, whales, elephants, dogs and horses; consider G Bateson, *Mind and Nature: A Necessary Unity* (Advances in Systems Theory, Complexity, and the Human Sciences), (Cresskill, NJ: Hampton Press, 2002), although deeper reflection (which involves the kind of self-evaluation important for Kierkegaard's differential) is of course philosophically 'given' as a true mark of humanness. I will leave human biologists to debate issues of our biological distinctness (for example our long nurture period, and post-natal brain development), especially in the light of the very recently discovered 'Lucy's child' (Ethiopia, at 3.3 Kyr BP): for example *Financial Times* [London] (21 Sept 2006): 8. This is not to be confused with the subject of a book pondering the progeny of the hominid named Lucy, found at Hadar, Ethiopa at 3 Kyr BP: D Johansaon and J Shreeve, *Lucy's Child: The Discovery of a Human Ancestor* (London: Viking, 1990).

11. For seminal works of relevance, start with FM Rosinski, 'Belief and Cult in Human Prehistory', in *The Realm of the Extra-human: Ideas and Actions*, edited by A Bharati, (World Anthropology), (The Hague: Mouton, 1976 [China]), 435; AC Blanc, 'Some Evidence for the Ideologies of Early Man', in *Social Life of Early Man*, edited by SL Washburn (Routledge Library Editions: Anthropology and Ethnography, 16), (London: Routledge, 2004 [Italy]), 119–25; W Stephenson, *The Ecological Development of Man* (Sydney: Angus and Robertson, 1972), 30–31 (weaponry); M Berenguer, *Prehistoric Man and his Art*, translated by M Heron (London: Souvenir, 1973), figures 10–11 (art); VG Childe, *Progress and Archaeology* (Thinker's Library, 102), (London: Watts & Co, 1944) (sacrifice); among many other works.

12. The Leakeys, quoted in *Time Magazine* 110, 19 (Nov 1977): 74; AC Leopold and Ardrey, 'Toxic Substances in Plants and the Food Habits of Early Man', *Science* 176, 4034 (1972): 512–4. For background, W Perry, 'Man the Primeval Pacifist', *Vincula* (14 Dec 1925): 64–71.

13. Note the project for the comparative study of male and female aggression at the University of Utrecht, 1980s, compare P Olivier, 'Serotonin and Aggression', for *Scientific Approaches to Youth Violence* (New York Academy of Sciences Symposium, New York, 2006) [sub no 4]; compare also very recent attempts to isolate a gene explaining violence in traditional warrior societies (in particular among the Maori): [AA], 'Once were Warriors: Gene linked to Maori Violence', *Sydney Morning Herald* (9 Aug 2006): 3. On female warriorhood, for example O Basirov, 'The Origin of the Pre-Imperial Iranian Peoples' (lecture delivered for the Zoroastrian Community, Sydney, 29 Dec 2002) (prehistory: Scythian cases); W Stevenson, 'Rebirth of Women Warriors', *Saskatchewan Indian* (March 1989): 15–18 (traditional societies). On related discussions in Biblical Studies, for example MJ

Selvidge, *Woman, Violence and the Bible* (Studies in Women and Religion 37), (Lewiston: Edwin Mellen Press, 1996).

14. See DM Lang, *Armenia: Cradle of Civilization* (London: Allen & Unwin, 1970), 70 (on the Mount Alagöz finds, bridging palaeo- and mesolithic times).

15. For example *Anatomies of Violence: An Interdisciplinary Investigation*, edited by R Walker, K Brass and J Byron (Sydney: Research Institute for Humanities and Social Sciences, University of Sydney, 2000).

16. For background, M Foucault, *Discipline and Punish: The Birth of the Prison*, translated by A Sheridan (London: Allen Lane, 1977); IM Wallerstein, *The Modern World-System* (Studies in Social Discontinuity), (New York: Academic Press, 1974–89), 3 volumes; G Greer, *The Female Eunuch* (London: Paladin, 1971), parts 1–2 and pages 263–72; P Singer, *Animal Liberation* (New York: Ecco, 2002).

17. For seminal ethnography, SR Steinmetz, *Ethnologische Studien zur erster Entwicklung der Strafe* (Leiden; SC Van Doesburgh, 1894); P Middelkoop, *Curse-Retribution-Enmity as Data in Natural Religion, especially in Timor, etc* (Amsterdam: J van Campen, 1960). Compare Trompf, *In Search of Origins: The Beginnings of Religion in Western Theory and Archaeological Practice* (Studies in World Religions, 1), (Delhi: New Dawn, 2005), 197–206; Trompf, *Payback: The Logic of Retribution in Melanesian Religions* (Cambridge: Cambridge University Press, 1994), 16–18.

18. Nietzsche, *On the Genealogy of Morals* (1887), translated by W Kaufmann and RJ Hollingdale (New York: Vintage Books, 1969), especially 70–74.

19. Nietzsche, *On the Genealogy of Morals*, 85–6, 113ff.

20. Note, for example, HH Turney-High, *Primitive War* (Columbia: University of South Carolina Press, 1971); B Malinowski, 'An Anthropological Analysis of War', in *Hostility and Violence: Nature or Nurture?*, edited by T Maple and DW Matheson (New York: Holt, Rinehart and Winston, 1973), 76–85; *War: The Anthropology of Armed Conflict and Aggression*, edited by M Fried, M Harris and R Murphy (Garden City, NY: Natural History Press, 1968).

21. For the Nazi appropriation of Nietzsche, see especially HF Peters, *Zarathustra's Sister: The Case of Elisabeth and Friedrich Nietzsche* (New York: Crown, 1977), chpaters 24–25.

22. Alluding to Rabrindanath Tagore, *Personality* (London: Macmillan & Co, 1919), 25. Self-defence, however, is a principle used to legitimate violence, one that extends from assumptions regarding self-preservation; see WT Vollmann, *Rising Up and Rising Down: Some Thoughts on Violence, Freedom and Urgent Means* (New York: Harper Collins, 2004), 145–356.

23. The art of balancing distinctly biological and distinctly learned (or socialised) aspects of violence will then be a constant matter for

reformulation as evidence comes to hand. There will also be theories about 'human types' coming into the equation, that is, not just races or national types (out of fashion among intellectuals now) but physiologies and temperaments that tertiary institutions' ethics committees demur giving permission to test any more. Note, for example, Julian Huxley's aggressive 'Somatotonics' who cannot do without war, based on William Sheldon's *The Varieties of Human Physique* (with SS Stevens and WB Tucker), (New York: Harper, 1940); and *Varieties of Temperament: A Psychology of Constitutional Differences* (with SS Stevens), (New York: Harper & Brothers, 1942); compare S Bedford, *Aldous Huxley: A Biography* (New York: Alfred A Knopf, 1973), 439–40.

24. Compare B Orme, *Anthropology for Archaeologists* (Ithaca, NY: Cornell University Press, 1981), 194–209.

25. Recently, on 'the big bang of human culture', S Mithen, *The Prehistory of the Mind* (London: Phoenix, 2003), chapter 9 (turning out to cover a 30,000 year time period! A common macrohistorical slide of language in prehistory; see critiques of RH Pfeiffer's *The Creative Explosion: An Enquiry into the Origin of Art and Religion* (New York: Harper & Row, 1982, mentioned in my *Origins*, 206–7).

26. See RV Munson, *Telling Wonders: Ethnographic and Political Discourse in the Work of Herodotus* (Ann Arbor: University of Michigan Press, 2001); and to Herodotus' work we might add the non-extant labours of Ephorus GL Barber (with MCJ Miller), *The Historian Ephorus* (Chicago: Ares, 1993), and Dicaearchus, see *Dikaiarchos* (Texte und Kommentar), edited by F Wehrli (Die Schule des Aristoteles, 1), (Basel, Stuttgart, [1967]). Compare ER Wolf, *Europe and the People without History* (Berkeley: University of California Press, 1982).

27. Bryce, *International Relations* (London: Macmillan, 1922), 3.

28. Trompf, in background comments to *Early Christian Historiography: Narratives of Retributive Justice* (Studies in Religion), (London: Continuum, 2000), 6.

29. Trompf, 'Salvation and Primal Religion', in *The Idea of Salvation*, edited by DW Dockrill and RG Tanner, Special Supplementary Issue of *Prudentia* (1988), 207–12.

30. Begin with J Ferguson, *The Religions of the Roman Empire* (Aspects of Greek and Roman Life), (London: Thames and Hudson, 1970), 72–73.

31. Comparative religion nonetheless has its early modern origins in apologetics about the universality of religion and such attempts at generalization. See, for instance, R Regnier, *Certitude des principes de la religion contre les nouveaux efforts des incrédules* (Lyon: Perisse, 1778), 175–6.

32. Curtius, *Hist Alex Magn Maced*, I, vii, 1ff, compare Arrian, *Vit Alex,* iv. Questioning whether Scythia was every a 'state' or 'empire', see EB Phillips, 'The Nomad Peoples of the Steppes', in *The Dawn of*

Civilization, edited by S Piggott (London: Thames and Hudson, 1962), 324–28.

33. Structuralism is a perfectly scientific method, championed especially by anthropologist Claude Lévi-Strauss, that rightly discerns motifs, patterns, or *structures* in thought and event-complexes that can be verified from data yet are not 'empirically given'; see, for instance, M Corvez, *Les Structuralistes* (Paris: Aubier–Montaigne, 1969), especially chapter 3. Post-modern *post*-structuralism (or Deconstruction) is confined to philosophical (and discursive) orientations and is not intended to 'leave behind' this scientific method; see especially V Descombes, *Modern French Philosophy*, translated by L Scott-Fox and JM Harding (Cambridge: Cambridge University Press, 1980), 77, 86.

34. For a relevant recent book on ancient imperialisms, try RL Fox, *The Classical World: An Epic History of Greece and Rome* (London: Penguin Books, 2006).

35. GWH Hegel, *Lectures on the Philosophy of Religions*, translated and edited by E Speirs and B Sanderson (London: Kegan Paul, Trench, Trübner & Co., 1895), volume 2, especially 125–6, 209–10, 228–9, 327–31; FM Müller, *Natural Religion* (Gifford Lectures 1889, in *Collected Works*, volume 1), (London: Longmans, Green & Co, 1898); CP Tiele, *Elements of the Science of Religion* (Gifford Lectures 1896), (Edinburgh: William Blackwood, 1897), chapter 5; H Siebeck, *Lehrbuch der Religionsphilosophie* (*Sammlung Theologischer Lehrbücher*, edited by Siebeck), (Freiburg: Mohr, 1893), chapter 5; A Kuenen, *National Religions and Universal Religions*, translated by P H Wicksteed (Hibbert Lectures 1882), (Edinburgh: Williams & Norgate, 1882); W Bousset, *Das Wesen der Religion* (Halle: Gebauer Schwetschke, 1903); N Söderblom, *Natürliche Theologie und Allgemeine Religionsgeschichte* (Beiträge zur Relgionwissenschaft 1 [1913–4]), (Leipzig: Hinrichs'sche, 1913, 54–58); Söderblom, *Uppenbarelsereligion* (1930), (Stockholm: Ronzo Boktryckeri, 1963); Moore, *The Birth and Growth of Religion* (Morse Lectures 1922), (Edinburgh: T&T Clark, 1923), 126–33 *et passim*; R Bellah, 'Religious Evolution', *American Sociological Review* 29 (1964): 358–74; compare Middelkoop, see above note 17.

36. Siebeck, *Lehrbuch*, chs 4–5. Siebeck is curiously not mentioned in EJ Sharpe's *Comparative Religion: A History* (London: Duckworth, 1986).

37. See Trompf, *Melanesian Religion* (Cambridge: Cambridge University Press, 1991), 73; and compare with F Tomasetti, *Religions of Melanesia: A Bibliographic Survey* (Bibliographies and Indexes in Religious Studies, 57), (Westport, CT: Praeger, 2006), *passim*.

38. To begin with, see SGF Brandon, *The Judgment of the Dead* (London: Weidenfeld and Nicolson, 1967), chs 4–9.

39. Beginning with Trompf, 'The Incarnation and Asian Traditions, or Do Hindus and Buddhists Carry a Christian Message?' in *That Our Joy*

May be Complete: Essays on the Incarnation for the New Millennium, edited by M Free *et al* (Adelaide: Openbook, 2000), 121–24.

40. For those who are surprised, I use the widely accepted revised date of Zoroaster; following especially M [SK] Marzbani, 'The Gathas Revisited: A Reappraisal of Zarathushtra's Vision' (doctoral dissertation, University of Sydney, Sydney, 2006), 27.

41. This proscription being first revealed to the wider world by Sir Richard Burton, see FM Brodie, *The Devil Drives: A Life of the Fabulous Explorer Sir Richard Burton* (Harmondsworth: Penguin, 1971), 120–21.

42. First, I believe, in 'Religion, Politics and the University', *Arts: Journal of the Sydney University Arts Association*, volume 21 (1999): 104.

43. A matter of interest, incidentally, in Max Weber's approach to the earliest religions: *The Sociology of Religions*, translated by E Fischoff (London: Methuen, 1965), especially 3–4.

44. This remains, however, a lively question, because, for one body of thought, psychoanalytical theory, tends to construe macrohistory as a very slow process from unconsciousness to self-consciousness

45. RW La Barre, *The Human Animal* (Chicago: University Chicago Press, 1955), 120–21, 239–47; *idem, The Ghost Dance: or The Origins of Religion* (New York: Delta, 1972), chapter 2; compare Trompf, *Origins*, 159–61.

46. For a recent insistence on the identity/violence connection, see A Sen, *Identity and Violence: The Illusion of Destiny* (London: Allen Lane, 2006).

47. For assistance, A Flew, *Hume's Philosophy of Belief* (London: Routledge & Kegan Paul, 1961), chapters 4–5; compare BL Whorf, *Language, Thought and Reality*, edited by JB Carroll (Cambridge, Mass: Massachusetts Institute of Technology, 1956).

48. Here I cannot forbear touching on suggestions of ritual life in animals (elephant graveyards, lyre-bird dancing grounds, etc): LJ Rogers and G Kaplan, *Not only Roars and Rituals: Communication in Animals* (Sydney: Allen & Unwin, 1998), 167–71.

49. Quoting JC Oliga, *Power, Ideology, and Control* (Contemporary Systems Thinking, 3), (New York: Plenum, 1996), 9, compare 268, using J Habermas' *The Theory of Communicative Action* (London: Heinemann, 1984).

50. Subtitled: *A Study in Sophocles and Greek Ethics* (Cambridge: Cambridge University Press, 1989).

51. R Girard, *Violence and the Sacred*, translated by P Gregory (Baltimore: Johns Hopkins University Press, 1977). Compare also W Burkert, R Girard and JZ Smith, *Violent Origins: Ritual Killing and Cultural Formation*, edited by R Hamerton-Kelly (Stanford: Stanford University Press, 1987); W Burkert, *Homo Necans: Interpretationen altgriechischer*

Opferriten und Mythen (De Guyter Studienbuch), (Berlin: Walter de Gruyter, 1997).

52. Especially because his theory is over-dependent on Greek sources and anthropologically limited; Trompf, 'On Sacrificing Girard: A view from Melanesia', *Threskeilogia* [Athens], volume 5 (2004): 131–40.

53. JG Frazer, *The Golden Bough: A Study in Magic and Religion* (London: Macmillan, 1911–15), volume 1, 222; and contemplate volume [13], part 8, 441. For the cases, JG Platvoet, *Comparing Religions: A Limitative Approach: An Analysis of Akan, Para-Creole, and IFO-Sananda Rites and Prayers* (Religion and Reason, 24), (The Hague: Mouton, 1982 [Akan]); Trompf, 'Bilalaf', in *Prophets of Melanesia*, edited by Trompf (Suva: Institute of Pacific Studies, 1986, 14–15 and fieldnotes [Fuyughe]).

54. For a famous 1803–6 Von Krusenstern Expedition lithograph of this phenomenon, see P Snow and S Waire, *The People from the Horizon* (Oxford: Phaidon, 1979), 130. Various Melanesian examples are given in Trompf, *Payback*, 26–28. The requirement of the initiates' ordeal has registered in Western imagination in Joseph Campbell's *Hero with a Thousand Faces* (London: Fontana, 1993).

55. Vico, *The New Science* [1744 edition], translated by TG Bergin and MH Fisch (Ithaca, NY: Cornell University Press, 1968), especially Book II.

56. Seminal for relevant analyses, H Cazelles, *Études sur la Code d'Alliance* (Paris: Letouzey et Ané, 1946), especially chapter 4; RE Clements, *God and Temple* (Philadelphia: Fortress Press, 1965); G von Rad, *Old Testament Theology,* translated by DMG Stalker (Edinburgh: Oliver and Boyd, 1962), part 1C, part 2C.

57. For useful sociological reflection, S Feuchtwang, *Popular Religion in China: The Imperial Metaphor* (Richmond, UK: Curzon, 2001); EL Davis, *Society and the Supernatural in Song China* (Honolulu: University of Hawai'i Press, 2001), especially chapter 9.

58. Or, 'find your own Refuge'; compare *Dhammapad* 12.4; *Cakkavattisîha-nâdasutta* 3.58. For meta-technology, note W Tremmel, *Religion: What is it?* (New York: Holt, Rinehart and Winston, 1976), 62–64.

59. Compare also RG Hamerton-Kelly, *Sacred Violence: Paul's Hermeneutic of the Cross* (Minneapolis: Fortress, 1992), on the way the cross as an 'epiphany of violence' transmutes into grace, salvation and *agapê* in Pauline theology.

60. A Steuco, *De perenni philosophia* (Basel: Nicolaus Bryling, 1542) (the 'ancient theology'); F Schuon, *De l'unité transcendante des religions* (Paris: Éditions du Seuil, 1979); SH Nasr, *Knowledge and the Sacred* (Gifford Lectures 1981), (Edinburgh: Edinburgh University Press, 1981) (modern [traditio-]perennialism); A Huxley, *The Perennial Philosophy* (London: Fontana, 1958). The perennial philosophy has also often been used of the tradition of natural theology in Catholic neo-scholasticism.

61. Consider A Sharma, *The Hindu* Gîtâ: *Ancient and Classical Interpretations of the* Bhagavadgîtâ (London: Duckworth, 1986), 254–6, compare EJ Sharpe, *The Universal* Gîtâ: *Western Images of the* Bhagavadgîtâ (London: Duckworth, 1985), 78, 129–30. The *Bhagavadgîtâ*, though composed much later than the *Mahâbhârata*, was placed in the middle of that great epic text.

62. A point somewhat missed in Dan Brown's *Da Vinci Code*! (or in *The Holy Blood and the Holy Grail* by Michael Baigent *et al*, that inspired his plot). See D Jeffries, 'The Justification of War and Malory's Tale of the Sangreal' (doctoral dissertation, University of Sydney, Sydney, 2007).

63. The complex history has been a neglected one, but see D Scott-Forbes, *Football* (London: Heinemann Educational, 1974), 51–56 (especially on war). For other dimensions, for example D Atyeo, *Blood and Guts: Violence in Sports* (New York: Paddington, 1979) (questions of physicality); D Williamson, 'Tribes set for September Warfare', *Sydney Morning Herald* (30 Sept–1 Oct, 2006): 9 (discourse).

64. Compare K Marx, *The Eighteenth Brumaire of Louis Bonaparte* (1869), i, in Marx–Engels, *Selected Works* (English translation), volume 1 (Moscow: Foreign Languages Publishing House, 1951), 225. For relevant reading on modern empires, try recent books by Niall Ferguson, for example *Empire: How Britain Made the Modern World* (London: Allen Lane, 2003).

65. I eschew the Ingersollian propensity to construe history as the recurrent duping of the masses by clerics and the 'religious class'; see RG Ingersoll, *Works* (New York: Dresden, 1900, 12 volumes), yet we simply have to face hideous facts. For the West, my allusion is to Aldous Huxley's *Grey Eminence: A Study in Religion and Politics* (London: Chatto & Windus: 1941), on Cardinal Richelieu's insidious assistant Fr François Leclerq de Tremblay ('Father Joseph'); for the case of a professional (from the Red Cross), see for example GL Posner and J Ware, *Mengele: The Complete Story* (New York: McGraw-Hill, 1986), chapters 1–2, especially 4, 6 (Nazi doctor Josef Mengele).

66. See G Bataille's article on Kojève in 'Hegel, la mort et le sacrifice', *Deucalion*, volume 5 (1955): 22.

67. See HG Wells, *The War that will End War* (London: F&C Palmer, 1914) (on World War [I]); L Trotsky, *Literature and Revolution*, translated by R Strunsky (London: G Allen & Unwin, 1925), 171 (on 'the new spiritual point of view'), compare G Malenkov, deputising for Stalin at the Nineteenth Congress of the Communist Part of the Soviet Union, 1952, extensively quoted in L Cantrell, 'Marxism and Literature', *Balcony: The Sydney Review* 6 (1967): 35 (regarding evil); P Berger, *Pyramids of Sacrifice: Political Ethics and Social Change* (New York: Basic Books, 1974); *Globalization and its Discontents*, edited by S McBride and J Wiseman (London: Macmillan, 2000).

68. To use John Bunyan's straightforward phrases, in *The Holy War* (1682), (Pittsburgh: Whitaker House, 1985), 6 (a sober reminder that the New Testament message of the Kingdom potentially carries this myth with it, whether into ecclesiastical triumphalism or political success).

69. A key turning point came with Reinhold Niebuhr's *Why the Christian Church is Not Pacifist* (London: SCM, 1940), a position later not acceptable to Martin Luther King, Jr, Desmond Tutu, Jim Wallis, etc. (let alone the Dalai Lama and others in other religious traditions) who confront the issue in action and extensive writing.

70. See the introduction of *The Moral of the Story: An Anthology of Ethics through Literature*, edited by P and R Singer (Oxford: Blackwell, 2005).

71. Shankara, *Viveka Chudamani*, I, *et passim* (*samadhi*); R Champakalakshmi and U Kris, *The Hindu Temple* (London: Roli and Janssen, 2001), 49–51 (on elephants in the Ekamresvara procession). Also, for his dichotomy between religions of initiatory disclosure and of discursive teaching, but overdoing it, see H Whitehouse, *Arguments and Icons: Divergent Modes of Religiosity* (Oxford: Oxford University Press, 2000).

72. Thus Anthony, in Aldous Huxley's *Eyeless in Gaza* (Harmondsworth: Penguin, 1955), 100.

73. Start with Lévi-Strauss, *The Raw and the Cooked,* translated by J and D Weightman (*Introduction to a Science of Mythology*, volume 1), (London: Cape, 1970) (notions of wild men); AJ Post, *Grundriss der ethnologischen Juriprudenz* (Oldenburg and Leipzig: Schulze'sche and A Schwartz, 1894–95, 2 volumes); R Redfield, 'Primitive Law', in *Law and Warfare: Studies in the Anthropology of Conflict*, edited by P Bohannan (American Museum Sourcebooks in Anthropology), (Garden City, NY: Natural History Press, 1967), 3–24 (legal issues).

74. J Campbell, with B Moyers, *The Power of Myth*, edited by S Flowers (New York: Doubleday, 1988), xvi.

75. Paulus Orosius, *Historia adversus Paganos* (*ca.* 418), compare Trompf, 'Retributive Logic in Orosius as Early Christian Social Theory', in *The World of Religions: Essays on Historical and Contemporary Issues in Honour of Professor Noel Quinton King, etc* edited by Trompf and G Hamel (Religion, Politics and Society, 1), (Delhi: ISPCK, 2002), 78–83.

76. I could be more cynical here. The days of encouraging the unemployed and school drops-out into the army as 'cannon fodder' have hardly gone; and throughout the world there are vestiges of dominance over armed forces by aristocratic, elite, rich-family and 'leisure class' elements. For background to the latter as the 'hunters and commanders' during most of modern history, see T Veblen, *The Theory of the Leisure Class* (London: Allen & Unwin, 1970). Reflect also on the Second Amendment of the Constitution of the United States of America (framed in 1791 and

frighteningly inadequate for technological advances in 'arms' borne in the twenty-first century); and also consider the problems for highly armed societies, for example Iraq.

77. For perspective, W Andres, *Bygone Punishments* (London: Philip Allen & Co, 1931); GR Scott, *The History of Capital Punishment* (London: Torchstream, 1950); H Potter, *Hanging in Judgment: Religion and the Death Penalty in England* (London: SCM, 1993).

78. Hume, 'Of the Original Contract', in *Essays: Moral Political and Literary*, edited by EF Miller, 471–4; compare Trompf, *The Idea of Historical Recurrence in Western Thought*, volume 2: *From the Later Renaissance to the Turn into the Third Millennium* (Berkeley: University of California Press, [forthcoming]), chapter 7.

79. For an unusual *entrée* into this thorny question by a 'religionist', G van der Leeuw, 'L'homme et la civilisation: Ce que peuit comprendre le terme: Évolution de l'homme', *Eranos Jahrbuch* 16 (1948): 141–82. Compare VF Lenzen, *Civilization* (Berkeley: University of California Press, 1959).

80. See Trompf, 'Salvation', 218–22; compare C Hayes, *Nationalism: A Religion* (New York: Macmillan, 1960) (surrogation); H Marcuse, *Eros and Civilization* (London: Sphere, 1969) (repression and civilisation).

81. SP Huntington, *The Clash of Civilizations and the New World Order* (New York: Simon & Schuster, 1996); *The Clash of Civilizations? Asian Responses*, edited by S Rashid (Oxford: Oxford University Press, 1997; compare *Islam and the West in the Mass Media: Fragmented Images in a Globalizing World*, edited by K Hafez (Cresskill, NJ: Hampton Press, 2000); *The New Crusades: Constructing the Muslim Enemy,* edited by E Qureshi and MA Sells (New York: Columbia University Press, 2003); W Cavanagh, *Does Religion Cause Violence?* (Helder Camara Lecture), (Sydney: Catholic Communications [Melbourne], 2006).

82. See J Lusthaus, 'The Logic of Violence: Legitimation Theory in Contemporary Judaism, Christianity and Islam' (honours sub-thesis, Studies in Religion, University of Sydney, Sydney, 2006); and for British political opinion to ban animal rights 'zealots', see *The Times* (UK) (26 July 2004): 3; *The Daily Telegraph* (UK) (30 July 2006): 13.

83. For example B Aadam, 'Orientalism Localised: An Australian Perspective' (honours sub-thesis, Studies in Religion, University of Sydney, Sydney, 2006) (on xenophobia and anti-Islamic mentalities in Australia, even in the media); *The American Gospel of Success: Individualism and Beyond*, edited by M Rischin (Chicago: Quadrangle, 1968) (American prosperity thinking); DV Biema and J Chu, 'Does God Want you to be Rich?', *Time Magazine* (Aus) (2 Oct, 2006): 50–57 (American properity gospel today).

84. E Fischer, with F Marek, *Marx in His Own Words*, translated by A Bostock (London: Allen Lane, 1970), 20. My thanks for suggestions and bibliographic advice on this chapter to Ania Szafjanska, State

Library of New South Wales, and Professor Cristiano Camporesi, University of Florence.

Conclusion

The papers delivered at this conference on scripture and violence have grappled with the problem of how to deal with the phenomenon of violence when it appears within the scriptures and traditions of particular religious faiths. Each contributor has approached the hermeneutical question which lies at the heart of the three 'religions of the book', and which is not unknown to adherents of other religions. When believers read their scriptures and encounter texts imbued with violence, they need to determine how it is that they will deal with those texts. 'How am I to deal with these violent words in my scripture?' is a question faced by Jews, Muslims and Christians alike. A range of answers to this question have been proposed in *Validating Violence—Violating Faith?*

The starting point adopted by every author in this volume has been to recognize the extent of violent language, imagery, stories, and ideologies which are imbedded within the text. There needs to be an honest recognition of the nature and character of the texts being read, heard, and appropriated as scripture. Such a recognition of violent elements within the text has been an essential first step in the context of this seminar. It is a step which is not always taken by interpreters of scriptural texts. The desire, or demand, to have a scriptural text speak with a holy voice, especially in the three 'religions of the book', can blind the interpreter to the reality of the text being approached, or influence the interpreter so that any such elements which are recognized, are explained as having minimal significance. Worse, the history of interpretation is littered with examples of violent accounts, or violent ideologies, being pressed into service in ways which cannot have been imagined by the authors of the text, and which appear to run counter to the higher ideals of the particular religion. So, the first step requires something of a 'reality check' about the nature and contents of the particular scripture.

This reality check begins with the simple act of description: what is seen in the text, what sits at the surface level of the narrative, what is explicitly stated or affirmed, must first be noted and expressed. Where violent actions or violent ideas are clear, they are to be acknowledged. Furthermore, where violent actions are commanded or violent behaviour is advocated, this too must be recognized and stated. Indeed, at this point, it may well be that the interpreter simply needs to declare that the text itself appears to praise or commend such violence. If this is the case, it can be seen that commendation can lead to validation: because the text describes violence in an approving manner, the violence gains credibility and is seen to be validated in itself. The holy text endorses the violent action. The implication is that the consequences of such violence are to be accepted, approved, applauded. Violence validated, becomes violence which violates.

Beyond the stage of description, then, comes the step of evaluation. What are we to make of the presence of violence within the text? In fact, the way that the text is constructed may itself provide some clues, or pointers, towards the way that we are to handle the text. Does the text place violent actions or behaviours alongside of other, non-violent, activities? In such a juxtaposition, is there any sense of internal dialogue or critique being developed within the text? Does the text bring 'peace' into relationship with 'violence'? If so, it may be that the text itself is attempting to establish a way of reading, such that violence and non-violence are each to be given their own distinctive weighting. The reader is thereby invited to make an assessment as to the relative value of each of these entities. The holy text, whilst describing violence, may be inviting a validation of that violence. Or it may be prodding the reader to violate the power of the violence itself, thereby leading to a validation of faith which can be crucial of, or stand independent of, such violence. Violence violated, enables faith to be validated.

The approach to the text will be vital in shaping the hermeneutical stance towards the text adopted by the interpreter. Description and evaluation each make their own invitation to consider the text in a specific way.

How, then, might the interpreter deal with violence in religious texts? The contributors to this volume have adopted a variety of approaches in deciding on what will be the fundamental mechanism for their dealing with these violent passages.

A starting point may be that of the story which is central to the particular scripture. Under the influence of historical-critical methods of reading, the interpreter may approach the text with a view that the text needs to be understood and appreciated as a literary artifact which came into being in a particular historical context. The social, cultural, political and religious dynamics of that context will influence and shape the way that the text is created; those dynamics will be evident, in one form or another, within the content of the text. Thus, Elizabeth Raine and John Squires locate their account of violence in the story of Jesus within the context of the first-century Roman-occupied Jewish homeland. The shape of the story emerges out of the imaginary narrative attributed to this ancient place and time; the elements of violence within the story are thus seen to be contingent upon the political, religious, and social situation. Critics of a rigorously historical approach might suggest that ancient words are inherently irrelevant to the present; the approach adopted in this chapter sets its face against such a conclusion. The hope implicit throughout this chapter is that this distancing of the story found within the scriptural text takes it away from our own time, and enables us to consider the issues without importing contemporary prejudices and hopes into the story. From the distanced story, then, observations may be made about violence and lessons might be learned (and, ultimately, applied to the present). Thus, the imaginary narrative concludes with comments and questions addressed to the present time.

A more explicit expression of relation of ancient text to contemporary situation can be observed in the contribution from Mehmet Ozalp. Setting the scriptural text (in this case, the Qur'an) into its historical context of seventh-century Arabia allows for a distanced, less biased view of the dynamics which are at work in the story which is told. The violent elements are able to be identified, explored, and appreciated within the nexus of this historical context. Ozalp is explicit about the steps to be taken once this context has been explored: it is necessary to apply insights gleaned from the seventh-century context to our world of the twenty-first century, through the process of analogy. A critic might argue that this approach leaves the text dangling in the air, as it were, waiting for an appropriate analogy to animate it in the present. Ozalp's expectation, on the contrary, is that the cultural analysis undertaken of the older context will illuminate features which cry out to be applied to contemporary understanding. When the cultural conditions are similar, then analogy is possible. Historical explanation provides an analogy for contemporary understanding.

Elements of this approach to scripture can also be seen in the chapter contributed by Anastasia Boniface-Malle. Her reading of Old Testament scripture is set firmly within the contemporary African context of societal violence; the process of analogy enables her to explain, evaluate, and contextualise, a number of scriptural passages relating to violence. Ancient stories and contemporary situations resonate with one another, so that the stance of the interpreter brings the scripture into the present and the present situation into the scripture. Once again, it is the process of analogy which best describes the hermeneutical process at work in this chapter. The strength of the parallels affirms the validity of the approach adopted. The same kind of process, interpreting by means of the analogy between ancient text and contemporary situation, is evident in the chapter by Rachael Kohn. The strident tones of violent texts sit alongside the horrors of recent experience and ongoing outbursts of violent action in the Middle East. One informs the other in an intuitive fashion. The fact that the texts form part of a canon of scripture within other religious traditions means that their potential for validating violence always looms large in the Jewish consciousness.

One step further on from this approach can be seen in the chapter by David Neville. Questions of morality become the primary factor at work in generating the hermeneutic of the interpreter. The fundamental question at the heart of Neville's exploration of Matthew's Gospel is a theological one: what does this scripture reveal about the nature of God? Yet the dynamic which impels his quest is a concern for the morality of the answer discovered: is it right, good, and satisfactory for believers to accept that the nature of God is that of a vengeful, violent personality? The eschatological passages considered would seem to paint God in this way; Neville's hermeneutic places alongside these texts those other passages which moderate, or dispute, this reading. It is the moral question, and the moral implications drawn, which shape the way that the text is read and interpreted. The essentially negative value of eschatological violence propels the interpreter to seek a positive moral quality by which to interpret the scripture. Heather Thomson brings a similar concern for morality into her reading of scripture through the lens of James Gilligan's work. The scriptural texts cited in this chapter point away from retribution, towards reconciliation. In seeking to expunge Christian theology of retribution and violence, Thomson proposes that justice be redefined so that is restorative, reconciling and healing. This concern for moral conclusions is what drives the hermeneutic adopted.

A different hermeneutical method is evident in the contributions of Christopher Stanley and Jione Havea. Critical evaluation of the range of scriptural content is what marks these chapters. Critical evaluation means, in the first instance, to allow equal space and equal time to our consideration of texts which have any apparent connection with the issue of violence. No scriptural passages should be excluded from consideration on the basis of an initial bias or prejudice, in one direction or another. This is what Stanley produces. In his survey of the scriptural texts of the three 'religions of the book', those texts advocating violence demand as much critical attention as texts which advocate peace. Only after a detailed accounting of the range of such texts, can conclusions be drawn. The task of the interpreter is to sift, assess, and evaluate; in the end, some texts are privileged over and against other texts, but this is done on the basis of comparison and analysis, and emerges out of the process of interpretation. This is one manifestation of a hermeneutic of 'critical consideration'.

Another example is to be found in the ruminations of Jione Havea. Here, the critical dimension emerges in the exploration of the nature of the scripture texts under consideration and, indeed, in the very act of interpretation itself. Havea's chapter presses the questions. To what extent does the scripture express violence in what is explicitly stated? To what extent is violence implicit in what is written? To what extent does the act of interpreting itself entail violence? To what extent does this violent process result in pleasure? And might that invite the interpreter to engage in the process without self-critical 'disapproval'? Such a conclusion invites further reflection on what is driving the interpreter. Havea's critical approach invites a constant reappraisal of the depth to which violence permeates the interpretive process. Nevertheless, whilst Havea and Stanley both adopt a professedly neutral tone in dealing with the scriptural texts, what drives their interpretations is the claim that the scriptures play a formative role in the communities of faith for which they are holy texts. The extensive critical appraisal results in conclusions in the service of the faith enterprise.

Three chapters in this current volume exemplify an approach which is oriented more towards the systematic than the hermeneutic, through the tendency to place critical analytical interpretation at the service of systematic exposition. The need to structure life in accordance with a greater principle is evident in this approach. Analytical arrangement and systematic exposition are to be found, in variant forms, in the studies of William Emilsen, Chris Budden and Garry Trompf. Each place a particular 'greater principle' at the heart of their analysis. Emilsen takes the Gandhian motif of non-violence as the central criterion by which all scriptures and all religiously-motivated behaviour are to be assessed. The scriptures are approached with a view to providing the data for considering religious behaviours; the principle of non-violence, found within the scriptures, becomes the norm by which all other elements of the scripture are to be evaluated. As Emilsen makes explicit how Gandhi viewed the matter, he also points to the process of centralizing and arranging around a central core which is fundamental to the task of systematic thinking.

In like fashion, Chris Budden provides a reading of the theological motif of atonement in which the myth of redemptive violence is placed under scrutiny. Budden argues that this myth is grounded in a particular understanding of the doctrine of God, expressed in a particular form of soteriology, and has been used to drive specific national policies in the contemporary era. The texts which are explored in this chapter are placed over against this understanding of atonement; they function as a critical corrective to the tradition and provide a basis for reworking the doctrine. In this way, a hermeneutic of analysis works in the service of the systematic agenda.

It is noteworthy that no contributors to this volume have employed another hermeneutical approach which might be proposed—namely, a form of revisionism in which the problematic texts (that is, texts which reflect or advocate violence) are simply excised, marginalized, or ignored. This is noteworthy simply because, all too often in the history of interpretation, an interpretive argument has been advanced by omitting to consider crucial passages. As we have already noted, this is not an option which is viable, in the contemporary context, when addressing the place of violence in religious scriptures. The lengthy analysis offered by Garry Trompf provides precisely the opposite approach—encompassing texts from a wide diversity of scriptures, mediated through a large number of religious traditions. Once again, the systematizing tendency is at work; all religious systems can be read within the framework of the relentless press of violent tendencies onto the desire for civilizing influences, coming especially from what Trompf characterizes as the 'salvation religions'. The tension is unresolved and incessant; the threat of violence remains high, and the call for understanding of scriptural imperatives remains. The text continues to play its role within the system.

To conclude our considerations, we might pose a final set of questions: What, then, is the shape of faith which emerges from the particular process we employ in interpreting scripture? What is it that we ultimately validate as 'true faith'? What role does violence play in this process of validation? Are faith and violence inextricably linked, or can faith be conceived without reference to violence? The essays in this volume provoke us to keep these questions at the forefront of our thinking in the contemporary age.

Index of Names

Index of Scriptural References

Genesis			22:2–3	13
1	88, 187		22:21–27	40
1:30	21		23:6–9	40
2:18	187		23:12	21
3:21–24	20		23:23–33	23
4:8	189		23:33	80
4:10–15	40		32:11–14	22
5:1	189		32:25–29	24
6:11–13	40		33:19	90
7 – 9	187		34:11–16	25
8:20–21	21			
9:1–4	21		Leviticus	
9:6	40		18:17–18	40
10:9	188		18:19	42
12	23		19:13–16	40
12:3–13	21		19:33–34	40
14:13–16	22		26:3–8	24
15	23		26:14–33	27
19	79			
19:22–33	22		Numbers	
22	23		5:11–31	25
26:17–33	41		11:33–34	24
31:19–55	41		14:20–32	24
33:1–15	41		14:20–35	25
45:4–15	41		16:23–50	24
49:5–6	40		20:14–21	41
			21:21–35	24
Exodus			22:31	187
3:7	91		25:1–5	80
4:24–26	40		25:1	85
14:14	92		25:6–8	24
15:3	91		27	78
17:8–16	22		31:1 – 32:42	24
21:12–27	40		31:14–17	80
21:23	40		33:50–56	23, 25
21:28–32	21		35:9–34	40
22:1	177		36	78